First Person Singular

FIRST PERSON SINGULAR
Writers on Their Craft

compiled by
JOYCE CAROL OATES

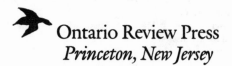
Ontario Review Press
Princeton, New Jersey

Library of Congress Cataloguing in Publication Data

Main entry under title:

First person singular.

   1. Authors, American—20th century—Interviews.
2. Authorship—Addresses, essays, lectures.   I. Oates,
Joyce Carol, 1938—
PS129.F5 1983   810'.9'0054   83-21927
ISBN 0-86538-037-6

Distributed by Persea Books, Inc.
225 Lafayette St.
New York, NY 10012

Saul Bellow: "Some Questions and Answers." Copyright © 1975 by Saul Bellow. Reprinted by permission of Harriet Wasserman Literary Agency, Inc., as agent for the author. First published in *The Ontario Review*.

Neal Bowers and Charles L. P. Silet: "An Interview with Howard Nemerov." Reprinted
from *The Massachusetts Review*, copyright © 1980 The Massachusetts Review, Inc. Reprinted by permission.

David Brooks: "A Conversation with Mark Strand." Copyright © 1978 by *The Ontario Review*. Reprinted by permission.

Hortense Calisher: excerpt from "Pushing Around the Pantheon" in *Herself* by Hortense
Calisher. Copyright © 1972 by Hortense Calisher. Reprinted by permission of Candida
Donadio & Associates, Inc.

Hayden Carruth: "The Question of Poetic Form." Reprinted from *Working Papers* by permission of the University of Georgia Press. Copyright © 1982 by the University of Georgia Press.

Gail Godwin: "A Diarist on Diarists." Copyright © 1976 by *Antaeus*. Reprinted by permission.

Mary Gordon: "The Parable of the Cave or: In Praise of Watercolors." Copyright © 1980
by Mary Gordon. Reprinted by permission of Literistic, Ltd.

Francine du Plessix Gray: "I Write for Revenge Against Reality." Copyright © 1982 by
Francine du Plessix Gray. Reprinted by permission.

Daniel Halpern: "The Pursuit of Suffering." Copyright © 1982 by *Antaeus*. Reprinted by
permission.

William Heyen: "A Memoir of John Berryman." Copyright © 1983 by William Heyen. First
published in *The Ohio Review*, Vol. XV, No. 2 (1974). Reprinted by permission.

John Hollander: "The Poetry of Everyday Life." Copyright © 1982 by *Raritan: a quarterly
review*. Reprinted by permission.

Colette Inez: "An Interview with Theodore Weiss." Copyright © 1977 by *Parnassus: Poetry
in Review*. Reprinted by permission.

Joyce Carol Oates: "A Conversation with Margaret Atwood." Copyright © 1978 by *The
Ontario Review*. Reprinted by permission.

Contents

Why Write?

JOHN UPDIKE

My title offers me an opportunity to set a record of brevity at this Festival of Arts; for an adequate treatment would be made were I to ask, in turn, "Why not?" and sit down.

But instead I hope to explore, for not too many minutes, the question from the inside of a man who, rather mysteriously to himself, has earned a livelihood for close to twenty years by engaging in the rather selfish and gratuitous activity called "writing." I do *not* propose to examine the rather different question of what use is writing to the society that surrounds and, if he is fortunate, supports the writer. The ancients said the purpose of poetry, of writing, was to entertain and to instruct; Aristotle put forward the still fascinating notion that a dramatic action, however terrible and piteous, carries off at the end, in catharsis, the morbid, personal, subjective impurities of our emotions. The enlargement of sympathy, through identification with the lives of fictional others, is frequently presented as an aim of narrative; D. H. Lawrence, with characteristic fervor, wrote, "And here lies the vast importance of the novel, properly handled. It can inform and lead into new places the flow of our sympathetic consciousness, and can lead our sympathy away in recoil from things that are dead." Kafka wrote that a book is an ax to break the frozen sea within us. The frozen sea within himself, he must have meant; though the ax of Kafka's own art (which, but for Max Brod's posthumous disobedience, Kafka would have taken with him into the grave), has served an analogous purpose for others. This note of pain, of saintly suffering, is a modern one, far removed from the serene and harmonious bards and poets of the courts of olden time. Listen to Flaubert, in one of his letters to Louise Colet:

> I love my work with a love that is frenzied and perverted, as an ascetic loves the hair shirt that scratches his belly. Sometimes, when I am empty, when words

Given in Adelaide, South Australia, in March 1974.

don't come, when I find I haven't written a single sentence after scribbling whole pages, I collapse on my couch and lie there dazed, bogged in a swamp of despair, hating myself and blaming myself for this demented pride which makes me pant after a chimera. A quarter of an hour later everything changes; my heart is pounding with joy. Last Wednesday I had to get up and fetch my handkerchief; tears were streaming down my face. I had been moved by my own writing; the emotion I had conceived, the phrase that rendered it, and satisfaction of having found the phrase—all were causing me to experience the most exquisite pleasure.

Well, if such is the writer at work, one wonders why he doesn't find a pleasanter job; and one also wonders why he appears himself to be the chief market for his own product.

Most people sensibly assume that writing is propaganda. Of course, they admit, there is bad propaganda, like the boy-meets-tractor novels of socialist realism, and old-fashioned propaganda, like Christian melodrama and the capitalist success stories of Horatio Alger or Samuel Smiles. But that some message is intended, wrapped in the story like a piece of crystal carefully mailed in cardboard and excelsior, is not doubted. Scarcely a day passes in my native land that I don't receive some letter from a student or teacher asking me *what I meant to say* in such a book, asking me to elaborate more fully on some sentence I deliberately whittled into minimal shape, or inviting me to speak on some topic, usually theological or sexual, on which it is pleasantly assumed I am an expert. The writer as hero, as Hemingway or Saint-Exupéry or D'Annunzio, a tradition of which Camus was perhaps the last example, has been replaced in America by the writer as educationist. Most writers teach, a great many teach writing; writing is furiously taught in the colleges even as the death knell of the book and the written word is monotonously tolled; any writer, it is assumed, can give a lecture, and the purer products of his academic mind, the "writings" themselves, are sifted and, if found of sufficient quality, installed in their places on the assembly belt of study, as objects of educational contemplation.

How dare one confess, to the politely but firmly inquiring letter-writer who takes for granted that as a remote but functioning element of his education you are duty-bound to provide the information and elucidating essay that will enable him to complete his term paper, or his Ph.D. thesis, or his critical *opus*—how dare one confess that the absence of a swiftly expressible message is, often, *the* message; that reticence is as important a tool to the writer as expression; that the hasty filling out of a questionnaire is not merely irrelevant but *inimical* to the writer's proper activity; that this activity is rather curiously private and finicking, a matter of exorcism and manufacture rather than of toplofty proclamation; that what he makes is ideally as ambiguous and opaque as life itself; that, to be blunt, the social usefulness of writing matters to him primarily in that it somehow creates a few job opportunities—in Australia, a few government grants—a few opportunities to live as a writer.

Not counting journalists and suppliers of scripts to the media, hardly a hundred American men and women earn their living by writing, in a wealthy nation of two hundred million. Does not then, you ask, such a tiny band of privileged spokesmen owe its country, if not the trophy of a Nobel Prize,* at least the benign services of a spiritual aristocracy? Is not the writer's role, indeed, to speak for humanity, as conscience and prophet and servant of the billions not able to speak for themselves? The conception is attractive, and there are some authors, mostly Russian, who have aspired to such grandeur without entirely compromising their gifts. But in general, when a writer such as Sartre or Faulkner becomes a great man, a well-intentioned garrulity replaces the specific witness that has been theirs to give.

The last time I dared appear on a platform in a foreign land, it was in Kenya, where I had to confess, under some vigorous questioning from a large white man in the audience, that the general betterment of mankind, and even the improvement of social conditions within my own violently imperfect nation, were *not* my basic motivation as a writer. To be sure, *as a citizen* one votes, attends meetings, subscribes to liberal pieties, pays or withholds taxes, and contributes to charities even more generously than— it turns out—one's own President. But as a writer, for me to attempt to extend my artistic scope into all the areas of my human concern, to substitute nobility of purpose for accuracy of execution, would certainly be to forfeit whatever social usefulness I *do* have. It has befallen a Solzhenitsyn to have experienced the Soviet labor camps; it has befallen Miss Gordimer and Mr. Mtshali † to suffer the tensions and paradoxes and outrages of a racist police state; social protest, and a hope of reform, is in the very fiber of their witness. But a writer's witness, surely, is of value in its circumstantiality. Solzhenitsyn's visible and brave defiance of the Soviet state is magnificent; but a novel like *The First Circle* affords us more than a blind flash of conditioned and—let's face it—chauvinistic indignation; it affords us entry into an unknown world, it offers a complex and only implicitly in-

---

* That year awarded to Australia's Patrick White.
† Oswald Mtshali, Zulu poet. Both he and Nadine Gordimer were present at the Adelaide Festival.

dignant portrait of how human beings live under a certain sort of political system. When I think of the claustrophobic and seething gray world of *The First Circle*, I am reminded in texture of Henry Miller's infamous Paris novels. Here, too, we have truth, and an undeniable passion to proclaim the truth—a seedy and repellent yet vital truth—though the human conditions Miller describes are far removed from any hope of political cure. And Miller, in his way, was also a martyr: as with Solzhenitsyn, his works could not be published in his native land.

We must write where we stand; wherever we do stand, there is life; and an imitation of the life we know, however narrow, is our only ground. As I sat on that stage in Kenya, a symbolic American in a corner of that immense range of peoples symbolically called The Third World, I felt guilty and bewildered that I could not hear in my formidable accuser's orotund phrases anything that had to do with my practice of the writer's profession; I was discomfited that my concerns—to survive, to improve, to make my microcosms amusing to me and then to others, to fail, if fail I must, through neither artistic cowardice nor laziness, to catch all the typographical errors in my proofs, to see that my books appear in jackets both striking and fairly representative of the contents, to arrange words and spaces and imagined realities in patterns never exactly achieved before, to be able to defend any sentence I publish—I was embarrassed that my concerns were so ignoble, compared to his. But, once off the stage (where a writer should rarely be), I tend to be less apologetic, and even to believe that my well-intentioned questioner, and the silent faces in the same audience looking to me to atone for America's sins real and supposed, and the touching schoolchildren begging me by letter to get them through the seventh grade—that none of these people have any felt comprehension of my vocation.

Why write: As soon ask, why rivet? Because a number of personal accidents drift us toward the occupation of riveter, which pre-exists, and, most importantly, the riveting-gun exists, and we love it.

Think of a pencil. What a quiet, nimble, slender and then stubby wonder-worker he is! At his touch, worlds leap into being; a tiger with no danger, a steam-roller with no weight, a palace at no cost. All children are alive to the spell of pencil and crayons, of making something, as it were, from nothing; a few children never move out from under this spell, and try to become artists. I was once a rapturous child drawing at the dining-room table, under a stained-glass chandelier that sat like a hat on the swollen orb of my excitement. What is exciting that child, so distant from us in time and space? He appears, from the vantage of this lectern unimaginable to him, to be in the grip of two philosophical perceptions.

One, mimesis demands no displacement; the cat I drew did not have to fight for food or love with the real cat that came to the back porch. I was in drawing *adding* to the world rather than rearranging the finite amount of goods within it. We were a family struggling on the poverty edge of the middle class during the Depression; I was keen to avoid my father's noisy plight within the plague of competition; pencil and paper were cheap, unlike most other toys.

And, Two, the world called into being on the pencilled paper admitted of connections. An early exercise, whose pleasure returns to me whenever I assemble a collection of prose or poetry or whenever, indeed, I work several disparate incidents or impressions into the shape of a single story, was this: I would draw on one sheet of paper an assortment of objects—flowers, animals, stars, toaster, chairs, comic-strip creatures, ghosts, noses—and connect them with lines, a path of two lines, so that they all became the fruit of a single impossible tree. The exact age when this creative act so powerfully pleased me I cannot recall; the wish to make collections, to assemble sets, is surely a deep urge of the human mind in its playful, artistic aspect. As deep, it may be, as the urge to hear a story from beginning to end, or the little ecstasy of extracting resemblances from different things. Proust, of course, made simile the cornerstone of his theory of aesthetic bliss, and Plato, if I understand him right, felt that that which a set of like objects have in common *must* have a separate existence in itself, as the *idea* which delivers us, in our perception of the world, from the nightmare of nominalism. At any rate, to make a man of pencil and paper is as much a magical act as painting a bison with blood on the wall of a cave; a child, frail and overshadowed, and groping for his fate, herein *captures* something and, further, brings down praise from on high.

I have described the artistic transaction as being between the awakening ego and the world of matter to which it awakes; but no doubt the wish to please one's parents enters early, and remains with the artist all his life, as a desire to please the world, however displeasing his behavior may seem, and however self-satisfying the work pretends to be. We are surprised to discover, for instance, that Henry James hoped to make lots of money, and that James Joyce read all of his reviews. The artist's personality has an awkward ambivalence: he is a cave dweller who yet hopes to be pursued into his cave. The need for privacy, the need for recognition: a child's vulnerability speaks in both needs, and in my own reaction to, say, the beseeching mail just described, I detect the live ambiguity—one is avid to receive the letters, and loath to answer them. Or (to make some reference to the literary scene I know best) consider the striking contrast between the eager, even breathless warmth of Saul Bellow's fiction, inviting our love and closeness with every phrase, and Bellow's own faintly haughty, distinctly edgy personal surface. Again, J. D. Salinger wrote a masterpiece, *The Catcher in the Rye*, recommending that readers who enjoy a book call up the author; then he spent his next twenty years avoiding the telephone. A writer, I would say, out of no doubt deficiencies of character, has constructed a cave-shaped organ, hollow more like a mouth than like an ear, through which he communicates with the world at one remove. Somewhat, perhaps, as his own subconscious communicates with him through dreams. Because the opportunities for feedback have been reduced to letters that need not be answered and telephones that can be unlisted, to an annual gauntlet of reviews and non-bestowal of prizes, the communication can be more honest than is any but the most trusting personal exchange; yet also great opportunities for distortion exist unchecked. For one more of these rather subterranean and reprehensible satisfactions of writing that I am here confessing is that the world, so balky and resistant and humiliating, can in the act of mimesis be rectified, adjusted, chastened, purified. Fantasies defeated in reality can be fully indulged; tendencies deflected by the cramp of circumstance can be followed to an end. In my own case I have noticed, so often it has ceased to surprise me, a prophetic quality of my fictions, even to the subsequent appearance in my life of originally fictional characters. We write, that is, out of latency as much as memory; and years later our laggard lives in reality act out, often with eerie fidelity, the patterns projected in our imaginings.

But we have come too far, too fast, from that ambitious child making his pencil move beneath the stained-glass chandelier. In my adolescence I discovered one could write with a pencil as well as draw, without the annoying need to consult reality so frequently. Also, the cave beneath the written page holds many more kinds of space than the one beneath the drawing pad. My writing tends, I think, to be pictorial, not only in its groping for visual precision but in the way the books are conceived, as objects in space, with events and persons composed within them like shapes on a canvas. I do not recommend this approach; it is perhaps a perversion of the primal narrative urge. Storytelling, for all its powers of depiction, shares with music the medium of time, and perhaps its genius, its most central transformation, has to do with time, with rhythm and echo and the sense of time not frozen as in a painting but channelled and harnessed as in a symphony.

But one can give no more than what one has received, and we try to create for others, in our writings, aesthetic sensations we have experienced. In my case, some of these would be: the graphic precision of a Dürer or a Vermeer, the offhand-and-backwards-feeling verbal and psychological accuracy of a Henry Green, the wonderful embowering metaphors of Proust, the enigmatic concreteness of Kafka and Joyce, the collapse into components of a solved mathematical problem, the unriddling of a scrupulous mystery story, the earth-scorning scope of science fiction, the tear-producing results of a truly humorous piece of writing. Writing, really, can make us do rather few substantial things: it can make us laugh, it can make us weep, and if it is pornography and we are rather young, it can make us come. It can also, of course, make us sleep; and though in the frequent discussion of the writer's social purpose this soporific effect is unfailingly ignored, I suspect it is the most widespread practical effect of writing—a book is less often a flaming sword or a beam of light than a bedtime toddy. Whatever the use, we hope that some members of society will find our product useful enough to purchase; but I think it would be a hypocrisy to pretend that these other people's welfare, or communication with them, or desire to ennoble or radicalize or terrify or lull them, is the primary reason why one writes.

No, what a writer wants, as every aspiring writer can tell you, is *to get into print*. To transform the changing shadows of one's dimly and fitfully lived life into print—into metal or, with the advent of offset printing, into rather mysteriously electrified rubber—to lift through the doubled magic of language and mechanical reproduction our own impressions and dreams and playful constructions into another realm of existence, a multiplied and far-flung existence, into a space far wider than that which we occupy, into a time theoretically eternal: *that* is the siren song that holds us to our desks, our dismal revisions, our insomnia panics, our dictionaries and encyclopedias, our lonely and, the odds long are, superfluous labor. "Of making many books there is no end; and much study is a weariness of the flesh." A weariness one can certainly feel entering even a modestly well-stocked bookstore. Yet is is just this involvement in the world of commerce and industry, this imposition of one's otherwise evanescent fancies upon the machinery of manufacture and distribution, that excites the writer's ego, and gives an illusion of triumph over his finitude.

Although, as a child, I lived what was to become my material and message, my wish to write did not begin with that material and message; rather, it was a wish to escape from it, into an altogether better world. When I was thirteen, a magazine came into the house, *The New Yorker* by name, and I loved that magazine so much I concentrated all my wishing

into an effort to make myself small and inky and intense enough to be
received into its pages. Once there, I imagined, some transfigured mode of
being, called a "writer's life," would begin for me. My fantasy was not
entirely fantastic, as my domineering position on this platform and the
first-class airplane tickets that brought me halfway around the world testify. But what I would not altogether insincerely ask you to accept is something shabby, precarious, and even craven about a writer's life.

Among artists, a writer's equipment is least out-of-reach—the language
we all more or less use, a little patience at grammar and spelling, the common adventures of blundering mortals. A painter must learn to paint; his
studio is redolent of alchemic substances and physical force. The musi-
cian's arcanum of specialized knowledge and personal dexterity is even
more intimidating, less accessible to the untrained, and therefore somehow less corruptible than the writer's craft. Though some painters and
musicians go bad in the prime of their lives, far fewer do, and few so
drastically, as writers. Our trick is treacherously thin; our art is so incor-
rigibly amateur that novices constantly set the world of letters on its ear,
and the very phrase "professional writer" has a grimy sound. Hilaire Belloc
said that the trouble with writing was that it was never meant to be a
profession, it was meant to be a hobby. An act of willful play, as I have
described it.

So I have not spoken up to now of language, of the joys of using it well,
of the role of the writer as a keeper of the keys of language, a guardian of
usage and enforcer of precision. This does not seem to me a very real
notion, however often it is put forward.* Language goes on evolving in
the street and in the spoken media, and well-written books are the last
places it looks for direction. The writer follows after the spoken language,
usually timidly. I see myself described in reviews as a doter upon words. It
is true, I am grateful to have been born into English, with its polyglot
flexibility and the happy accident, in the wake of two empires, of its world-
wide currency. But what I am conscious of doting on is not English *per se,*
its pliable grammar and abundant synonyms, but its potential, for the
space of some phrases or paragraphs, of becoming reality, of engendering
out of imitation another reality, infinitely lesser but thoroughly possessed,
thoroughly human.

Pascal says, "When a natural discourse paints a passion or an effect, one
feels within oneself the truth of what one reads, which was there before,
although one did not know it. Hence one is inclined to love him who
makes us feel it, for he has not shown us his own riches, but ours." The

---

* As, say, by Iris Murdoch, in the 1972 Blashfield Address.

writer's strength is not his own; he is a conduit who so positions himself that the world at his back flows through to the readers on the other side of the page. To keep this conduit scoured is his laborious task; to be, in the act of writing, anonymous, the end of his quest for fame.

Beginning, then, with cunning private ambitions and a childish fascination with the implements of graphic representation, I find myself arrived, in this audible search for self-justification, at an embarrassed altruism. Beginning with the wish to make an impression, one ends wishing to erase the impression, to make of it a perfect transparency, to make of oneself a point of focus purely, as selfless as a lens. One begins by seeking celebrity and ends by feeling a terrible impatience with everything—every flattering attention, every invitation to speak and to impersonate a wise man, every hunger of the ego and of the body—an impatience with everything that clouds and clots our rapt witness to the world that surrounds and transcends us. A writer begins with his personal truth, with that obscure but vulnerable and, once lost, precious life that he lived before becoming a writer; but, those first impressions discharged—a process of years—he finds himself, though empty, still posed in the role of a writer, with it may be an expectant audience of sorts and certainly a habit of communion. It is then that he dies as a writer, and becomes an inert cultural object merely, or is born again, by resubmitting his ego, as it were, to fresh drafts of experience and refined operations of his mind. *To remain interested*—of American novelists, only Henry James continued in old age to advance his art; most, indeed, wrote their best novels first, or virtually first. Energy ebbs as we live; success breeds disillusion as surely as failure; the power of hope to generate action and vision lessens. Almost alone the writer can reap profit from this loss. An opportunity to sing louder from within the slackening ego is his. For his song has never been all his own: he has been its excuse as much as its source. The little tyrant's delight in wielding a pencil always carried with it an empathy into the condition of *being* a pencil; more and more the writer thinks of himself as an instrument, a means whereby a time and a place make their mark. To become less and transmit more, to replenish energy with wisdom—some such hope, at this more than mid-point of my life, is the reason why I write.

The Lesson of the Master

CYNTHIA OZICK

There was a period in my life—to purloin a famous Jamesian title, "The Middle Years"—when I used to say, with as much ferocity as I could muster, "I hate Henry James and I wish he was dead."

I was not to have my disgruntled way. The dislike did not last and turned once again to adoration, ecstasy, and awe; and no one is more alive than Henry James, or more likely to sustain literary immortality. He is among the angels, as he meant to be.

But in earlier days I felt I had been betrayed by Henry James. I was like the youthful writer in "The Lesson of the Master" who believed in the Master's call to live immaculately, unspoiled by what we mean when we say "life"—relationship, family mess, distraction, exhaustion, anxiety, above all disappointment. Here is the Master, St. George, speaking to his young disciple, Paul Overt:

> "One has no business to have any children," St. George placidly declared. "I mean, of course, if one wants to do anything good."
> "But aren't they an inspiration—an incentive?"
> "An incentive to damnation, artistically speaking."

And later Paul inquires:

> "Is it deceptive that I find you living with every appearance of domestic felicity—blest with a devoted, accomplished wife, with children whose acquaintance I haven't yet had the pleasure of making, but who *must* be delightful young people, from what I know of their parents?"
> St. George smiled as for the candour of his question. "It's all excellent, my dear fellow—heaven forbid I should deny it. . . . I've got a loaf on the shelf; I've got everything in fact but the great thing."
> "And the great thing?" Paul kept echoing.
> "The sense of having done the best—the sense which is the real life of the artist and the absence of which is his death, of having drawn from his intellectual instrument the finest music that nature had hidden in it, of having played it as it

should be played. He either does that or he doesn't—and if he doesn't he isn't worth speaking of."

Paul pursues:

> "Then what did you mean . . . by saying that children are a curse?"
> "My dear youth, on what basis are we talking?" and St. George dropped upon the sofa at a short distance from him. . . . "On the supposition that a certain perfection's possible and even desirable—isn't it so? Well, all I say is that one's children interfere with perfection. One's wife interferes. Marriage interferes."
> "You think, then, the artist shouldn't marry?"
> "He does so at his peril—he does so at his cost."

Yet the Master who declares all this is himself profoundly, inextricably, married; and when his wife dies, he hastens to marry again, choosing Life over Art. Very properly James sees marriage as symbol and summary of the passion for ordinary human entanglement, as experience of the most commonplace, most fated kind.

But we are also given to understand, in the desolation of this comic tale, that the young artist, the Master's trusting disciple, is left both perplexed and bereft: the Master's second wife is the young artist's first love, and the Master has stolen away his disciple's chance for ordinary human entanglement.

So the Lesson of the Master is a double one: choose ordinary human entanglement, and live; or choose Art, and give up the vitality of life's passions and panics and endurances. What I am going to tell now is a stupidity, a misunderstanding, a great Jamesian life-mistake: an embarrassment and a life-shame. (Imagine that we are in one of those lavishly adorned Jamesian chambers where intimate confessions not accidentally but suspensefully take place.) As I have said, I felt myself betrayed by a Jamesian trickery. Trusting in James, believing, like Paul Overt, in the overtness of the Jamesian lesson, I chose Art, and ended by blaming Henry James. It seemed to me James had left out the one important thing I ought to have known, even though he was saying it again and again. The trouble was that I was listening to the Lesson of the Master at the wrong time, paying powerful and excessive attention at the wrong time; and this cost me my youth.

I suppose a case can be made that it is certainly inappropriate for anyone to moan about the loss of youth and how it is all Henry James's fault. All of us will lose our youth, and some of us, alas, have lost it already; but not all of us will pin the loss on Henry James.

I, however, do. I blame Henry James.

Never mind the sublime position of Henry James in American letters. Never mind the Jamesian prose style—never mind that it, too, is sublime, nuanced, imbricated with a thousand distinctions and observations (the reason H.G. Wells mocked it), and as idiosyncratically and ecstatically red-olent of the spirals of past and future as a garlic clove. Set aside also the Jamesian impatience with idols, the moral seriousness active both in the work and the life. (I am thinking, for example, of Edith Wharton's compliance in the face of their mutual friend Paul Bourget's anti-Semitism and James's noble and definitive dissent.) Neglect all this, including every other beam that flies out from the stupendous Jamesian lantern to keep generations reading in rapture (which is all right), or else scribbling away at dissertation after dissertation (which is not so good). I myself, after all, committed a Master's thesis, long ago, called "Parable in Henry James," in which I tried to catch up all of James in the net of a single idea. Before that, I lived many months in the black hole of a microfilm cell, transcribing every letter James ever wrote to Mr. Pinker, his London agent, for a professorial book; but the professor drank, and died, and after thirty years the letters still lie in the dark.

All that while I sat cramped in that black bleak microfilm cell, and all that while I was writing that thesis, James was sinking me and despoiling my youth, and I did not know it.

I want, parenthetically, to recommend to the Henry James Society—there is such an assemblage—that membership be limited: no one under age forty-two-and-three-quarters need apply. Proof of age via birth certificate should be mandatory; otherwise the consequences may be harsh and horrible. I offer myself as an Extreme and Hideous Example of Premature Exposure to Henry James. I was about seventeen, I recall, when my brother brought home from the public library a science fiction anthology, which, through an odd perspective that perplexes me still, included "The Beast in the Jungle." It was in this anthology, and at that age, that I first read James—fell, I should say, into the jaws of James. I had never heard of him before. I read "The Beast in the Jungle" and creepily thought: here, here is my autobiography.

From that time forward, gradually but compellingly—and now I yield my scary confession—I became Henry James. Leaving graduate school at the age of twenty-two, disdaining the Ph.D. as an acquisition surely beneath the concerns of literary seriousness, I was already Henry James. When I say I "became" Henry James, you must understand this: though I was a near-sighted twenty-two-year-old young woman infected with the commonplace intention of writing a novel, I was *also* the elderly bald-headed Henry James. Even without close examination, you could see the light glancing off my pate; you could see my heavy chin, my watch-chain, my walking stick, my tender paunch.

I had become Henry James, and for years and years I remained Henry James. There was no doubt about it: it was my own clear and faithful truth. Of course, there were some small differences: for one thing, I was not a genius. For another, even in my own insignificant scribbler class, I was not prolific. But I carried the Jamesian idea, I was of his cult, I was a worshipper of literature, literature was my single altar; I was, like the elderly bald-headed James, a priest at that altar; and that altar was all of my life. Like John Marcher in "The Beast in the Jungle," I let everything pass me by for the sake of waiting for the Beast to spring—but unlike John Marcher, I knew what the Beast was, I knew exactly, I even knew the Beast's name: the Beast was literature itself, the sinewy grand undulations of some unraveling fiction, meticulously dreamed out in a language of masterly resplendence, which was to pounce on me and turn me into an enchanted and glorious Being, as enchanted and glorious as the elderly bald-headed Henry James himself.

But though the years spent themselves extravagantly, that ambush never occurred: the ambush of Sacred and Sublime Literature. The great shining Beast of Sacred and Sublime Literature did not pounce. Instead, other beasts, lesser ones, unseemly and misshapen, sprang out—all the beasts of ordinary life: sorrow, disease, death, guilt, responsibility, envy, grievance, grief, disillusionment—the beasts that are chained to human experience, and have nothing to do with Art except to interrupt and impede it, exactly according to the Lesson of the Master.

It was not until I read a certain vast and subtle book that I understood what had happened to me. The book was not by Henry James, but about him. Nowadays we give this sort of work a special name: we call it a nonfiction novel. I am referring, of course, to Leon Edel's ingenious and beautiful biography of Henry James, which is as much the possession of Edel's imagination as it is of the exhilaratingly reported facts of James's life. In Edel's rendering, I learned what I had never before taken in—but the knowledge came, in the Jamesian way, too late. What I learned was that Henry James himself had not always been the elderly bald-headed Henry James!—that he, too, had once been twenty-two years old.

This terrible and secret knowledge instantly set me against James. From that point forward I was determined to eradicate him. And for a long while I succeeded.

What had happened was this: in early young womanhood I believed, with all the rigor and force and stunned ardor of religious belief, in the old

Henry James, in his scepter and his authority. I believed that what *he* knew at sixty I was to encompass at twenty-two; at twenty-two I lived like the elderly bald-headed Henry James. I thought it was necessary—it was imperative, there was no other path!—to be, all at once, with no progression or evolution, the author of the equivalent of *The Ambassadors* or *The Wings of the Dove,* just as if "A Bundle of Letters," or "Four Meetings," or the golden little "The Europeans" had never preceded the great late Master.

For me, the Lesson of the Master was a horror, a Jamesian tale of a life of mishap and mistake and misconceiving. Though the Master himself was saying, in *The Ambassadors,* in Gloriani's garden, to Little Bilham, through the urgent cry of Strether, "Live, live!"—and though the Master himself was saying, in "The Beast in the Jungle," through May Bartram, how ghastly, how ghostly, it is to eschew, to evade, to turn from, to miss absolutely and irrevocably what is all the time there for you to seize—I mistook him, I misheard him, I missed, absolutely and irrevocably, his essential note. What I heard instead was: *Become a Master.*

Now the truth is it could not have been done, even by a writer of genius; and what a pitiful flicker of the flame of high ambition for a writer who is no more than the ordinary article! No one—not even James himself—springs all at once in early youth into full Mastery, and no writer, whether robustly gifted, or only little and pale, should hope for this implausible fate.

All this, I suppose, is not at all a "secret" knowledge, as I have characterized it, but is, rather, as James named it in the very person of his naive young artist, most emphatically *overt*—so obvious that it is a mere access of foolishness even to talk about it. Still, I offer the implausible and preposterous model of myself to demonstrate the proposition that the Lesson of the Master is not a lesson about genius, or even about immense ambition; it is a lesson about misreading—about what happens when we misread the great voices of Art, and suppose that, because they speak of Art, they *mean* Art. The great voices of Art never mean *only* Art; they also mean Life, they always mean Life, and Henry James, when he evolved into the Master we revere, finally meant nothing else.

The true Lesson of the Master, then, is, simply, never to venerate what is complete, burnished, whole, in its grand organic flowering or finish—never to look toward the admirable and dazzling end; never to be ravished by the goal; never to worship ripe Art or the ripened artist; but instead to seek to be young while young, primitive while primitive, ungainly when ungainly—to look for crudeness and rudeness, to husband one's own stupidity or ungenius.

There *is* this mix-up most of us have between ourselves and what we admire or triumphantly cherish. We see this mix-up, this mishap, this mishmash, most often in writers: the writer of a new generation ravished by the genius writer of a classical generation, who begins to dream herself, or himself, as powerful, vigorous and original—as if being filled up by the genius writer's images, scenes, and stratagems were the same as having the capacity to pull off the identical magic. To be any sort of competent writer one must keep one's psychological distance from the supreme artists.

If I were twenty-two now, I would not undertake a cannibalistically ambitious Jamesian novel to begin with; I would look into the eyes of Henry James at twenty-two, and see the diffident hope, the uncertainty, the marveling tentativeness, the dream that is still only a dream; the young man still learning to fashion the Scene. Or I would go back still further, to the boy of seventeen, misplaced in a Swiss Polytechnic School, who re-called in old age that "I so feared and abhorred mathematics that the sim-plest arithmetical operation had always found and kept me helpless and blank." It is not to the Master in his fullness I would give my awed, stricken, desperate fealty, but to the faltering, imperfect, dreaming youth.

If these words should happen to reach the ears of any young writer dumbstruck by the elderly bald-headed Henry James, one who has hun-grily heard and ambitiously assimilated the voluptuous cathedral-tones of the developed organ-master, I would say to her or him: put out your lean and clumsy forefinger and strike your paltry, oafish, feeble, simple, skele-tal, single note. Try for what Henry James at sixty would scorn—just as he scorned the work of his own earliness, and revised it and revised it in the manner of his later pen in that grand chastisement of youth known as the New York Edition. Trying, in youth, for what the Master in his mastery would condemn—that is the only road to modest mastery. Rapture and homage are not the way. Influence is perdition.

Some Questions and Answers

SAUL BELLOW

Q. How do you, a novelist from Chicago, fit yourself into American Life?
Is there a literary world to which you belong?

A. When I entered the Restaurant Voltaire in Paris with the novelist Louis
Guilloux some years ago, the waiter addressed him as "Maître." I didn't
know whether to envy him or to smile. No one had ever treated me so
reverentially. And as a student I had sat in Chicago reading of *salons* and
cénacles, of evenings at Magny's with Flaubert and Turgeniev and Sainte-
Beuve—reading and sighing. What glorious times! But Guilloux himself,
a Breton and a former leftwinger, seemed uncomfortable with his title. It
may be that even in Paris literary culture is now preserved by smarmy
headwaiters. I am not altogether sure of that. What is certain is that we
have nothing like it in America—no Maîtres except in dining rooms, no
literary world, no literary public. Many of us read, many love literature but
the traditions and institutions of literary culture are lacking. I do not say
that this is bad, I only state it as a fact that ours is not a society which
creates such things. Any modern country that has not inherited them simply does not have them.

American writers are not neglected, they mingle occasionally with the
great, they may even be asked to the White House but no one there will
talk literature to them. Mr. Nixon disliked writers and refused flatly to
have them in, but Mr. Ford has invited them together with actors, musicians, television newscasters and politicians. On these great evenings the
East Room fills with celebrities who become ecstatic at the sight of other
celebrities. Secretary Kissinger and Danny Kaye fall into each other's
arms. Cary Grant is surrounded by Senators' wives who find him wonderfully preserved, as handsome in the flesh as on film, and they can hardly
bear the excitement of personal contact with greatness. People speak of
their diets, of travel and holidays, of vitamins and the problems of aging.
Questions of language or style, the structure of novels, trends in painting

are not discussed. The writer finds this a wonderful Pop occasion. Senator Fulbright seems almost to recognize his name and says, "You write essays, don't you? I think I can remember one of them." But the Senator, as everyone knows, was once a Rhodes Scholar.

It is actually pleasant on such an evening for a writer to pass half disembodied and unmolested by small talk from room to room, looking and listening. He knows that active public men can't combine government with literature, art and philosophy. Theirs is a world of high-tension wires not of primroses on the river's brim. Ten years ago Mayor Daley in a little City Hall ceremony gave me a five hundred dollar check on behalf of the Midland Authors' Society. "Mr. Mayor, have you read *Herzog?*" asked one of the reporters standing by. "I've looked into it," said Daley, yielding no ground. Art is not the Mayor's dish. But then why should it be? I much prefer his neglect to the sort of interest Stalin took in poetry, phoning Pasternak to chat with him about Mandelstam and, shortly afterwards, sending Mandelstam to die.

Q. Are you saying that a modern industrial society dismisses art?

A. Not at all. Art is one of those good things towards which it feels friendly. It is quite receptive. But what Ruskin said about the English public in 1871 applies perfectly to us. "No reading is possible for a people with its mind in this state. No sentence of any great writer is intelligible to them." Ruskin blames avarice. ". . . so incapable of thought has it [the public] become in its insanity of avarice. Happily, our disease is, as yet, little worse than this incapacity of thought; it is not corruption of the inner nature; we ring true still, when anything strikes home to us . . . though the idea that everything should 'pay' has infected our every purpose so deeply . . . ."

Q. You don't see avarice as the problem, do you?

A. No. "A people with its mind in this state," is where I lay the stress. We are in a peculiarly revolutionary state, a critical state that never ends. Yesterday I came upon a description of a medical technique for bringing patients to themselves. They are exposed for some minutes to high-frequency sounds until they are calm enough to think and to feel out their symptoms. To possess your soul in peace for a few moments you need the help of medical technology. It is easy to observe in bars, at dinner tables, everywhere, that from flop house to White House Americans are preoccupied by the same questions. Our own American life is our passion, our social and national life against a world background, an immense spectacle presented daily by the papers and the television networks—our cities, our crime, our housing, our automobiles, our sports, our weather, our technology, our politics, our problems of sex and race and diplomacy and international relations. These realities are real enough. But what of the formulae, the jargon, the principles of selection the media prefer? TV creates the exciting fictions, the heightened and dramatized shadow events accepted by the great public and believed by almost everyone to be real. Is reading possible for a people with its mind in this state?

Q. Still a book of good quality can find a hundred thousand readers. But you say that there is no literary public.

A. An influential book appears to create its own public. When *Herzog* was published I became aware that there were some fifty thousand people in the United States who wanted to read my novel. They had evidently been waiting for something like it. Other writers have certainly had the same experience. But such a public is a temporary one. There is no literary culture that permanently contains all of these readers. Remarkably steady and intelligent people emerge from the heaving wastes of the American educational system. They survive by strength, luck and cunning.

Q. What do they do while waiting for the next important event?

A. Exactly. What can they read month in, month out? In what journals do they keep up with what matters in contemporary literature?

Q. What about the universities? Haven't they done anything to train judgment and develop taste?

A. To most Professors of English a novel is an object of the highest cultural importance. Its ideas, its symbolic structure, its position in the history of Romanticism or Realism or Modernism, its higher relevance require devout study. But what has this sort of cultural study to do with novelists and readers? What they want is the living moment, they want men and women alive, and a circumambient world. The teaching of literature has been a disaster. Between the student and the book he reads lies a gloomy preparatory region, a perfect swamp. He must cross this cultural swamp before he is allowed to open his *Moby Dick* and read, "Call me Ishmael." He is made to feel ignorant before masterpieces, unworthy, he is frightened and repelled. And if the method succeeds it produces B.A.'s who can tell you why the *Pequod* leaves port on Christmas morning. What else can they tell you? No feeling for the book has been communicated, only a lot of pseudolearned interpretation. What has been substituted for the novel itself is what can be said about the novel by the "educated." Some professors find educated discourse of this kind more interesting by far than novels. They take the attitude towards fiction that one of the Church Fathers took towards the Bible. Origen of Alexandria asked whether we were really to imagine that God walked in a Garden while Adam and Eve hid under a bush. Scripture could not be taken literally. It must yield higher meanings.

Q. Are you equating Church Fathers with Professors of Literature?

A. Not exactly. The Fathers had sublime conceptions of God and Man. If Professors of Humanities were moved by the sublimity of the poets and philosophers they teach they would be the most powerful men in the university and the most fervent. But they are at the lower end of the hierarchy, at the bottom of the pile.

Q. Then why are there so many writers at the universities?

A. A good question. Writers have no independent ground to stand on. They belong to institutions. They work for newsmagazines and publishing houses, for cultural foundations, advertising agencies, television networks. And they teach. There are only a few literary journals left and those are now academic quarterlies. The big national magazines don't want to publish fiction. Their editors want to discuss only the most significant national and international questions and concentrate on "relevant" cultural matters. By "relevant" they mean political. The "real" questions facing us are questions of business and politics—energy, war, sex, race, cities, education, technology, ecology, the fate of the automobile industry, the Middle East crisis, the dominoes of Southeast Asia, the moves of the Russian politburo. These are, of course, matters of the highest importance. More accurately, there are questions of life and death at the heart of such important public matters. But these life and death questions are not discussed. What we hear and read is crisis-chatter. And it is the business of the cultural-intelligentsia (professors, commentators, editors) to produce such chatter. Our intelligentsia, completely politicized and analytical in temper, does not take much interest in literature. The members of this elite *had* literature in their student days and are now well beyond it. At Harvard or Columbia they read, studied, absorbed the classics, especially the modernist classics. These prepared them for the important, the essential, the incomparable tasks they were destined to perform as functionaries in the media, the managers of scores of new enterprises. Sometimes I sense that they feel they have replaced writers. The cultural business they do is tinged by literature, or rather the memory of literature. I said before that our common life had become our most passionate concern. Can an individual, the subject of a novel, compete in interest with corporate destinies, with the rise of a new class, a cultural intelligentsia?

Q. Do you suggest that when we become so extremely politicized we lose interest in the individual?

A. Exactly. And that a liberal society so intensely political can't remain liberal for very long. I take it for granted that an attack on the novel is also an attack on liberal principles. I view "activist" art theories in the same way. The power of a true work of art is such that it induces a temporary suspension of activities. It leads to contemplative states, to wonderful and, to my mind, sacred states of the soul.

Q. And what you call crisis-chatter creates a contrary condition?

A. I should like to add that the truth is not loved because it is *better* for us. We hunger and thirst for it. And the appetite for truthful books is greater than ever, sharpened by privation.

Q. To return for a moment to the subject of a literary world . . .

A. No tea at Gertrude Stein's, no Closerie de Lilas, no Bloomsbury evenings, no charming and wicked encounters between George Moore and W. B. Yeats. Reading of such things is very pleasant indeed. I can't say that I miss them, because I never knew anything like them. I miss certain dead friends. Writers. That Molière put on the plays of Corneille, that Louis XIV himself may have appeared, disguised, in one of Molière's farces—such facts are lovely to read in books. I'd hardly expect Mayor Daley to take part in any farce of mine. He performs in his own farces only. I have, however, visited writers' clubs in Communist countries and can't say that I'm sorry we have no such institutions here. When I was in Addis Ababa I went to the Emperor's Zoo. As Selassie was the Lion of Judah he was perhaps bound to keep a large collection of lions. These poor animals lay in the filth of dim green cages too small for pacing, mere coops. The leonine brown of their eyes had turned blank and yellow, their heads were on their paws and they were sighing. Bad as things are here they are not so bad as in the Emperor's Zoo or in writers' centers behind the Iron Curtain.

A. Not so bad is not the same as good. What of the disadvantages of your condition?

A. There are moments of sorrow, I admit. George Sand wrote to Flaubert, in a collection of letters I looked into the other day, that she hoped he would bring his copy of her latest book on his next visit. "Put in it all the criticisms which occur to you," she said. "That will be very good for me. People ought to do that for each other as Balzac and I used to do. That doesn't make one person alter the other; quite the contrary, for in general one gets more determined in one's *moi*, one completes it, explains it better, entirely develops it, and that is why friendship is good, even in literature, where the first condition of any worth is to be one's self." How nice it would be to hear this from a writer. But no such letters arrive. Friendships and a common purpose belong to a nineteenth-century French dream world. The physicist Heisenberg in a recent article in *Encounter* speaks of the kindly and even brotherly collaboration among scientists of the generation of Einstein and Bohr. Their personal letters were quoted in seminars and discussed by the entire scientific community. Heisenberg believes that in the musical world something of the same spirit appeared in the eighteenth century. Haydn's relations with Mozart were of this generous affectionate kind. But when large creative opportunities are lacking there is no generosity visible. Heisenberg says nothing about the malice and hostility of less lucky times. Writers today seldom wish other writers well. Critics use strength gathered from the past to pummel the present. Edmund Wilson wouldn't read his contemporaries at all. He stopped with Eliot and Hemingway. The rest he dismissed. This lack of goodwill, to put it at its mildest, was much admired. That fact speaks for itself. Curious about Canadians, Indians, Haitians, Russians, studying Marxism and the Dead Sea scrolls, he was the Protestant majority's big literary figure. I have sometimes thought that he was challenged by Marxism or Modernism in the same way that I have seen the descendants of Orthodox Jews challenged by oysters. Historical progress demands that our revulsions be overcome. A man like Wilson might have done much to strengthen literary culture, but he dismissed all that, he would have nothing to do with it. For temperamental reasons. Or Protestant majority reasons. Or perhaps the Heisenberg principle applies—men are generous when there are creative opportunities, and when such opportunities dwindle they are . . . something else. But it would have made little difference.

At this moment in human evolution, so miraculous, atrocious, glorious and hellish, the firmly established literary cultures of France and England, Italy and Germany can originate nothing. They look to us, to the "disadvantaged" Americans, and to the Russians. From America have come a number of great irrepressible solitaries like Poe or Melville or Whitman, alcoholics, obscure government employees. In busy America there was no Weimar, there were no cultivated princes. There were only these obstinate geniuses writing—why? For whom? There is the real *acte gratuite* for you. Unthanked, these writers augmented life marvelously. They did not emerge from a literary culture nor did they create any such thing. Irrepressible individuals of a similar type have lately begun to show themselves in Russia. There Stalinism utterly destroyed a thriving literary culture and replaced it with a horrible bureaucracy. But in spite of this and in spite of forced labor and murder the feeling for what is true and just has not been put out. I don't see, in short, why we should continue to dream of what we have never had. To have it would not help us. Perhaps if we were to purge ourselves of nostalgia and stopped longing for a literary world we would see a fresh opportunity to extend the imagination and resume imaginative contact with nature and society.

Q. Other people, scholars and scientists, know a great deal about nature and society. More than you know.

A. True. And I suppose I sound like a fool but I nevertheless object that their knowledge is defective—something is lacking. That something poetry. Huizinga, the Dutch historian, in his recently published book on America says that the learned Americans he met in the Twenties could speak fluently and stimulatingly, but he adds, "More than once I could not recognize in what he wrote the living man who had held my interest. Frequently repeated experience makes me hold the view that my personal reaction to American scholarly prose must still rest upon the qualities of the prose itself. I read it with the greatest difficulty; I have no sense of contact with it and cannot keep my attention fixed on it. It is for me as if I had to do with a deviant system of expression in which the concepts are not equivalent to mine, or are arranged differently." The system has become more deviant during the last fifty years. I want information and ideas, and I know that certain highly trained and intelligent people have it—economists, sociologists, lawyers, historians, natural scientists. But I read them with the greatest difficulty, exasperated, tormented, despairing. And I say to myself, "These writers are part of the educated public, your readers. You make your best efforts for them, these unpoetic or antipoetic people. You've forgotten Ortega's philistine professional, the educated Mass Man . . . etcetera." But none of this matters. Philistine intellectuals don't make you stop writing. Writing is your *acte gratuite*. Besides, those you address are there. If you exist, then they exist. You can be more certain of their existence than of your own.

Q. But whether or not a literary culture exists . . .

A. Excuse me for interrupting but it occurs to me that Tolstoi would probably have approved of this and seen new opportunities in it. He had no use for literary culture and detested professionalism in the arts.

Q. But should writers make their peace with the academic Ivory Tower?

A. In his essay "Bethink Yourselves" Tolstoi advises each man to begin at the point at which he finds himself. Better such Towers than the Cellar alternatives some writers choose. Besides, the university is no more an Ivory Tower than *Time* magazine with its strangely artificial approach to the world, its remote-making managerial arrangements. A writer is offered more money, bigger pensions, richer security-plans by Luce enterprises than by any university. The Ivory Tower is one of those platitudes that haunt the uneasy minds of writers. Since we have none of the advantages of a literary world we may as well free ourselves from its banalities. Spiritual independence requires that we bethink ourselves. The university is as good a place for such thinking as any other. But while we think hard about the next step we should avoid becoming academics. Teachers, yes. Some are even moved to become scholars. The great danger for writers in the university is the academic danger.

Q. Can you conveniently give a brief definition of academic?

A. I limit myself arbitrarily to a professorial type to be found in the Humanities. Owen Barfield refers in one of his books to "the everlasting professional device for substituting a plethora of *talk*" about what matters for—what actually matters. He is sick of it, he says. Many of us are sick of it.

A Diarist on Diarists

GAIL GODWIN

This inescapable duty to observe oneself: if someone else is observing me, naturally I have to observe myself too; if none observes me, I have to observe myself all the closer.
—Kafka, *November 7, 1921*

I fall back on this journal just as some other poor devil takes to drink.
—Barbellion

I am enamoured of my journal.
—Sir Walter Scott

Diarists: that shrewdly innocent breed, those secret exhibitionists and incomparable purveyors of sequential, self-conscious life: how they fascinate me and endear themselves to me by what they say and do not say. If my friends kept diaries, and if I read them, would I know them as well as I know Kafka, standing in front of his mirror, playing with his hair? And Virginia Woolf, languishing because of a snide remark made about her novels by an undergraduate. And poor Dorothy Wordsworth, trying valiantly to stick to descriptions of sunsets while losing all her teeth. And Pepys, giving a colorful account of his latest fight with his wife. And Camus, coolly observing, "Whatever does not kill me strengthens me." Or plantation owner William Byrd, "dancing his dances" and "rogering his wife" (code words for bowel movements and sexual intercourse). Or the anonymous Irish scribe driven to confide into the margin of a medieval text: "I am very cold without fire or covering . . . the robin is singing gloriously, but though its red breast is beautiful I am all alone. Oh God be gracious to my soul and grant me a better handwriting."

In the old days everybody kept diaries. That's how we know that "Carlyle wandered down to tea looking dusky and aggrieved at having to live in such a generation": from Caroline Fox's diary; and that Henry James "kept up a perpetual vocal search for words even when he wasn't saying anything": from his nineteen-year-old nephew's diary; and that when Liszt played, he compressed his lips, dilated his nostrils and, when the music expressed quiet rapture, "a sweet smile flitted over his features": from George Eliot's diary. People came home from their dinners and visits and wrote down what others said and how the great men looked and who wore what and who made an ass or a pig of himself ("A little swinish at dinner," the diligent Dr. Rutty wrote of himself in his eighteenth-century diary). Those who stayed home alone also documented their evenings. ("I dined by myself and read an execrably stupid novel called 'Tylney Hall.' Why do I read such stuff?" wrote Macaulay.) Even a literate body-snatcher gave an account of himself before he turned in at night: "March 16, 1812, Went to Harps got 3 Large and 1 Large Small, 1 Small & 1 Foetus, took 2 Large to St. Thomas's, 1 Large to Guy's."

Are there fewer diarists now? It seems so, to me, but perhaps I'm unusual in that I have not one friend who keeps a diary—or at least who admits to it. Sometimes I'll happen upon a diarist and we greet each other like lonely explorers. Last spring I discovered a fellow diarist over lunch, and what a time we had discussing the intricacies of our venture-in-common, our avocation . . . specialty . . . compulsion? We confessed eccentricities (he has a pseudonymn for the self that gambles; I often reread old journals and make notes to my former selves in the margin). We examined our motives: why keep these records, year after year? What would happen if we stopped? *Could* we stop? We indulged in shop-talk: hardbound or softcover? lined or unlined? about how many pages a night? proportion of external events to internal? Did one write more on bad days than on good? More or less on quiet days? (More, we both decided.) Did we feel honor-bound to report in at night, even when exhausted—or intoxicated? Ah, it was a good lunch we had.

"I should live no more than I can record, as one should not have more corn growing than one can get at. There is a waste of good if it be not preserved." This, from Boswell, expresses the aspect of duty that many diarists typically feel. Queen Victoria continued her diary strictly as a duty from the age of thirteen to eighty-two. Unfortunately, much of it reads like it. Many diaries, left by long-forgotten owners in attic trunks, describe neither affairs of state nor the table talk of great geniuses nor the growing pains of profound souls. But a sense of *accountability* emanates from these old books. ("Went with Maud to Chok's for a soda. J. L. lost two heifers from shipping disease . . . nothing of interest to record today.") Man and woman were beholden to the *recording* of God's hours, be they interesting or not.

No mighty deeds, just common things,
The tasks and pleasures each day brings.
And yet I hope that when I look
Over the pages of this book,
Twill be (and, if so, I'm content)
The record of five years well spent.

This, from the title page of my mother's college diary, offers captured memory as incentive to daily diligence. *Nulla dies sine linea,* it orders, and my mother obeyed, detailing in tiny handwriting, in a variety of inks, the social and mental highlights of 1932–36. People seemed to go to the movies every day, sometimes twice in one day. They ate a lot of spaghetti—but, of course, there was a Depression. No longer a diarist, my mother offered the little blue and gold book to me (we had to pick the lock—she had no idea it was even hers until we opened it). Her parents had given her the five-year diary as a going-away present for college, and she felt she owed it to them to write in it. I'm glad she did. How many daughters can read—in purple ink—about the night they were conceived?

Now I'm the only practicing diarist in my family. Not one of my friends keeps a diary, as I've mentioned. "To tell the truth, I've never thought I was that interesting," says one. "I'm not a *writer,*" says another. A third writes letters, sometimes three or four every evening, and says this serves the purpose of a diary. Another person who is a very prolific writer has advised me to "put all that material into stories rather than hide it in your journals. When you feel haunted or sad, write a story about a person, not necessarily yourself, who feels haunted or sad. Because, you see, it's the feelings that are universal, not the person."

Art, fiction, if it is to be public, must tap the universal. A diary by its very nature is the unfolding of the private, personal story—whether that story be told from a distance (the "I" in a political diary, observing affairs of state; the "I" in the captain's log, marking latitude, longitude, and the moods of the sea) or with the subjectivity of a person whose politics and moods and sea-changes exist inside his own head. I need to write a diary, just as I need to write fiction, but the two needs come from very different sources. I write fiction because I need to organize the clutter of too many details into some meaning, because I enjoy turning something promising into something marvelous; I keep a diary because it keeps my mind fresh and open. Once the details of being me are safely stored away every night, I can get on with what isn't just me. So, as I explained to my friend, the fictional and the diary-making processes are not interchangeable. I had to keep a diary for many years before I could begin writing fiction.

Like Victoria, I, too, began keeping track of my days at the age of thirteen. But it was not because I felt the young queen, whose comings and goings would one day be read by the world. Nor did anyone make me a present of a sumptuous diary with a lock and key that cried out to be made the repository of secrets. I made my first diary, with half-sheets of notebook paper, cardboard, and yarn, and I wrote in it passionately, because I felt there was nobody else like me and I had to know why—or why not. "I don't believe people exist whose inner plight resembles mine; still, it is possible for me to imagine such people—but that the secret raven forever flaps about their head as it does about mine, even to imagine that is impossible." That is Kafka at thirty-eight, speaking for me at thirteen—and for diarists not yet born.

There are many books about diarists, and some of them make fascinating reading. What is odd, however, is that many of the authors do not seem to be diarists themselves: they write with the air of scientists, observing this peculiar organism called a "diarist" from the other side of a polished lens. F. A. Spalding states in *Self-Harvest, a Study of Diaries and Diarists* that we seldom if ever find development within the individual diary, either in what is recorded or in the manner of recording it. Also that "diarists who hope to aid memory continue to the end to complain of the lack of it." Also that diaries do not seem to teach diarists "how the better to spend my time for the future," even if they read over their diaries, "and few do so." Spalding also says that, except for Scott and Byron, "there is hardly an example of a diary written out of a first class creative mind." "We cannot imagine a Shakespeare keeping a diary," he says. In fairness to Mr. Spalding, he wrote his book before access to the Kafka diaries was possible—or Virginia Woolf's; though maybe he wouldn't have considered these writers first class creative minds. As for Shakespeare, that enigma, who can say with certainty whether he did not jot down his moods and plots for plays into a little book that lies crumbling in the earth or awaiting its finder in some forgotten cranny?

Every true diarist knows that having a relationship with a diary is like having a relationship with anyone or anything else: the longer it lasts, the more it is bound to change. When I began my diary, at age thirteen, I traversed that naked space between my mind and my little book's pages as hesitantly as a virgin approaching a man who may or may not prove trustworthy. Now, two-and-a-half decades later, my diary and I have an old marriage. The space between us is gone. I hardly *see* my diary anymore. And yet, there is a confident sense that we are working together. We have been down many roads together, my diary and I (I used the singular, but what I call "my diary" resides in many separate books—some of them lost, others maimed or destroyed [more on this later]), and I have been neglectful and insincere and offhand and have not always shown respect in regard to this fellow-traveler of mine. In adolescence, I weighed him down with feelings of gloom and doom; in late teens, I wasted his pages cataloguing the boys who fell into, or eluded, my snare; in my twenties, I drove him to near death-from-boredom with my lists of resolutions, budgets, and abortive plans for "the future." Sometimes I shunned the sight of him, and I wrote my secrets on sheets of loose paper—not wanting to be bound by him—and, of course, those pages are now lost. In my thirties, as my craft of fiction was consolidated and I felt I had "something of my own," I returned to him with new respect. I told him when good things happened, and shared ideas for future work. As I became less trapped in my universe of moods and recognized my likeness to other people and other things in the universe-at-large, my entries began to include more space. Now there are animals and flowers and sunsets in my diary, as well as other people's problems. As a rule, I complain less and describe more; even my complaints I try to lace with memorable description, because . . . yes, Mr. Spalding, diarists do reread their diaries, and how many times I have exclaimed aloud with rage when I looked up a year or a day, hoping to catch the fever or the flavor of the past, and found only a meager, grudging, "I feel awful today." So now I write for my future self, as well as my present mood. And sometimes, to set the record straight, I jot down a word or two in old diaries to my former self—to encourage, to scold, to correct, or to set things in perspective.

As for memory, I don't complain of the lack of it or use my diary to improve it, as Mr. S. would have me do. It is rather that I know one of us has it—my diary or me—and so, if I can't remember something, I look it up. (Though, as I've said, sometimes nothing's there except a mood nobody wants anymore.) Yet, though I frequently look things up, or sometimes browse through a year, I have never read my diaries straight through, and possibly never will. I have tried, a couple of times, but there are simply too many of them, and, after a while, I get the peculiar dizziness that comes from watching a moving train while on another moving train. One cannot live two lives at once, for long periods of time.

Early, or late, there comes a time in every diarist's life when he asks himself: "What if someone should read this?" If he truly recoils at the thought, he might take measures to prevent it, writing in cipher like Pepys, or in mirror-writing (da Vinci's notebooks) or in a mixture of foreign languages. One seventeenth-century schoolmaster wrote his diary in a notebook so small as to be illegible without a magnifying glass, the whole in abbreviated Latin. (The diary was four inches by two and a half inches; and there were seventy lines to the page!)

But far, far more prevalent, I think, is the breed of diarist who writes for *some* form of audience. This audience may be God, it may be a friendly (or unfriendly) spirit (witness the way some diarists must justify their self-contradictions and shortcomings); or it may be one's future self (at thirty-eight, Virginia Woolf wrote in her journal that she was hoping to entertain herself at fifty) or . . . in many cases, more often than we may care to admit . . . we write for some form of posterity. How many diarists can honestly say they have never once imagined their diaries being "discovered," either before or after their deaths? Many of us hope we will make good reading. (I occasionally catch myself "explaining," in my diary: putting in that extra bit of information that I know quite well but cannot expect a stranger to know.)

In *The Golden Notebook* Doris Lessing writes about a pair of lovers, each of whom keeps two diaries. It is understood tacitly between them that one diary must be "secretly read" but the second diary, the really private one, may not. Of course, one of the partners cheats and the couple is sundered forever because of this unpardonable breach. I know perfectly well that if I had a partner who kept a diary (or two diaries) I would probably cheat. Several times over my diary-keeping years, people have read my journals. Some sneaked and were caught (perhaps other sneaked and were not); a few let me know about it, in a variety of ways. One left a cheerful note: "Enjoy the halcyon days!" Another tore out a handful of pages. Another tossed the whole book into the Atlantic Ocean. On several occasions I have actually read parts of my diary aloud to someone. But too much "publicity" is destructive to a diary, because the diarist begins, unconsciously perhaps, to leave out, to tone down, to pep up, to falsify experience, and the *raison d'être* of the undertaking becomes buried beneath posings.

The prospect of people reading my diaries after I am dead does not disturb me in the least. I like to think of pooling myself with other introspective hearts: madmen (and women), prudes, profligates, celebrities, outcasts, heroes, artists, saints, the lovelorn and the lucky, the foolish and the proud. I have found so many sides of myself in the diaries of others. I would like it if I someday reflect future readers to themselves, provide them with examples, warnings, courage, amusement even. In these unedited glimpses of the self in others, of others in the self, is another proof of our ongoing survival, another of the covenants eternity makes with the day-to-day.

The Poetry of Everyday Life

JOHN HOLLANDER

The finest poetry was first experience; but the thought has suffered a transformation since it was an experience. Cultivated men often attain a good degree of skill in writing verses; but it is easy to read, through their poems, their personal history: any one acquainted with the parties can name every figure; this is Andrew and that is Rachel. The sense thus remains prosaic. It is a caterpillar with wings, and not yet a butterfly. In the poet's mind the fact has gone quite over into the new element of thought, and has lost all that is exuvial. . . .

—Emerson, "Shakespeare; or, The Poet"

I hope that my title is not too misleading, and this is just to say that by "the poetry of everyday life" I do not mean casual verses of the sort that W. C. Williams tacked up on the refrigerator door to explain the missing plums. (Mrs. Williams's longing might have been filled by a trope of the eaten fruit; Dr. Williams's excuse could never flower, in this case, into true poetry, but only literature.) That genre is indeed a common one, and no discussion of contemporary poetry could fail to remark upon it. But in these few pages I must forbear to discuss the everyday life of poetry in America—the secular religiosity which has overcome the production and reception of banal verse; the religiosity with which any printout with an unjustified right-hand edge is sanctified as poetry; the fashions—formal, gestural, ideological—into which falls the stuff, not of fiction or poetry, but of literary verse today. I shall treat of this in detail elsewhere; but even though it is late in the spring, and my dooryard is as yet unraked of last winter's leaves, I shall forgo the clearing away of the debris of last season's inane discourse to dig at one corner of the lawn, down to the heart of the matter. Analyzing the relations of journalism, religion, modernism's role in the formation of literary canons and college curricula, the rise and spread of inept free verse as the contemporary American replacement of inept rhymed jingle (even as an easy rusty irony has displaced an earlier sentimentality), the cultural politics of vulgarity generally—I shall attend to all this later. (And I must do it myself: there is no hiring of earnest students to do this work any more—even at outrageous wages—for none have been taught to know leaves or to hold a rake at the right angle.) For now, I shall dig at the poetry itself.

"The subject of a poem," said Hobbes, "is the manners of men, not natural causes." But the manners of men, and of women, is what contemporary verse, for all its mythological gestures and clichéd figures of pathos, is all about. We should rather reply to Hobbes that it is what lies between "the manners of men" and the "natural causes"—connecting, mediating, mutually transforming them—that is both the subject and object of poetry. All the rest is literature, as Verlaine declared after having insisted that poetry was music before all else—a symbolist song about poetry being trope before all else. In "the poetry of everyday life" we can take "of" in the sense of "about" or "on the subject of," and the whole phrase to denote some of this literature, reportage, versified journalism. But poetry is a matter of figuration; and I have made "of" in "the poetry of everyday life" to be genitive and attributive. In my phrase, I denote the poetry that everyday life *is*, rather than providing little topics and themes for. In order more immediately to distinguish literature about daily life from the poetry of it, I shall now direct the reader's attention to a number of examples of this poetry, and to some procedures for discerning it, momentarily free of its usual envelope, or carapace, or costume, or whatever its formal or casual literary duds.

Talking to Our Cats It is their very independence of us, their mythical self-sufficiency, which makes them so malleable, like language itself. They do not possess, but rather *are*, a kind of language, and one is always taking cats figuratively. We interpret them when we address, and then respond to, their silences, whereas we merely come to understand, without intervening fables, models, or metaphors, our dogs. Cats are named differently from dogs, not in that "Fido," "Rags," or "Spot" would be inappropriate (there are cats so named, cats who have been made clowns), but because feline names are never in a true grammatical vocative. Cats never respond to their *names* per se, as do dogs. Their names are the titles of poetic texts, the names of tropes, into which all of the uncharacterizable life of each particular cat seems to grow. We read the cat as we do an unfolding book, and our glossing of its invisible expressions is like moralizing a dark, pregnant myth. Our discourse is with a fable we have invented, albeit in order to explain one of the most compelling of presences, a domestic spirit. Its response to us, and ours to it, are both parts of a parable.

The Eternal Mutual Impingements of the Weather and Our Consciousness of It   That consciousness may or may not include a recognition of the traditional, proverbial givens of such impingements—the willowy arch of the long hair of the weeping girl, the rain falling in the heart of the rueful town. Reading the text of the book of daily life, in which the weather— and the separate sense we have of ourselves as living in its domain—are both major fictions, whether of person or of place: this is itself to write a new book. Which same may be heroic, as when we seem to be subjects of the weathery kingdom, living under the reign of a sunless king, or, in a later age, moving in the republic of our own sunlight. The force with which a fine day confirms our elation or mocks our despair is the same one with which a starry night causes even a caressing hand to shiver, or opens up the heavy atlas of understanding. There is no end to this mutual rereading, ours of the unending emblem of the weather, of the mysterious high- and low-pressure areas in ourselves.

Revelations of the Priority of Meaning   —And how American this is! We, whose surrounding waters were Lethean, who dwell among effacements of where we have been, must always feel that origins are secondary, are derived, and that what has descended from them is primary rather, and thereby prior. Our forebears are rooted in ourselves, trace back to us, and blossom in our chronicles as well-made artificial flowers. Our common words originally came into the world as embodiments of our uses of them; the belated fables composed by etymologists are charming and compelling, but they come into the world so many ages after the fact of our experience. *Silly* means "silly," which we know well in childhood: the assertion that it once meant "innocent" and before that, "blessed" and "lucky," is the derivative, ironic epigram stretched by a modern poet to cast a shadow across our sophistication. This is what we feel we know, living in the world of our words. But then we are translated.

Long ago, musing on the shores of childhood, I considered the names of my friends and classmates; the more I read and heard of, the more I wondered that so many English families of the past should have acquired what were so obviously, and originally, American boys' first names— Herbert, Howard; Irving, Milton, Morris; Russell, Sidney; Wayne and Dwight—as surnames. New priorities seemed to arise. What dawned was not merely more light but, each morning, a few more degrees of horizon reaching around behind my ears until I could hear the echoes of history, and learn how, in the matter of names, it was the new discoveries which came first. And so with all the other words, aside from proper names. And so with the unending tournament of the two champions of a word's "real" meaning—What it Means locked in shadowy combat with What it Once Meant. *Clear* and *obscure* contend with their semantic ancestors, radiance and darkness. Once we have tripped over some pavement of meaning and learned of their mental fight, we have changed for the world as much as it has for us, and neither can ever get together in quite the same way any more.

The Wonder, Not at the Matter of Being, But at How Questions of Being Explode into Galaxies of Other Matter —Becoming, that is, questions of being this or that; when or then; here now in a midnight field of high stubble reaching into the star-flawed darkness of summer sky, or there, then, in the artificial light of the figurative kindergarten, seriously pasting a gold star on blue paper. And of being in the world of multiplicities of modes of worldliness, those which shape the meanings of "being," those which cause the sky and the paper to bend toward each other and with extended hands to exchange the gifts of resemblance.

The Marriage of the Wandering Mind to the Attentive One The wedding was a secret, and neither wears a ring. The partners are generally known separately, and both are ordinary candidates for representative in the un-acknowledged legislature. The Wanderer? He who drops the scrubbing brush from unhurried fingers into the soapy kettle, and stares out into acres of virtual space, as a strong-winged irrelevancy of far delight or near loss comes homing across the fields at him. Or who drops his hurried fingers from the keyboard, vacating the place of labor that there may be space for flight. The Attentive One? She who cleaves to the loom, making up her mind in a fabric of figurations that draws the world into place around her. Or she who perceives the shaded lowliness of the mushrooms in their sombreros, flicking it into focus with the brush of phrase. We have heard much of both of them, but it is their marriage in us that we usually fail to acknowledge, but that can overcome us with moments of its domesticity. That is when the Task and the Desire, momentarily wearied of hounding each other, of dodging the flung pots and pans, sink into a wide bed, canopied with figures accepted from the street lamps through drawn shades.

Consider the Space You Inhabit When You Can See Nothing Lie in the sun, suspended, preferably, by a deck chair, lest the curving hardness of

ground, the scratching of grass against your back, be too touching a reminder of all that earth, the horizontality of death, the vulnerability of our
surfaces, has come to mean. Inhabit for a while, instead, another region of
bodily experience: let the heat of the sun on your closed eyes and left
shoulder blend in a most painterly fashion with the faint, cool breeze leak-
ing out of the stand of invisible trees over your right shoulder. (If you cry
out for color, smell the tincture of mown grass in it, then.) This is the
checkered shade of paradise. Not the ruled squares of light and dark, into
each of which we run seeking relief from the eventual tyranny of the other,
but the experience of heat and shade as themselves and as phases of something major, meeting in a zone of indeterminacy halfway across your chest.

There is no room for the eye here. The space of your world is more
enclosed than the contingent openness into which our eyes keep finding,
and poking, holes. But it extends across the front of us, it is shaped to fit
the delicate landscape of our own curvature, whereas the eye's just but
imaginative compass traces out its horizontal circle around us with such
unfailing constancy that we trust it to have completed the task always
behind our backs. The rest of the circle is always there, and we do not, in
fact, jut out of some flat background; space does not terminate behind us,
but this is only what we have had to come to believe. The dog's space is
not that of his eye, and what he sees are only appearances screened and
distanced by his skepticism. His nose invites and confirms his knowing,
whereas for us scent is a chink in our walls, a spyhole open to rumor, hint,
and, of course, memory. The dog's space of awareness extends three hundred and sixty degrees around him, and smelling is as seeing through a
band of eyes encircling his whole frame. Thus it is not a matter of trust for
him that he inhabits the center of his room. He knows that he does;
whereas we know too much else of and about ourselves in the world, let
alone too much and too little about knowing itself. We know that we are
not centers but trivial epicenters; that all of the Emersonian circles we
make and inhabit crowd available space and, intersected and overlaid like
far too many engraved lines, create a cosmos of murk; that our eyes are all
fussy landscape painters after all, academic in their systems of illusion,
derivative and anxious in their allusiveness to various kinds of picture. All
this we know from scholarly works in the same library of inference whose
children's reference room reassures that our hundred and twenty degrees
of visible arc is completed behind us.

Your eyes have opened, now, onto the painting before you. Near
greens, both yellowed by sunlight and darkened, move off into layers of
distance, through archways cut among dark pines, into further layers. The
painter has colored the distant spruces blue, and the gouache at your feet

gives way to the wash of the farthest hills. But return for a moment to the near but far from spherical space of the heat and the cool: your own sweat and the rising breeze have altered the way it contains you, yet it remains the same realm of total knowledge of our world. If a bee stings now, or a backache seizes, it goes to show how shattery, how fragile that realm is. But unfractured, the skin's profoundest grasp of space itself reigns supreme, and perspective, inference, extrapolation, puzzlement, and wonder lie rusted against the garden wall, like outgrown perambulators, seesaws and swings, like wheelchairs, crutches and leg-braces for cripples long since healed.

The Riddle of the Sphinx It is a mistake to think that this was a question that had been formerly posed to a finite series of travellers ending with the Correct Answerer. Not to realize that we must continue to try to answer it is the mistake we all continue to make. The Riddle of the Sphinx is the Sphinx herself; her apparent historical and formal existence is a trap; her continuing presence is like the puns we overlook in a conundrum, the alternative we reject in a solution or proof, only to wail or snarl when it is pointed out to us later as the right path we refused to take. For she is always here, now, with us, lurking in puzzling and ambiguous reflections on water or in windows we pass, inhering in double-exposed photographs or staring out of areas of erasure in uncompleted drawings.

You may see her even in the apparently unambiguous representations, the ones we should least expect her to inhabit. An academy painting glistening with the inauthenticity of its high finish, actually purporting to show her in the original scene—she will in fact be there, at least once, for each of us. Consider such a painting: the famous crossroads, framed by unremarkable hills untransformed even by the strangely whitened but sunless sky, the kind of daylight that gives the air some of the density of night, revealing everything as if momentarily, as if all vision were about to be withdrawn. The light of showdowns. And there, frightful in the cheesy frightfulness of her form, as in the certain violence of her action should we fail, making an obscenity of our very canniness, she sits in a bad picture, putting forth her riddle with the same old answer: "What are the Astonishing and the nauseatingly Ordinary both examples of?"

Learn to inspect the snapshots of our attention; it is only by misreading those discrete moments of vision for their apparent continuity that the illusion of motion can occur, with its consequent frauds of the quotidian, its lies of the ordinary. These snapshots are not the grotesque freeze-frames plucked out of movie film, presenting pictures we never see at all

(and yet, we are shocked to observe, are part of what we have been seeing); these snapshots are those unposed, unarranged pictures which become emblems of our consciousness. Consider, for example:

You rush down a corridor, message in hand, turn into a room, and
behold from the side a young woman, star ̇ naked, standing in a shallow,
rectangular puddle of sunlight, down at which she gazes as if in meditation, off toward the right. Her skin is winter-pale, her long, dark hair falls
halfway down her back, and her left hand is extended, slightly curved and
palm downward. You immediately frame snapshots of surprise and desire;
but these are soon followed by other, broader and more complex pictures.
Down the room, to your right, is the artist, working away at his reddish
clay. It appears that you have not "caught" the girl in a moment of meditation, after all; she has rather caught you in a moment of extrapolated as-
tonishment, and even as your heart beats wildly for a moment in wonder
and then warmth, you are turned to a kind of stone by the click of her
shutter. She is not a person being herself, espied in a moment of contemplation of something beyond her—the pool of sunlight obstructing
the window on the floor—that is yet herself. No: she is a model; she
stands for—as one may be said to "sit for"—the artist. His finished piece
will stand for her as well, but in another sense, a way that recircles the
meanings, and even the priorities, of object and image. She stands for the
modelling process, which will produce an image which will stand for her.
And yet even here the two senses of the phrase are again reversed: the
finished image will stand for the modelling of the girl's gaze, the gaze of a
model who represents her image.

This is what you see in those later snapshots, those that take in the artist,
the modelled figure growing in particularity through several successive
phases, the changing rectangles of sunlight on the floor. They will, however, illustrate no dusty tales that one might tell of artists and models—
such as that of the model who turned slowly to stone as her completed,
carved figure came gradually alive; or of the model who felt each movement of the painter's brush along the surface of the unseen figure of herself
on the canvas as a caress so passionate that she had to seize her body with
her hands and give way to her own, not to the painter's, desire; or of the
model who was literally consumed as her image grew—not bit by bit,
fingers, toes, ears dissolving into the afternoon light, but in a reversed
recapitulation of the act of modelling, losing detail and specificity, shrink-
ing or ballooning into general form and, finally, into a huge lump of the
stuff of earth; or of the model whose own work of art consisted of this
séance: herself in this room with an artist (enacted by a friend), playing at
representing something of her. For these tales one needs the illustrative

hand of shadowy mezzotints and stilted engravings. The Fable your snapshots take up—perhaps attested to in legends scrawled lightly across their
backs—is too large and open: the Fable of what goes on, the tale that
interprets itself.

Keep them, for what it is that they are snapshots of will vanish, even as
the snapshots themselves will vanish like now-unfrozen frames in an un-
reeling array. You cough. The artist looks up. The model complains of the
cold and breaks her pose. You enter the room with paper in extended hand
and say, "This came for you." The paper is taken, read, understood or
misunderstood, as the case may be; and there are consequences of this. But
they are black and blank, like the covers of the old album in which snapshots used to be kept, and speak of nothing but their closure.

*Take one of the forgotten books that has been propping up one corner of the
sagging table, dust it off, and read it.* Very well: here is an old, dusty
volume—not very old, really, but certainly dated. *The Book of Airplanes.*
Reading it is to ask, "What is the parable of the aircraft and our flight in
it?" Flight is surely our contemporary version of the old moralists' road,
The Way. Well, we may learn from the airplane
    1) that dark clouds gleam brightly when seen from above;
    2) that the fastest motion forward through the air is the least
    eventful;
    3) that, one way or another, we will descend.

Consider the young person kneeling over the pond.   (Look at him, yes, with
any of the particular desires—to touch and know, or to remember, or to
organize available visual space with the curve of bending back, the face
averted and hidden below the line of sight. Succumb to any of these if you
will—call out a name, walk over and caress, turn away to look into the
shade falling on the far lawn, reach for your sketchbook and pencil. Then
go away. Now, the rest of you who are still here, consider the young
person kneeling over the pond:) There are several schools of consideration, and it is well to know of them before falling into reflective depths
oneself. One of these maintains that the young man is studying the
pond—the slanting sunlight on the far surface, the agitation of wavelet
nearby, the several depths of water, rock, and mud and the discursive
weeds moving among them, the large, pausing fish and the minute, van-
ishing ones—and that not only is he therefore a serious person, but that he
is being considered with seriousness.

Another view is that he studies nothing but his image in the water—
knowing it to be an image only and something other than himself, mind-

ful of old fables, but nonetheless (or perhaps all the more) absorbed in the half-presence that is on the water, or in it, or whatever. Such a view holds that there is nothing else to be seen anymore, and that if the young person claimed to be investigating the pond he would either be lying or, more likely, unwittingly frivolous. As frivolous, indeed, as the first school considers the second to be.

But our tales are told out of school, and our fables spring from their own antiquities. We are latecomers enough to this spot to realize that if he sees the pond—its shallows and its bottom, its room and the objects in it—he can only do so by looking down through the shadow of his own motionless, searching head. Only within the bounds of the cool darkness of its contemplative shade will the water's surface not defy any gaze with the derision of ripples, the laughter of returning sunlight that so charmingly parodies reflection, and turns it away. Only within that darkened frame will rock, fish, weed, and the silt below them rise slowly into perceptibility, as if the eye, breathing deeply, were slowly quickening.

Perhaps that is enough of a lesson, and those who have learned it—or have learned that, indeed, they knew it already—may leave. (There are so few of us left now that I might as well whisper—the truth is too perplexing and fragile to shout or even to proclaim.) Very well. Look at the water-gazer again: he does indeed see into and through and in and among the regions of water; he does, in fact, do so by means of his own reflection. But in this wise: he sees his image but does not, as in the previous interpretation, look through it. Rather, in the dim, mirrored versions of his eyes swimming in the dark green, he sees, magnified in their pupils, the whole realm that lies below, beyond, his image—lighter and darker darks; forms, shapes, stillnesses; algae and pebbles; a lost and rusted hook flying a wisp of line; and, deeper in the cold gray below, two sunken perch, fins barely breathing in the slow stream. All this is truly there, but there by means of the seer's own image, and by far different means from those offered by the happy accident of science we spoke of before, that allows a reflection to hold up a shading and elucidating hand to dazzled eyes.

But this will be impossible to explain to the two schools of fishing and Narcissus.

Confound the rhetorician. Take his fussing, his distinctions, his protestations that the glories of what we see, the horrors of what we fear, the pleasures and the pains that touch us are all mere tropes. Take these with you on your morning walk into the country, and—No: do not throw them away, down into the first abyss you pass, or in the last metal garbage can provided by the town. For then the rhetorician will have confounded you: his trope will have been realized in your trash, and he will have won whatever combat you sought to wage between the troops of common-sense and nonsense. No: take them with you, all his tools and toys, but take them seriously, more seriously, perhaps, than the rhetorician could.

I know what the antiquarians will now say: "Yes, yes: you, not the rhetorician, will find true language in the woods—run-on sentences in rivers, synecdoches in trees, *midrash* in the underbrush, footnotes to ser-mons in the stones, and trope in everything." How charming, and how falsifyingly literal! But the antiquary and the rhetorician, though they may quarrel in public, embrace sweatily and breathlessly in closets; and to fol-low such advice, however at once fresh and venerable it may seem, is once again to confirm all the fuss and bother, to help augment with real figures the empty ledgers of the rhetorician, he "who seemèd busyer than he was."

No, no: confound him and his kind. Take his precious and widely used utensil—for example, the distinction between metaphor and synecdoche. It is a distinction which contrives to lump together on one side parts for wholes, wholes for parts, labels for containers, handles for chests, cousins for siblings, opposites for opposites, and a multitude of others. In the light—or, rather the darkness—of it, if, enraged, I fling my dinner napkin at the rhetorician instead of the cast-iron pot, I do so in metaphor; but if the matching cloth pot-holder, then in metonymy. Take this distinction, then, with you on your walk. Go up into the low hills, and find the first point of prospect you come to from which to regard the road along—and up—which you have come, and the higher hills far around and beyond. Look across at the hills: consider the graying and bluing that goes on in the water color of what you see, the array of tints that makes for layer on layer of distant height. Then look down along the path you have taken: observe the three tiny walkers, at various removes behind and below where you are now, one moving like a bug as seen from above, the others strokes of moving color at a level distance.

Now is the time to take out your utensil to cut up the appearances into portions of truth. Is the bluing of the hills then a metaphor for distance? Or a metonymy? What of the conventions of perspective that shrink your following travellers to minuscules or even dots? They alter by trope, but which one? And the ultimate question that emerges from these, the ques-tion that reigns over all such subjects: does the two-dimensional world of drawing make its representations of three-dimensional space by meton-ymy, the two for the three? Or by metaphor? The world of the plane cannot imagine, even on the analogy of its own perception of the relations of point, line, and polygon within it, the for us inevitable step into solid space. For the plane, that would be the wildest metaphorical leap. Which, then?

Carry the question home with you from your walk. The question itself—preserved from the rotting of easy answer by your botanizing care—will be more fruitful than a dozen dry verses or a dozen dry deconstructions. Keep such questions: the poet will taste of their sweetness, long after they have dried. The rhetorician will experience their bitterness, and his own acute indigestion.

We can reclaim truth from the lies of writing. The scribbler of verses will have it, for instance, that "Morning is a shopping list." By this he or she will mean to employ a once pointed and poignant device—that of the widow lamenting in springtime who says "Sorrow is my own yard," now rotted into the foul cuteness of "Happiness is a cuddly kitten," or the like. For such a scribbler the morning will indeed shrink to something short, fragile, injunctive, and reproachful, in a grossly literal kind of contraction. But when one is free of the foolishness of writing, one can awaken and seize the morning, take it in hand like a shopping list, and read it as a prophecy whose continuation is its own fulfillment. This is a list whereon necessities and superflux, designs and impulses, are all present; a list whereon the very orders of priority, or of implicit route through the day's avenues, themselves embody yet another order of choice and chance. Some lists contain works and plays all mingled higgledy-piggledy, that messiness being the greatest of self-indulgences in itself; some will start or end with what one buys laughing, some with the shops one visits in pain and tears. The lists will thus represent the rarities and repetitions of each new day, each old morning—one of the new, more of the old. And the "is" of the bad writer's little nastiness will be turned toward the noble work of trope: shuttling back and forth between identity and predication, touching neither, but humming away in the energy of its doings, the "is" will truly couple. And the list itself will have been written—even the dreadful reminder of one, black item—by you and necessity together, setting out, even if not to end the day, hand in hand.

A Conversation with
Bernard Malamud

Bernard Malamud lives in a white clapboard house in Bennington, Vermont. Spacious and comfortable, it sits on a gentle downward slope, behind it the rise of the Green Mountains. To this house on April 26, 1974, came friends, family, colleagues and the children of friends—to celebrate Malamud's sixtieth birthday. It was a sunny weekend, the weather and ambience, benign, friendly.

There were about a half dozen young people taking their rest in sleeping bags in various bedrooms and in a home volunteered by a friend and neighbor. Three of them, from nearby universities, were children of friends on the faculty of Oregon State University more than a dozen years ago.

On Saturday night there was a birthday party, with champagne, birthday cake and dancing. At the end of the evening the young people drummed up a show of slides: scenes of past travels; in particular, scenes of Corvallis, Oregon, where Malamud had lived and taught for twelve years before returning East.

Bernard Malamud is a slender man with a graying mustache and inquisitive brown eyes that search and hide a little at the same time. He is a quiet man who listens a lot, and responds freely. His wife, Anne, an attractive, articulate woman of Italian descent, had planned the party, assisted by the young people from Oregon, and the Malamuds' son, Paul, and daughter, Janna.

The taping of the interview began late Friday morning, on the back porch which overlooks a long descending sweep of lawn and, in the distance, the encircling mountains. It was continued, later, in the book-filled study where Malamud writes. (He also writes in his office at Bennington College.) At first he was conscious of the tape-recorder, but grew less so as the session—and the weekend—continued. He has a quick laugh and found it easy to discourse on the questions asked. An ironic humor would seem to be his mother tongue.

[Daniel Stern is the interviewer.]

INTERVIEWER: Why sixty? I understand that when *The Paris Review* asked you to do an interview after the publication of *The Fixer* you suggested doing it when you hit sixty?

MALAMUD: Right. It's a respectable round number and when it becomes your age you look at it with both eyes. It's a good time to see from. In the past I sometimes resisted interviews because I had no desire to talk about myself in relation to my fiction. There are people who always want to make you a character in your stories and want you to confirm it. Of course there's some truth to it: Every character you invent takes his essence from you; therefore you're in them as Flaubert was in Emma—but, peace to him, you are not those you imagine. They are your fictions. And I don't like questions of explication: What did I mean by this or that?—I want the books to speak for themselves. You can read?—all right, tell me what my books mean. Astonish me.

INTERVIEWER: What about a little personal history? There's been little written about your life.

MALAMUD: That's how I wanted it—I like privacy and as much as possible to stay out of my books. I know that's disadvantageous to certain legitimate kinds of criticism of literature, but my needs come first. Still I have here and there talked a little about my life: My father was a grocer; my mother, who helped him, after a long illness, died young. I had a younger brother who lived a hard and lonely life and died in his fifties. My mother and father were gentle, honest, kindly people, and who they were and their affection for me to some degree made up for the cultural deprivation I felt as a child. They weren't educated but their values were stable. Though my father always managed to make a living they were comparatively poor, especially in the Depression, and yet I never heard a word in praise of the buck. On the other hand, there were no books that I remember in the house, no records, music, pictures on the wall. On Sundays I listened to somebody's piano through the window. At nine I caught pneumonia and when I was convalescing my father bought me *The Book of Knowledge*, twenty volumes where there had been none. That was, considering the circumstances, an act of great generosity. When I was in high school he bought a radio. As a kid, for entertainment I turned to the movies and dime novels. Maybe *The Natural* derives from Frank Merriwell as well as the adventures of the Brooklyn Dodgers in Ebbets Field. Anyway, my parents stayed close to the store. Once in while, on Jewish holidays, we went visiting, or saw a Jewish play—Sholem Aleichem, Peretz, and others. My mother's brother, Charles Fidelman, and their cousin, Isidore Cashier, were in the Yiddish theatre.

Around the neighborhood the kids played Chase the White Horse, Ringolevio, Buck-Buck, punchball and one o'cat. Occasionally we stole tomatoes from the Italian dirt farmers, gypped the El to ride to Coney Island, smoked in cellars and played blackjack. I wore sneakers every summer. My education at home derived mostly from the presence and example of good, feelingful, hardworking people. They were worriers, with other faults I wasn't much conscious of until I recognized them in myself. I learned from books, in the public schools. I had some fine teachers in grammar school, Erasmus Hall High School, and later in City College, in New York. I took to literature and early wanted to be a writer.

INTERVIEWER: How early?

MALAMUD: At eight or nine I was writing little stories in school and feeling the glow. To anyone of my friends who'd listen I'd recapitulate at tedious length the story of the last movie I'd seen. The movies tickled my imagination. As a writer I learned from Charlie Chaplin.

INTERVIEWER: What in particular?

MALAMUD: Let's say the rhythm, the snap of comedy; the reserved comic presence—that beautiful distancing; the funny with sad; the surprise of surprise.

INTERVIEWER: Please go on about your life.

MALAMUD: Schools meant a lot to me, those I went to and taught at. You learn what you teach and you learn from those you teach. In 1942 I met my wife and we were married in 1945. We have two children and have lived in Oregon, Rome, Bennington, Cambridge, London, New York, and have traveled a fair amount. In sum, once I was twenty and not so young, now I'm sixty inclined on the young side.

INTERVIEWER: Which means?

MALAMUD: Largely, the life of imagination, and doing pretty much what I set out to do. I made my mistakes, took my lumps, learned. I resisted my ignorance, limitations, obsessions. I'm freer than I was. I'd rather write it than talk. I love the privileges of form.

INTERVIEWER: You've taught during the time you were a professional writer?

MALAMUD: Thirty-five years—

INTERVIEWER: There are some who say teaching doesn't do the writer much good; in fact it restricts life and homogenizes experience. Isn't a writer better off on the staff of *The New Yorker,* or working for the BBC? Faulkner fed a furnace and wrote for the movies.

MALAMUD: Doesn't it depend on the writer? People experience similar things differently. Sometimes I've regretted the time I've given to teaching but not teaching itself. And a community of serious readers is a miraculous thing. Some of the most extraordinary people I've met were students of mine, or colleagues. Still I ought to say I teach only a single class of prose fiction, one term a year. I've taught since I was twenty-five and though I need more time for reading and writing I also want to keep on doing what I can do well and enjoy doing.

INTERVIEWER: Do you teach literature?

MALAMUD: If you teach prose fiction you are teaching literature. You teach those who want to write to read fiction, even their own work, with greater understanding. Sometimes they're surprised to find out how much they've said or not said that they didn't know they had.

INTERVIEWER: Can one, indeed, teach writing?

MALAMUD: You teach writers—assuming a talent. At the beginning young writers pour it out without much knowing the nature of their talent. What you try to do is hold a mirror up to their fiction so, in a sense, they can see what they're showing. Not all who come forth are fully armed. Some are gifted in narrative, some shun it. Some show a richness of metaphor, some have to dig for it. Some writers think language is all they need; they mistake it for subject matter. Some rely on whimsy. Some on gut feeling. Some of them don't make the effort to create a significant form. They do automatic writing and think they're probing themselves. The odd thing is most young writers write traditional narrative until you introduce them to the experimental writers—not for experiment's sake, but to try something for size. Let the writer attempt whatever he can. There's no telling where he will come out stronger than before. Art is in life but the realm is endless.

INTERVIEWER: Experiment at the beginning?

MALAMUD: Sometimes a new technique excites a flood of fictional ideas. Some, after experimenting, realize their strength is in traditional modes. Some, after trying several things, may give up the thought of writing fiction—not a bad thing. Writing—the problems, the commitment, the effort, scares them. Some may decide to try poetry or criticism. Some turn to painting—why not? I have no kick against those who use writing, or another art, to test themselves, to find themselves. Sometimes I have to tell them their talents are thin—not to waste their lives writing third-rate fiction.

INTERVIEWER: Fidelman as a painter? The doubtful talent?

MALAMUD: Yes. Among other things it is a book about finding a vocation. Forgive the soft impeachment.

INTERVIEWER: In *Fidelman* and *The Tenants* you deal with artists who can't produce, or produce badly. Why does the subject interest you so much? Have you ever been blocked?

MALAMUD: Never. Even in anxiety I've written, though anxiety, because it is monochromatic, may limit effects. I like the drama of non-productivity, especially where there may be talent. It's an interesting ambiguity: the force of the creative versus the paralysis caused by the insults, the confusions of life.

INTERVIEWER: What about work habits? Some writers, especially at the beginning, have problems settling how to do it.

MALAMUD: There's no one way—there's so much drivel about this subject. You're who you are, not Fitzgerald or Thomas Wolfe. You write by sitting down and writing. There's no particular time or place—you suit yourself, your nature. How one works, assuming he's disciplined, doesn't matter. If he or she is not disciplined, no sympathetic magic will help. The trick is to make time—not steal it—and produce the fiction. If the stories come, you get them written, you're on the right track. Eventually everyone learns his or her own best way. The real mystery to crack is you.

INTERVIEWER: What about the number of drafts? Some writers write only one.

MALAMUD: They're cheating themselves. First drafts are for learning what your novel or story is about. Revision is working with that knowledge to enlarge and enhance an idea, to re-form it. D. H. Lawrence, for instance, did seven or eight drafts of *The Rainbow*. The first draft of a book is the most uncertain—where you need guts, the ability to accept the imperfect until it is better. Revision is one of the true pleasures of writing. "The men and things of today are wont to lie fairer and truer in tomorrow's memory," Thoreau said.

INTERVIEWER: Do you teach your own writing?

MALAMUD: No, I teach what I know about writing.

INTERVIEWER: What specific piece of advice would you give to young writers?

MALAMUD: Write your heart out.

INTERVIEWER: Anything else?

MALAMUD: Watch out for self-deceit in fiction. Write truthfully but with cunning.

INTERVIEWER: Anything special to more experienced types?

MALAMUD: To any writer: Teach yourself to work in uncertainty. Many writers are anxious when they begin, or try something new. Even Matisse painted some of his fauvist pictures in anxiety. Maybe that helped him to simplify. Character, discipline, negative capability count. Write, complete, revise. If it doesn't work begin something else.

INTERVIEWER: And if it doesn't work twenty or thirty times?

MALAMUD: You live your life as best you can.

INTERVIEWER: I've heard you talk about the importance of subject matter?

MALAMUD: It's always a problem. Very young writers who don't know themselves obviously often don't know what they have to say. Sometimes by staying with it they write themselves into a fairly rich vein. Some, by the time they find what they're capable of writing about, no longer want to write. Some go through psychoanalysis or a job in a paint factory and begin to write again. One hopes they then have something worth saying. Nothing is guaranteed. Some writers have problems with subject matter not in their first book, which may mine childhood experience, or an obsession, or fantasy, or the story they've carried in their minds and imagination to this point, but after that—after this first yield—often they run into trouble with their next few books. Especially if the first book is unfortunately a best seller. And some writers run into difficulties at the end, particularly if they exclude important areas of personal experience from their writing. Hemingway would not touch his family beyond glimpses in short stories, mostly the Nick Adams pieces. He once wrote his brother that their mother was a bitch and father a suicide— who'd want to read about them? Obviously not all his experience is available to a writer for purposes of fiction, but I feel that if Hemingway had tried during his last five years, let's say, to write about his father rather than the bulls once more, or the big fish, he mightn't have committed suicide. Mailer, after *The Naked and the Dead,* ran into trouble he couldn't resolve until he invented his mirror image, Aquarius, Prisoner of Sex, Doppelgänger, without whom he can't write. After he had invented "Norman Mailer" he produced *The Armies of the Night,* a beautiful feat of prestidigitation, if not fiction. He has still to write, Richard Poirier says, his *Moby Dick.* To write a good big novel he will have to invent other selves, richly felt selves. Roth, since *Portnoy,* has been hunting for a fruitful subject. He's tried various strategies to defeat the obsession of the hated wife he almost never ceases to write about. He'll have at last to bury her to come up with a new comedy.

INTERVIEWER: What about yourself?

MALAMUD: I say the same thing in different words.

INTERVIEWER: Anything else to say to writers—basic stuff?

MALAMUD: Take chances. "Dare to do," Eudora Welty says. She's right. One drags around a bag of fears he has to throw to the winds every so often if he expects to take off in his writing. I'm glad Virginia Woolf did *Orlando,* though it isn't my favorite of her books, and in essence she was avoiding a subject. Still, you don't have to tell everything you know. I like Updike's *Centaur,* Bellow's *Henderson.* Genius, after it has got itself together, may give out with a *Ulysses* or *Remembrance of Things Past.* One doesn't have to imitate the devices of Joyce or Proust, but if you're not a genius imitate the daring. If you are a genius assert yourself, in art and humanity.

INTERVIEWER: Humanity? Are you suggesting art is moral?

MALAMUD: It tends toward morality. It values life. Even when it doesn't it tends to. My former colleague, Stanley Edgar Hyman, used to say that even the act of creating a form is a moral act. That leaves out something, but I understand and like what he was driving at. It's close to Frost's definition of a poem as "a momentary stay against confusion." Morality begins with an awareness of the sanctity of one's life, hence the lives of others—even Hitler's to begin with—the sheer privilege of being, in this miraculous cosmos, and trying to figure out why. Art, in essence, celebrates life and gives us our measure.

INTERVIEWER: It changes the world?

MALAMUD: It changes me. It affirms me.

INTERVIEWER: Really?

MALAMUD: *(laughs)* It helps.

INTERVIEWER: Let's get to your books. In *The Natural,* why the baseball-mythology combination?

MALAMUD: Baseball flat is baseball flat. I had to do something else to enrich the subject. I love metaphor. It provides two loaves where there seems to be one. Sometimes it throws in a load of fish. The mythological analogy is a system of metaphor. It enriches the vision without resorting to montage. This guy gets up with his baseball bat and all at once he is, through the ages, a knight—somewhat battered—with a lance; not to mention a guy with a blackjack, or someone attempting murder with a flower. You relate to the past and predict the future. I'm not talented as a conceptual thinker but I am in the uses of metaphor. The mythological and symbolic excite my imagination. Incidentally, Keats said: "I am not a conceptual thinker, I am a man of ideas."

INTERVIEWER: Is *The Assistant* mythological?

MALAMUD: Some, I understand, find it so.

INTERVIEWER: Did you set it up as a mythology?

MALAMUD: No. If it's mythological to some readers I have no objection. You read the book and write your ticket. I can't tell you how the words fall, though I know what I mean. Your interpretation—*pace*, S. Sontag— may enrich the book or denude it. All I ask is that it be consistent and make sense.

INTERVIEWER: Is it a moral allegory?

MALAMUD: You have to squeeze your brain to come up with that. The spirit is more than moral! and by the same token there's more than morality in a good man. One must make room in those he creates. So far as range is concerned, ultimately a writer's mind and heart, if any, are revealed in his fiction.

INTERVIEWER: What is the source of *The Assistant?*

MALAMUD: Source questions are piddling but you're my friend so I'll tell you. Mostly my father's life as a grocer, though not necessarily my father. Plus three short stories, sort of annealed in a single narrative: "The Cost of Living" and "The First Seven Years"—both in *The Magic Barrel.* And a story I wrote in the forties, "The Place Is Different Now," which I've not included in my story collections.

INTERVIEWER: Is *The Fixer* also related to your father's life?

MALAMUD: Indirectly. My father told me the Mendel Beilis story when I was a kid. I carried it around almost forty years and decided to use it after I gave up the idea of a Sacco and Vanzetti novel. When I began to read for the Sacco and Vanzetti it had all the quality of a structured fiction, all the necessary elements of theme and narrative. I couldn't see any way of re- forming it. I was very much interested in the idea of prison as a source of the self's freedom and thought of Dreyfus next, but he was a dullish man, and though he endured well he did not suffer well. Neither did Beilis for that matter but his drama was more interesting—his experiences; so I invented Yakov Bok, with perhaps the thought of him as a potential Van- zetti. Beilis, incidentally, died a bitter man, in New York—after leaving Palestine, because he thought he hadn't been adequately reimbursed for his suffering.

INTERVIEWER: Some critics have commented on this prison motif in your work.

MALAMUD: Perhaps I use it as a metaphor for the dilemma of all men:

necessity, whose bars we look through and try not to see. Social injustice, apathy, ignorance. The personal prison of entrapment in past experience, guilt, obsession—the somewhat blind or blinded self, in other words. A man has to construct, invent, his freedom. Imagination helps. A truly great man or woman extends it for others in the process of creating his/her own.

INTERVIEWER: Does this idea or theme, as you call it, come out of your experience as a Jew?

MALAMUD: That's probably in it—a heightened sense of prisoner of history, but there's more to it than that. I conceive this as the major battle in life, to transcend the self—extend one's realm of freedom.

INTERVIEWER: Not all your characters do.

MALAMUD: Obviously. But they're all more or less engaged in the enterprise.

INTERVIEWER: Humor is so much a part of your work. Is this an easy quality to deal with? Is one problem that the response to humor is so much a question of individual taste?

MALAMUD: The funny bone is universal. I doubt humorists think of individual taste when they're enticing the laugh. With me humor comes unexpectedly, usually in defense of a character, sometimes because I need cheering up. When something starts funny I can feel my imagination eating and running. I love the distancing—the guise of invention—that humor gives fiction. Comedy, I imagine, is harder to do consistently than tragedy, but I like it spiced in the wine of sadness.

INTERVIEWER: What about suffering? It's a subject much in your early work.

MALAMUD: I'm against it but when it occurs why waste the experience?

INTERVIEWER: Are you a Jewish writer?

MALAMUD: What is the question asking?

INTERVIEWER: One hears various definitions and insistences, for instance, that one is primarily a writer and any subject matter is secondary; or that one is an American-Jewish writer. There are qualifications, by Bellow, Roth, others.

MALAMUD: I'm an American, I'm a Jew, and I write for all men. A novelist has to or he's built himself a cage. I write about Jews, when I write about Jews, because they set my imagination going. I know something about their history, the quality of their experience and belief, and of their literature, though not as much as I would like. Like many writers I'm influenced especially by the Bible, both Testaments. I respond in particular to the East European immigrants of my father's and mother's generation; many of them were Jews of the Pale as described by the classic Yiddish writers. And of course I've been deeply moved by the Jews of the concentration camps, and the refugees wandering from nowhere to nowhere. I'm concerned about Israel. Nevertheless, Jews like Rabbis Kahane and Korrf set my teeth on edge. Sometimes I make characters Jewish because I think I will understand them better as people, not because I am out to prove anything. That's a qualification. Still another is that I know that, as a writer, I've been influenced by Hawthorne, James, Mark Twain, Hemingway, more than I have been by Sholem Aleichem and I. L. Peretz, whom I read with pleasure. Of course I admire and have been moved by other writers, Dostoyevsky and Chekhov, for instance, but the point I'm making is that I was born in America and respond, in American life, to more than Jewish experience. I write for those who read.

INTERVIEWER: Thus S. Levin is Jewish and not much is made of it?

MALAMUD: He was a gent who interested me in a place that interested me. He was out to be educated.

INTERVIEWER: Occasionally I see a remark to the effect that he has more than a spoonful of you in him.

MALAMUD: So have Roy Hobbs, Helen Bober, Willie Spearmint and Talking Horse. More to the point—I prefer autobiographical essence to autobiographical history. Events from life may creep into the narrative but it isn't necessarily my life history.

INTERVIEWER: How much of a book is set in your mind when you begin? Do you begin at the beginning? Does its course ever change markedly from what you had in the original concept?

MALAMUD: When I start I have a pretty well developed idea what the book is about and how it ought to go, because generally I've been thinking about it and making notes for months if not years. Generally I have the ending in mind, usually the last paragraph almost verbatim. I begin at the beginning and stay close to the track, if it is a track and not a whalepath. If it turns out I'm in the open sea, my compass is my narrative instinct, with an assist by that astrolabe, theme. The destination, wherever it is, is, as I said, already defined. If I go astray it's not a long excursus, good for getting to know the ocean if not the world. The original idea, altered but recognizable, on the whole remains.

INTERVIEWER: Do characters ever run away from you and take on identities you hadn't expected?

MALAMUD: My characters run away but not far. Their guise is surprises.

INTERVIEWER: Let's go to Fidelman. You seem to like to write about painters?

MALAMUD: I know a few. I love painting.

INTERVIEWER: Rembrandt and who else?

MALAMUD: Too many to name, but Cezanne, Monet, and Matisse, very much, among Modernists.

INTERVIEWER: Chagall?

MALAMUD: Not that much. He rides his nostalgic nag to death.

INTERVIEWER: Some have called you a Chagallean writer.

MALAMUD: Their problem. I used Chagallean imagery intentionally in one story, "The Magic Barrel," and that's it. My quality is not much like his.

INTERVIEWER: Fidelman first appears in "The Last Mohican," a short story. Did you already have in mind that there would be an extended work on him?

MALAMUD: After I wrote the story in Rome I jotted down ideas for several incidents in the form of a picaresque novel. I was out to loosen up—experiment a little—with narrative structure. And I wanted to see, if I wrote it at intervals—as I did from 1957 to 1968—whether the passing of time and mores would influence his life. I did not think of the narrative as merely a series of related stories because almost at once I had the structure of a novel in mind and each part had to fit that form. Robert Scholes in *The Saturday Review* has best explained what I was up to in Fidelman.

INTERVIEWER: Did you use all the incidents you jotted down?

MALAMUD: No.

INTERVIEWER: Can you give me an example of one you left out?

MALAMUD: Yes, Fidelman administering to the dying Keats in Rome—doing Severn's job, one of the few times in his life our boy is engaged in a purely unselfish act, or acts. But I felt I had no need to predict a change in him, especially in a sort of dream sequence, so I dropped the idea. The painting element was to come in via some feverish watercolors of John Keats, dying.

INTERVIEWER: Fidelman is characterized by some critics as a schlemiel.

MALAMUD: Not accurately. Peter Schlemiel lost his shadow and suffered the consequences for all time. Not Fidelman. He does better. He escapes his worst fate. I dislike the schlemiel characterization as a taxonomical device. I said somewhere that it reduces to stereotypes people of complex motivations and fates. One can often behave like a schlemiel without being one.

INTERVIEWER: Do you read criticism of your work?

MALAMUD: When it hits me in the eye, even some reviews.

INTERVIEWER: Does it affect you?

MALAMUD: Some of it must. Not the crap, the self-serving pieces, but an occasional insightful criticism, favorable or unfavorable, that confirms my judgment of my work. While I'm on the subject, I dislike particularly those critics who preach their esthetic or ideological doctrines at you. What's important to them is not what the writer has done but how it fits, or doesn't fit, the thesis they want to develop. Nobody can tell a writer what can or ought to be done or not done, in his fiction. A living death if you fall for it.

INTERVIEWER: That narration, for instance, is dead or dying?

MALAMUD: It'll be dead when the penis is.

INTERVIEWER: What about the death of the novel?

MALAMUD: The novel could disappear but it won't die.

INTERVIEWER: How does that go?

MALAMUD: I'm not saying it will disappear, just entertaining the idea. Assume it does; then someday a talented writer writes himself a long heartfelt letter and the form reappears. The human race needs the novel. We need all the experience we can get. Those who say the novel is dead can't write them.

INTERVIEWER: You've done two short stories and a novel about blacks. Where do you get your material?

MALAMUD: Experience and books. I lived on the edge of a black neighborhood in Brooklyn when I was a boy. I played with blacks in the Flatbush Boys Club. I had a friend—Buster; we used to go to his house every so often. I swiped dimes so we could go to the movies together on a couple of Saturday afternoons. After I was married I taught for a year in a black evening high school in Harlem. The short stories derive from that period. I also read black fiction and history.

INTERVIEWER: What set off *The Tenants*?

MALAMUD: Jews and blacks, the period of the troubles in New York City; the teachers' strike, the rise of black activism, the mix-up of cause and effect. I thought I'd say a word.

INTERVIEWER: Why the three endings?

MALAMUD: Because one wouldn't do.

INTERVIEWER: Will you predict how it will be between blacks and Jews in the future?

MALAMUD: How can one? All I know is that American blacks have been badly treated. We, as a society, have to redress the balance. Those who want for others must expect to give up something. What we get in return is the affirmation of what we believe in.

INTERVIEWER You give a sense in your fiction that you try not to repeat yourself?

MALAMUD Good. In my books I go along the same paths in different worlds.

INTERVIEWER: What's the path—theme?

MALAMUD: Derived from one's sense of values, it's a vision of life, a feeling for people—real qualities in imaginary worlds.

INTERVIEWER: Do you like writing short stories more than you do novels?

MALAMUD: Just as much, though the short story has its own pleasures. I like packing a self or two into a few pages, predicating lifetimes. The drama is terse, happens faster, and is often outlandish. A short story is a way of indicating the complexity of life in a few pages, producing the surprise and effect of a profound knowledge in a short time. There's, among other things, a drama, a resonance, of the reconciliation of opposites: much to say, little time to say it, something like the effect of a poem.

INTERVIEWER: You write them between novels?

MALAMUD: Yes, to breathe, and give myself time to think what's in the next book. Sometimes I'll try out a character or situation similar to that in a new novel.

INTERVIEWER: How many drafts do you usually do of a novel?

MALAMUD: Many more than I call three. Usually the last of the first puts it in place. The second focuses, develops, subtilizes. By the third most of the dross is gone. I work with language. I love the flowers of afterthought.

INTERVIEWER: Your style has always seemed so individual, so recognizable. Is this a natural gift, or is it contrived and honed?

MALAMUD: My style flows from the fingers. The eye and ear approve or amend.

INTERVIEWER: Let's wind up. Are you optimistic about the future?

MALAMUD: My nature is optimistic but not the evidence—population misery, famine, politics of desperation, the proliferation of the atom bomb. Mylai, one minute after Hiroshima in history, was ordained. We're going through long, involved, transformations of world society, ongoing upheavals of colonialism, old modes of distribution, mores, overthrowing the slave mentality. With luck we may end up in a society with a larger share of the world's goods, opportunities for education, freedom, going to the presently underprivileged. Without luck there may be a vast economic redistribution without political freedom. In the Soviet Union, as it is presently constituted, that's meant the kiss of death to freedom in art and literature. I worry that democracy which has protected us from this indignity, especially in the United States, suffers from a terrifying inadequacy of leadership, and the apathy, unimaginativeness, and hard-core selfishness of too many of us. I worry about technology rampant. I fear those who are by nature beastly.

INTERVIEWER: What does one write novels about nowadays?

MALAMUD: Whatever wants to be written.

INTERVIEWER: Is there something I haven't asked you that you might want to comment on?

MALAMUD: No.

INTERVIEWER: For instance, what writing has meant to you?

MALAMUD: I'd be too moved to say.

Words into Fiction

EUDORA WELTY

We start from scratch, and words don't; which is the thing that matters—matters over and over again. For though we grow up in the language, when we begin using words to make a piece of fiction, that is of course as different from using even the same words to say hello on the telephone as putting paint on canvas is. This very leap in the dark is exactly what writers write fiction in order to try. And surely they discovered that daring, and developed that wish, from reading. My feeling is that it's when reading begins to impress on us what degrees and degrees and degrees of communication are possible between novelists and ourselves as readers that we surmise what it has meant, can mean, to write novels.

Indeed, learning to write may be a part of learning to read. For all I know, writing comes out of a superior devotion to reading. I feel sure that serious writing does come, must come, out of devotion to the thing itself, to fiction as an art. Both reading and writing are experiences—lifelong—in the course of which we who encounter words used in certain ways are persuaded by them to be brought mind and heart within the presence, the power, of the imagination. This we find to be above all the power to reveal, with nothing barred.

But of course writing fiction, which comes out of life and has the object of showing it, can't be learned from copying out of books. Imitation, or what is in any respect secondhand, is precisely what writing is not. How it is learned can only remain in general—like all else that is personal—an open question; and if ever it's called settled, or solved, the day of fiction is already over. The solution will be the last rites at the funeral. Only the writing of fiction keeps fiction alive. Regardless of whether or not it is reading that gives writing birth, a society that no longer writes novels is not very likely to read any novels at all.

Since we must and do write each our own way, we may during actual writing get more lasting instruction not from another's work, whatever its blessings, however better it is than ours, but from our own poor scratched-over pages. For these we can hold up to life. That is, we are born with a mind and heart to hold each page up to, and to ask: is it valid?

Reading the work of other writers and in the whole, and our long thoughts in retrospect, can tell us all we are able to know of fiction and at firsthand, but this is about *reading.*

The writer himself studies intensely how to do it while he is in the thick of doing it; then when the particular novel or story is done, he is likely to forget how; he does well to. Each work is new. Mercifully, the question of *how* abides less in the abstract, and less in the past, than in the specific, in the work at hand; I chance saying this is so with most writers. Maybe some particular problems, with their confusions and might-have-beens, could be seen into with profit just at the windup, but more likely it's already too late. Already the *working* insight, which is what counts, is gone—along with the story it made, that made it.

And rightly. Fiction finished has to bear the responsibility of its own meaning, it is its own memory. It is now a thing apart from the writer; like a letter mailed, it is nearer by now to its reader. If the writer has had luck, it has something of its own to travel on, something that can make it persist for a while, an identity, before it must fade.

How can I express outside fiction what I think this reality of fiction is?

As a child I was led, an unwilling sightseer, into Mammoth Cave in Kentucky, and after our party had been halted in the blackest hole yet and our guide had let us wait guessing in cold dark what would happen to us, suddenly a light was struck. And we stood in a prism. The chamber was bathed in color, and there was nothing else, we and our guide alike were blotted out by radiance. As I remember, nobody said boo. Gradually we could make out that there was a river in the floor, black as night, which appeared to come out of a closet in the wall; and then, on it, a common rowboat, with ordinary countrified people like ourselves sitting in it, mute, wearing hats, came floating out and on by, and exited into the closet in the opposite wall. I suppose they were simply a party taking the more expensive tour. As we tourists mutually and silently stared, our guide treated us to a recitation on bats, how they lived in uncounted numbers down here and reached light by shooting up winding mile-high chimneys through rock, never touching by so much as the crook of a wing. He had memorized the speech, and we didn't see a bat. Then the light was put out—just as it is after you've had your two cents' worth in the Baptistry of Florence, where of course more happens: the thing I'm trying here to leave out. As again we stood damp and cold and not able to see our feet, while we each now had something of our own out of it, presumably, what I for one remember is how right I had been in telling my parents it would be a bore. For I was too ignorant to know there might be more, or even less, in there than I could see unaided.

Fiction is not the cave; and human life, fiction's territory, merely contains caves. I am only trying to express what I think the so-called raw material is *without its interpretation;* without its artist. Without the act of human understanding—and it is a double act through which we make sense to each other—experience is the worst kind of emptiness; it is obliteration, black or prismatic, as meaningless as was indeed that loveless cave. Before there is meaning, there has to occur some personal act of vision. And it is this that is continuously projected as the novelist writes, and again as we, each to ourselves, read.

If this makes fiction sound full of mystery, I think it's fuller than I know how to say. Plot, characters, setting, and so forth, are not what I'm referring to now; we all deal with those as best we can. The mystery lies in the use of language to express human life.

In writing, do we try to solve this mystery? No, I think we take hold of the other end of the stick. In very practical ways, we rediscover the mystery. We even, I might say, take advantage of it.

As we know, a body of criticism stands ready to provide its solution, which is a kind of translation of fiction into another language. It offers us close analysis, like a headphone we can clamp on at the U.N. when they are speaking the Arabian tongue. I feel that we can accept this but only with distinct reservations—not about its brilliance or its worth, but about its time and place of application. While we are in the middle of reading some novel, the possibility of the critical phrase "in other words" is one to destroy, rather than make for, a real—that is, imaginative—understanding of the author. Indeed, it is one sure way to break off his carefully laid connection.

Fiction is made to show forth human life, in some chosen part and aspect. A year or so of one writer's life has gone into the writing of a novel, and then to the reader—so long at least as he is reading it—it may be something in his life. There is a remarkable chance of give-and-take. Does this not suggest that, in the novel at least, words have been found for which there may be no other words? If fiction matters—and many lives are at stake that it does—there can be, for the duration of the book, *no* other words.

The point for us if we write is that nearly everything we can learn about writing can be set down only in fiction's terms. What we know about writing the novel *is* the novel.

Try to tear it down, take it back to its beginning, and you are not so much lost as simply nowhere. Some things once done you can't undo, and

I hope and believe fiction is one of them. What its own author knows about a novel is flexible till the end; it changes as it goes, and more than that, it will not be the same knowledge he has by the time the work ends as he had when it began. There is a difference not so much in measure of knowledge, which you would take for granted, as in kind of knowledge. The idea is now the object. The idea is something that you or I might just conceivably have had in common with the author, in the vague free air of the everyday. But not by the wildest chance should we be able to duplicate by one sentence what happened to the idea; neither could the author himself write the same novel again. As he works, his own revision, even though he throws away his changes, can never be wholly undone. The novel has passed through that station on its track. And as readers, we too proceed by the author's arbitrary direction to his one-time-only destination: a journey rather strange, hardly in a straight line, altogether personal.

*   *   *

There has occurred the experience of the writer in writing the novel, and now there occurs the experience of the reader in reading it. More than one mind and heart go into this. We may even hope to follow into a kind of future with a novel that to us seems good, drawn forward by what the long unfolding has promised and so far revealed. By yielding to what has been, by all his available means, *suggested*, we are able to see for ourselves a certain distance beyond what is possible for him simply to *say*. So that, although nobody else ought to say this, the novelist *has* said, "In other words . . ."

Thus all fiction may be seen as a symbol, if this is desired—and how often it is, so it seems. But surely the novel exists within the big symbol of fiction itself—not the other way round, as a conglomeration of little symbols. I think that fiction is the hen, not the egg, and that the good live hen came first.

Certainly symbols fill our daily lives, our busily communicative, if not always communicating, world; and any number of them come with perfect naturalness into our daily conversation and our behavior. And they are a legitimate part of fiction, as they have always been of every art—desirable as any device is, so long as it serves art. Symbols have to spring from the work direct, and stay alive. Symbols for the sake of symbols are counterfeit, and were they all stamped on the page in red they couldn't any more quickly give themselves away. So are symbols failing their purpose when they don't keep to proportion in the book. However alive they are, they should never call for an emphasis greater than the emotional reality they serve, in their moment, to illuminate. One way of looking at Moby Dick is that his task as a symbol was so big and strenuous that he *had* to be a whale.

Most symbols that a fiction writers uses, however carefully, today are apt to be as swiftly spotted by his reader as the smoke signals that once crossed our plains from Indian to Indian. Using symbols and—still worse—finding symbols is such a habit. It follows that too little comes to be suggested, and this, as can never be affirmed often enough, is the purpose of every word that goes into a piece of fiction. The imagination has to be involved, and more—ignited.

How much brighter than the symbol can be the explicit observation that springs firsthand from deep and present feeling in one breast. Indeed, it is something like this, spontaneous in effect, pure in effect, that takes on the emotional value of a symbol when it was first minted, but which as time passes shrinks to become only a counter.

When Chekhov says there were so many stars out that one could not have put a finger between them, he gives us more than night, he gives us *that* night. For symbols can only grow to be the same when the same experiences on which fiction is based are more and more partaken of by us all. But Chekhov's stars, some as large as a goose's egg and some as small as hempseed, are still exactly where they were, in the sky of his story "Easter Eve." And from them to us that night still travels—for, so much more than symbols, they are Chekhov looking at his sky.

Communication through fiction frequently happens, I believe, in ways that are small—a word is not too small; that are unannounced; that are less direct than we might first suppose on seeing how important they are. It isn't communication happening when you as the reader follow or predict the novel's plot or agree with, or anticipate, or could even quote the characters; when you hail the symbols; even when its whole landscape and climate have picked you up and transported you where it happens. But communication is going on, and regardless of all the rest, when you believe the writer.

Then is plausibility at the bottom of it? When we can read and say, "Oh, how right, I think so too," has the writer come through? Only stop to think how often simple plausibility, if put to measure a good story, falls down, while the story stands up, never wavers. And agreement isn't always, by any means, a mark of having been reached.

As a reader who never held a gun, I risk saying that it isn't exactly plausible that Old Ben, the bear in Faulkner's story, when he was finally brought down by a knife-thrust, had already in him fifty-two little hard lumps which were old bullets that had had no effect on him. Yet as a reader caught in the story, I think I qualify to bear witness that nothing less than fifty-two bullets could have been embedded in Old Ben or Old Ben he would not be. Old Ben and every one of his bullets along with him are parts of the truth in this story, William Faulkner's particular truth.

Belief doesn't depend on plausibility, but it seems to be a fact that validity of a kind, and this is of course a subjective kind, gained in whatever way that had to be, is the quality that makes a work reliable as art. This reliability comes straight out of the writer himself. In the end, it is another personal quotient in writing fiction; it is something inimitable. It is that by which each writer *lets us believe*—doesn't ask us to, can't make us, simply lets us.

To a large extent a writer cannot help the material of his fiction. That is, he cannot help where and when he happened to be born; then he has to live somewhere and somehow and with others, and survive through some history or other if he is here to write at all. But it is not to escape his life but more to pin it down that he writes fiction (though by pinning it down he no doubt does escape it a little). And so certainly he does choose his subject. It's not really quibbling to say that a writer's subject, in due time, chooses the writer—not of course *as* a writer, but as the man or woman who comes across it by living and has it to struggle with. That person may come on it by seeming accident, like falling over a chair in a dark room. But he may invite it with wide-open arms, so that it eventually walks in. Or his subject may accrue, build up and build up inside him until it's intolerable to him not to try to write it in terms he can understand: he submits it to the imagination, he finds names, sets something down. "In other words . . ."

So he does choose his subject, though not without compulsion, and now not too much stands in the way of the writer's learning something for himself about his own writing. For he has taken the fatal step when he put himself into his subject's hands. He might even do well to feel some misgivings: he and his fiction were never strangers, but at moments he may wonder at the ruthlessness of the relationship, which is honesty, between it and himself.

His inspiration, so-called, may very easily, then, be personal desperation—painful or pleasurable. All kinds of desperation get to be one in the work. But it will be the particular desperation that the particular writer is heir to, subject to, out of which he learns in daily life, by which, in that year, he is driven, on which he can feel, think, construct something, write out in as many drafts as he likes and then not get to much of an end. What he checks his work against remains, all the way, not books, not lore, neither another's writing nor in the large his own, but life that breathes in his face. Still, he may get to *his* end, have *his* say.

It really is his say. We have the writer's own vision of everything in the world when we place his novel in the center. Then so much is clear: how he sees life and death, how much he thinks people matter to each other and to themselves, how much he would like you to know what he finds beautiful or strange or awful or absurd, what he can do without, how well he has learned to see, hear, touch, smell—all as his sentences go by and in their time and sequence mount up. It grows clear how he imposes order and structure on his fictional world; and it is terribly clear, in the end, whether, when he calls for understanding, he gets any.

And of course he knew this would be so: he has been, and he is, a *reader*. Furthermore, all his past is in his point of view; his novel, whatever its subject, is the history itself of his life's experience in feeling. He has invited us, while we are his readers, to see with his point of view. Can we see? And what does he feel passionately about? Is it honest passion? The answer to that we know from the opening page. For some reason, honesty is one thing that it's almost impossible to make a mistake about in reading fiction.

Let us not think, however, that we ever plumb it all—not one whole novel; and I am not speaking of the great ones exclusively. It is for quite other reasons that we never know all of a single person. But the finished novel transcends the personal in art. Indeed, that has been its end in view.

For fiction, ideally, is highly personal but objective. It is something which only you can write but which is not, necessarily, *about* you. Style, I think, is whatever it is in the prose which has constantly pressed to give the writing its objectivity. Style does not obtrude but exists as the sum total of all the ways that have been taken to make the work stand on its own, apart. Born subjective, we learn what our own idea of the objective is as we go along.

Style is a product of highly conscious effort but is not self-conscious. Even with esthetic reasons aside, the self-consciousness would not be justified. For if you have worked in any serious way, you *have* your style—like the smoke from a fired cannon, like the ring in the water after the fish is pulled out or jumps back in. I can't see that a writer deserves praise in particular for his style, however good: in order for him to have written what he must have very much wanted to write, a way had to be found. A reader's understanding of his style—as the picture, or the reflection, or the proof of a way in which communication tried to happen—is more to be wished for than any praise; and when communication does happen, the style is in effect beyond praise.

*   *   *

What you write about is in the public domain. Subject you can choose, but your mind and heart compel you. Point of view you develop in order to transcend it. Style you acquire in the pursuit of something else which may turn out to be the impossible. Now let me mention shape.

In fiction, as we know, the shapes the work takes are marvelous, and vary most marvelously in our minds. It is hard to speak further about them. Specific in the work, in the mind, but not describable anywhere else—or not by me; shape is something felt. It is the form of the work that you feel to be under way as you write and as you read. At the end, instead of farewell, it tells over the whole, as a whole, to the reader's memory.

In sculpture, this shape is left in rock itself and stands self-identifying and self-announcing. Fiction is made of words to travel under the reading eye, and made to go in one sequence and one direction, slowly, accumulating; time is an element. The words follow the contours of some continuous relationship between what can be told and what cannot be told, to be in the silence of reading the lightest of the hammers that tap their way along this side of chaos.

Fiction's progress is of course not tactile, though at once you might rejoin by saying that some of Lawrence's stories, for instance, *are*—as much as a stroke of the hand down a horse's neck. Neither is shape necessarily, or even often, formal, though James, for example, was so fond of making it so. There is no more limit to the kinds of shape a fictional work may take than there appears to be to the range and character of our minds.

The novel or story ended, shape must have made its own impression on the reader, so that he feels that some design in life (by which I mean esthetic pattern, not purpose) has just been discovered there. And this pattern, shape, form that emerges for you then, a reader at the end of the book, may do the greatest thing that fiction does: it may move you. And however you have been moved by the parts, this still has to happen from the whole before you know what indeed you have met with in that book.

From the writer's view, we might say that shape is most closely connected with the work itself, is the course it ran. From the reader's view, we might say that shape is connected with recognition; it is what allows us to know and remember what in the world of feeling we have been living through in that novel. The part of the mind in both reader and writer that form speaks to may be the deep-seated perception we all carry in us of the beauty of order imposed, of structure rising and building upon itself, and finally of this coming to rest.

It is through the shaping of the work in the hands of the artist that you most nearly come to know what can be known, on the page, of his mind and heart, and his as apart from the others. No other saw life in an ordering exactly like this. So shape begins and ends subjectively. And that the two concepts, writer's and reader's, may differ, since all of us differ, is neither so strange nor so important as the vital fact that a connection has been made between them. Our whole reading lives testify to the astonishing degree to which this can happen.

This ordering, or shape, a felt thing that emerges whole for us at the very last, as we close the novel to think back, was to the writer, I think, known first thing of all. It was surmised. And this is above all what nobody else knew or could have taught or told him. Besides, at that point he was not their listener. He could not, it seems, have cast his work except in the mold it's in, which was there in his mind all the hard way through. And this notwithstanding thousands of other things that life crowded into his head, parts of the characters that we shall never meet, flashes of action that yielded to other flashes, conversations drowned out, pieces of days and nights, all to be given up, and rightly.

For we have to remember what the novel is. Made by the imagination for the imagination, it is an illusion come full circle—a very exclusive thing, for all it seems to include a good deal of the world. It was wholly for the sake of illusion, made by art out of, and in order to show, and to be, some human truth, that the novelist took all he knew with him and made that leap in the dark.

For he must already have apprehended and come to his own jumping-off place before he could put down on paper that ever-miraculous thing, the opening sentence.

A Memoir of John Berryman

WILLIAM HEYEN

John, at least here
I hold you in mid-air.

In 1964 I was teaching at the S.U.N.Y. College at Cortland. One of my colleagues was Jerome Mazzaro. One day Jerry came back from somewhere with a copy of *77 Dream Songs*, which had just appeared. I remember thinking the dustjacket very striking. I borrowed the book and read it, or tried to. It was difficult going. I hadn't read Berryman before this, but soon looked up *Homage to Mistress Bradstreet*, which I *studied*. Now *that*, I felt until a couple of years ago, was a language to envy.

It was about this time that Jerry and I drove to Syracuse University to hear a reading by W. D. Snodgrass, who began by reciting several of the seventy-seven songs of the man who had been his teacher. Snodgrass' high-pitched voice carried Berryman's voices through their levels of irony and pain and humor perfectly. From that time on, although I never felt able to write anything on Berryman (except for a brief review for *Southern Review* of *Berryman's Sonnets* when it appeared in 1967), few days went by when I did not read at least a little while from one of his books. I became convinced that he was one of the great ones that he was so determined to be.

Against my real will and better judgement, I became Director of the Brockport Writers Forum at the S.U.N.Y. College at Brockport in 1970. My first thought was to write to John Berryman. I was to take over the Forum beginning that September, but I wrote Berryman in late April or early May. I don't have my letter, or subsequent ones, but I have his. The first note from him is postmarked May 9, 1970: "Dear Mr. Heyen," it goes, "How do you get to Brockport, from Kennedy airport? I travel a good deal but hate it. Could somebody pick me up? The first Wednesday in November wd be best for me." I must have written back, and very happily, simply to tell him either to fly into Buffalo, just an hour's drive away, or into Rochester, just twenty minutes away, where I could pick him up. Kennedy is a seven-hour drive from Brockport. His next note is dated 6 June: "I've been in hospital five weeks & I'm afraid my doctors have forbidden anything until next Spring. Perhaps we can arrange something later." I'm not sure whether or not I answered right away. I know that his next note came as a surprise. No doubt, he'd forgotten he'd just written me. This note is dated 18 June 70: "I'm just home after a long spell in hospital & my doctors advise against any more trips this year. Could your attractive invitation be extended to some time next Spring?" That was fine with me, certainly. I must have written him back to tell him I would hold onto the $1,000 of our budget that I'd offered him until he could appear for a Spring reading and television interview.

A surprise note dated 19 Aug 70 arrived: "I'll be at Loyola College in Montreal from mid-Sept. to mid-Dec, more convenient to you than here. If you want to propose a date or dates, do. Peter Stitt wd. be fine for the interview." I'd thought of flying Peter Stitt in from Vermont for the interview—I felt it best, when possible, to ask one of the poet's friends to co-interview: Allen DeLoach helped me interview Allen Ginsberg, and Jerry Mazzaro helped make James Wright comfortable—but Stitt's visit didn't work out. In any case, I wrote back to Berryman and proposed some dates. His next note makes it clear that he still expected to be in residence at Loyola in the Fall: "Oct 7th sounds all right, if Loyola schedules me Mon-Tues as I suggested—but this is tentative: you haven't stated a fee yet ever, have you? My soc. sec. no. is 104-20-1374, and I'll look out a photograph." His next note is from 7 Sept 70: "I'm on Mohawk flight #196 arriving (fr. Buffalo) at Rochester 5:52 p.m. Wed. Oct 8th. That gives time for dinner—anyway, can't anyone who wants to meet me do so at a party somewhere (or just at a coffee shop or bar) after the reading?"

The problem here was that Wednesday was October 7, not 8. I wasn't sure what day he was arriving, and needed to know for television studio and room, program, and dinner arrangements. I wrote him. No answer. I had to call, and dreaded it. I hated the phone, and I hated to bother him. My memory blurs. I had to talk to him two or three times. It was incredible and baffling, but one of our conversations ended when he hung up immediately after saying he would fly into Kennedy. Another one left me with the feeling that he'd be flying to Pittsburgh (perhaps mistaking our Forum for the International Poetry Forum). But I never ascribed any of these confusions to his drinking. I felt that a man as brilliant and sensitive as Berryman ought to be distracted. I felt sure that if I had not been so awed and flustered and embarrassed on the phone, I could have made things clear.

Somehow, things became settled. October 7th it would be. Worrying about J.B.'s visit, I hadn't slept well in weeks. I was particularly worried about the television tape, and hoped he would be easy to interview. The morning arrived. Around noon, my wife got a call from Berryman at the Minneapolis airport. I got back from school and he called again. He was drunk, and had missed his plane, and would try to charter one, etc., etc. I said that if he could get to Brockport, even too late for the reading, we could schedule him for the next day. He was relieved. He said fine, because he hated to miss an engagement, and he'd see what he could do. We talked on the phone three or four times. Then he didn't call. At eight in the evening, still hoping that he would descend on us like a miracle, I drove over to the college and announced to a couple of hundred people that the poet had not arrived. I invited lots of friends over to my house for drinks and consolation. We sat around. Some of us played poker. Our hopes were dwindling when J.B. called to say he was in Buffalo. I was elated, and told him to sit tight, that Jerry Mazzaro would be there to pick him up within a half hour. I called Jerry, who was standing by at his house in Buffalo. I began drinking in earnest and losing at poker and didn't care. All of us waiting for the man. At about the time I hoped Jerry would be pulling into my driveway, a call came through from Berryman from the airport. He'd seen Mazzaro, but Mazzaro, it seems, had left him! I told him to sit tight, that Jerry must only have gone to the bathroom. I was afraid Berryman and Mazzaro had had an argument. Somehow, I began winning at poker. At one in the morning I heard a crash outside. Jerry had hit a boulder that edges my driveway. Yes, I saw a silhouette on the other side of the front seat. Berryman had made it to Brockport.

The two days of his visit remain central to my life in ways I can only hope to suggest. It was not just that Berryman's visit, at mid-week, had all the qualities of the proverbial lost weekend. This had something to do, once and for all for me, with the reality of poetry in this life. This had something to do with Berryman's presence as a presence committed to the life of poetry. I kept feeling that Berryman was spending for vast returns, was driving himself toward the next poem in a necessary frenzy, and that he had been born to do this. He was always noting lines, sounding out lines, pulling one of his new short poems from one of his pockets. His moods were mercurial, and he always wrenched me with him. Lawrence Lieberman has described Berryman's voice as a "superarticulate mental wail." He was brilliant, dazzling, this man who had met Yeats and had written *Homage,* the *Sonnets,* and *The Dream Songs.* I still feel that he was the only genius I've ever met. (In the Emersonian sense, Genius as opposed to Talent, inspired form as opposed to the somewhat pedestrian ability to make meters and rhymes.) It is my feeling that he came to this Genius at the end of his life in *Love & Fame* (1970) and *Delusions, Etc.* (1972), that we will find this out, and that this will take a long time.

In his essay on Whitman, Randall Jarrell quotes some lines and says that either someone with a tin ear and no art at all wrote those lines, or someone with an incredibly sensitive ear. We know the truth by now. In the same way, I feel that those poems of *Love & Fame* and *Delusions, Etc.*, received with general suspicion and dislike, need us to catch up to them. Their sounds are odd. We will have to tune up to them, and it will take some doing. As Berryman wrote of Stephen Crane's poems, "They are not like literary compositions. They are like things just seen and said, *said for use.*" Those late Berryman poems are deceptively excellent. He was making a violent break, and wanted to trust himself (that constant protesting "Isn't that good?" "Isn't that good?"), but was at the same time caught up in a horror of suspicion that his alcoholism had already destroyed his ability to function without delusion. He was shedding the self in these poems, dealing directly with his life in order to get away from it. He wanted to be of *use*. And he began to find God, even in "a motor hotel in Wallace Stevens' town," as he said in "The Facts & Issues."

We were up all the night that Berryman arrived in Brockport. We made the television tape the next morning, had lunch at the college and dinner at my house that day, and Berryman read that evening. We were up all night long again, and he left by plane that morning. As his plane took off, I cried. Exhaustion and relief. I'd never been through anything like that before. I know that I felt, after he left Brockport, that he would not live for long, and I began to write out some impressions and memories of his visit. I felt a sense of history in his presence. Some of these notes are now embarrassing or naive or otherwise silly. For better or worse, here is what I wrote:

He said at dinner that when he left a town everyone went to sleep and he checked into a hospital. We laughed. How long could he last. For two days, 48 sleepless hours, I wondered about his heart, miraculous machine: kept him going through fifty-six years, his chain-smoking, alcoholism, insomnia, rages and crying jags and a memory that would not let the dead die. His heart. Hard as a fist. Himself seeming to be all bone. What it must be like to live inside his head. Dream as the panorama of the whole mental life: in one of his four or five calls from the Minneapolis and Buffalo airports on Wed. as he was missing his reading here he spoke of the latest dream: a snake curled in a gold box that was half of his mother-in-law's

French door. "What do you think it means," he asked me. I said, could you get to Syracuse? Sunday morning: his wife just called saying she does not know where he is, she is trying to retrace his steps. I told her I put him on a plane Friday morning at 9:00 to New York where he was going to meet Robert Giroux and have lunch, and spend the afternoon with friends, and fly back to Minneapolis at night, because he could not miss a talk he had to give in St. Paul on Saturday morning. Kate said she would call again. She said he *did* call her Friday night but she did not know where he was calling from. My wife just emptied out one of his ashtrays of Herbert Tarreyton butts. His lips would snap the cigarette with each drag, forced, hurried, driven. He left one of his shirts here with, like his others, cigarette burns and holes along its left side. Too absent-minded now to drive he said, and too absorbed ever to use an ash-tray. Sugar that my daughter spilled and his ashes now to vacuum from our shag rugs. All of this, the sleeplessness, an effort to murder time. His marriage is what he had to have it, a storm, he said. He kept telling me that he had one very fine piece of advice for me: to focus on my wife, write about her, but to see her from someone else's perspective, his, perhaps. This was the key. Wms. must have been much the same in both ways: incredible physical stamina and need to talk and write, living the 24 hr. day; to focus on his wife through 3 novels and many poems culminating in "Of Asphodel." I wanted, Friday morning, to send him to Minneapolis and not New York: he replied: "No. I will negotiate from a position of strength, not weakness." The last time he had called her (5 in the morning) her line was busy. He believed she had taken it off the hook. He screamed, even to himself when I left him alone in the living room for a minute: "She'll get out of the house. Out. I will not live with her." "She hates me." "She cannot bear my fame." "She is waiting for me to die." He kept telling me he could not convince her that he loved her. He arrived, finally, from Buffalo with Jerry Mazzaro, at midnight on Wednesday. Fifteen or 20 of us at my house. He took over. Wanted, at first, only to talk to my wife and Sis Rock. Shut the rest of us out. I played cards with Bill Rock, Ned Grade, Allen DeLoach, Mirko. Won $125. Kept going into the living room to talk to him. He did not see the rest of us. Did not look like the pictures on *His Toy, His Dream, His Rest.* Beard trimmed, hair not as wild, or high. Glasses on. More professorial, academic. Charming, disputatious, dominating, brilliant. What it must be like to live in his head, to walk drunk into a living room filled with strangers half-way across the country, and to talk. Magnificent conceit. We were awed. "I won that round" after destroying someone trying to be friendly. He had a bad foot, pinched or displaced nerve. Went shoeless. Raged as we were going down steps into the television studio, saying he had not contracted to go up and down steps. Disdained a hand or shoulder to lean on. . . . He disliked Jerry though Jerry tried to be kind, flattered him, showing him his rare *The Dispossessed* bought with money from a poetry prize which Jerry spent on those books important to him. Shrug. He liked me, did not even hear me when I said I would have knocked his block off had he insulted and attacked me the way he did a student at the Thursday night party. Said the student had condescended to him. Egads. Sunday morning: I just called Mrs. Berryman to find out whether she has found him yet. She said he was in Minneapolis all the time. I was stupid enough to say I was glad things were all right. She said, well, things weren't all right: he had to go to the hospital again. But, at least, he was safe. There were people talking in the background, friends, no doubt, who got hold of him and checked him in. In my easy chair Friday morning, stretched out straight, he seemed unreal, his clothes much too big for him, or so it seemed, as though there were nothing under his clothes. And before the reading he came out of the bathroom shirtless, all bone, I thought of Ezra Pound as I'd seen him in photos. He was cute. The last thing my wife said to him at the airport was: Mr. Berryman, your pants are open. And he laughed and zipped his fly. He cried twice: early Thursday morning, over Dylan Thomas; Thursday afternoon, over R. P. Blackmur and Auschwitz & Belsen & Dachau. The reading Thursday night: incredible, powerful, he said later he hadn't done so well in a long time, that he had people in the audience he liked and wanted to read to. He went on past where he usually quits, he said. The six dream songs he read knocked me over. He's better than Thomas. Imagine, to have written *The Dream Songs,* and *Homage.* He asked me, Wed. night-Thurs. morning, where I lived. I said do you mean here, in my house, or spiritually. Yes, he nodded. I said someday I hope to write a poem as fine as *Homage.* He said: "I want you to." I said that stanza beginning "It is Spring's New England . . ." choked me up. He said it was the best in the poem. Yes. He was "hot as a pistol" these days, writing like hell. Explained the Dickinson origin of his new style, the unrhymed quatrains he's been writing w. a short 4th line. I realize as I write this he is in the hospital, probably in a dead sleep. What it must be like to live in his head. He stuck the $1,000 check in his jacket pocket without opening the envelope. Dream Song #282 was his current favorite. He said God must have spoken to him when he wrote that one. Yes. He liked Dickey. Jerry told him, on their drive from Buffalo, that Dickey didn't know what to do with detail. He disliked Jerry. Told me on the phone, when he'd wandered away from Jerry, that he couldn't imagine Mazzaro wd. write another book on Lowell. His love-hate for Lowell always apparent. Screwed up all my plans for the tape. I threw away my notes as soon as we started or, rather, didn't get to use them. Read, to begin, "The Song of the Tortured Girl." Best single reading of any poem I've ever heard. Impossible to interview. Sometimes 15 second pauses and then continuing, interrupting our next question; once saying we'd have to ask him a question. His obliviousness: to cigarette ashes; to being in one back-straight position at the party for 6 hrs; to traffic as we crossed streets; to anything but poems. When he 1st got here he gripped my hand long & hard. The "strain" and "torsion" in his work is the man. We did get him to eat: a cup of chicken soup Wed. night; a ham & cheese sandwich Th. noon; a decent dinner Thurs. night. Constant bourbon, water, no ice. "Mr. Heyen, I'm an alcoholic. I'd like another drink." I'd say sure. Betrayer, I suppose. He wrote my wife a poem out, which we'll frame: "After you went to bed,/Your tall sweet husband and I talked all night,/until there was no more to be said." Jerry went to bed in Kristen's room around 6 Thurs. morning. J.B. gripped my wrist hard, told me what I had to do to join the great ones: focus on my wife, write sonnets, suffer. Told me I was a late starter. Said he read my book and didn't like it. I don't think he read it—he talked as though he'd read something by a beat. We talked in the car as I tried to drop him off at the motel, about Wilbur. Wilbur said one of his new poems was "low voltage." He respected Wilbur. "No one" had done the perfect the way Wilbur had. "Walking to Sleep" a very great poem, he said. I asked him how Henry was: O.K.—hard to leave him behind. When he sat down he did not want to move. He wanted to talk and drink. He was content talking for hours. His rage at the television taping was not that he was to be interviewed, but that they didn't start quickly enough for him and that he would be cued, told when to begin. This he couldn't bear, but once we did begin he would have been content to sit and talk and say poems for ten hours. This is no exaggeration. Swore on the phone to kiss my wife's left ear when he saw her, and he hadn't done this, he said, since 1940. It was too powerful. Angry at his own body—the brilliant mind having to be borne by the dying animal, the clumsy partner. Now, I'm a famous man, was his usual preface to a story. Now it is three days after he left and I can't get over him. Told me he had been unfaithful only once in his nine years of marriage, but that Kate didn't trust him, hated him, envied him, wanted him dead. In the same breath admitted he was a masochist, and smiled. Tortured himself into poems. Had to stay hot as a pistol. "I haven't finished my coffee. Sit down." Late to everything but lucky to get anywhere. And a little child shall lead them as Kristen led him to dinner. Mr. Berryman talks silly, she said. He has a daughter my son's age. Billy was very quiet. / When he broke into an imitation of Maurice Chevalier, Kristen said: "Mr. Berryman, are you talking or singing?" Han remembers that he cried a third time: Wed. night when he called up an Yvonne, read his new poem to her, and, apparently, she didn't like it. About 6:30 Thurs. morning I drove him to the motel, had to come back for his suitcase, drove him there again, drove him back to my house again when he found there was no phone in his room. He told the woman: "Know that your accommodations are totally unsatisfactory." She winked at me as we left./Two weeks later I travel to Rochester to hear John Logan read: before dinner, over drinks, Anthony Hecht says that he heard a great Berryman story from Bill Merwin: it seems that a couple of weeks before, Berryman was at the Minneapolis airport and couldn't remember whether he was supposed to go to Pittsburgh or Buffalo and. . . . Nov. 5: I travel to Buffalo to hear Robert Bly read. Later, at a party, Allen DeLoach says that Merwin and someone else *were* waiting in Pittsburgh for Berryman. A postcard arrives from Berryman in the hospital: he seems happy, has written 12 or 15 poems, promises to send *Love and Fame* when copies are available, remembers Patti Hancock, "beautiful and serene," sends us all his love. I have written all this out of love.

I kept in loose touch with him after his visit, but never saw him again, except on the television tape we made. I sent him books and programs of his reading to sign. I have a letter from August 21, 1971 that ends: "I hope you both, & the kids, are flourishing. I am." And there's a postscript: "Reading in Rotterdam 1st wk. in June, back for new baby due 2nd wk. June. So it goes . . ." I thought he was healthy and happy again, and I was glad.

By September of 1971 I was walking the streets and woodpaths of a suburb of Hanover, Germany, where I'd gone for a year as a Fulbright lecturer. I was with my family, but I felt lost, gloomy. A whole year stretched darkly in front of me. I wrote to J.B. and asked him to write out a poem. A card arrived dated 16 Oct 71: "You think *you-all* are lonely. Listen to *this* poor guy I invented in Wisconsin & N Y C & back here last Dec." He wrote out "Old Man Goes South Again Alone" which would appear posthumously in *Delusions, Etc.* (1972). Even though he is heading for the beaches of exotic Trinidad, the old man of the poem is sad "without the one // I would bring with me. . . ." Berryman knew that his own solitary trips tore him apart. He was telling me that I had enough not to be lonely. The *you-all* was emphatic. It was the same message he'd given me that night when he told me to focus on Han, study her, write about her, lose myself in her—love was the only way out of the lonely reaches of the ego.

The high ones die. He chose the frozen Mississippi. I received this telegram from Al Poulin, Jr. Han and I knew what it meant. I walked for miles through the woods that day, trying to will him back to life, playing mental tricks, trying to wake up earlier in the day than the telegram had arrived, often fighting back tears and losing, trying to believe his death. Over the next days, clippings came from friends.

This death struck / strikes us so hard. We are still hurt. We cannot *understand* why he died. His suicide has deepened every question I have asked myself about poetry. W. D. Snodgrass once said to me that he would rather be happy than write great poems. I suspect that Berryman would not have said this, that he felt, although in the Brockport interview he denies this, that intense suffering led to the greatest poetry, and, certainly, he wanted nothing less than to write masterpieces. His horrible admission in the *Paris Review* interview that perhaps he needed something like cancer to get on with his writing, confirms this. "I hope to be nearly crucified," he says. I say *No* to this. *No.*

And now we have *Recovery* (1973), a powerful reading experience, certainly, for those who knew him. It lays bare the terrible dimensions of the battle Berryman fought against the forces that finally killed him. That he could not, or *would not* (I have to say this: if it is a delusion, it is a necessary one) cure himself and finish the book—this says something chilling about the death of art, and about where several other poets a decade younger than Berryman was when he died are now headed. Berryman's suicide, for me, has cast a pall over much of his work, the darkest and most painful of it. It may be true, as Lionel Trilling said of Robert Frost, that it takes a poet who terrifies us to satisfy us. But, I would think, there exists a line between truth-telling and morbidity. For Roethke, finally, the dead seemed to *help*.

I have come to feel that as magnificent as *The Dream Songs* is, it is a great deathflower, held in full bloom by Berryman's elegiac genius. I read the songs saying to myself, "Yes, yes, but poetry does not have to be what this is. It can be, but it does not have to be." I turn for comfort to Stevens and Wilbur: Stevens, who wrote at the end of his life about the "planet's encouragement," and Wilbur, to whom Sylvia Plath's "brilliant negative" is, finally, "unjust." I have come to feel that I have to find my own life in Stevens and Wilbur. There are lives of obsession and frenzy, and there are lives of gentleness and grace and control. And it may be that our lives are to a great extent what we wish and will them to be. Stevens, Wilbur, William Stafford. This is one of Stafford's "Stories to Live in the World With":

> At a little pond in the woods
> I decided: this is the center of my life.
> I threw a big stick far out, to be
> all the burdens from earlier years.
> Ever since, I have been walking
> lightly, looking around, out of the woods.

In the *Paris Review* interview, Berryman says that he had absolutely no observation of nature. Observation of nature, he said, "makes possible a world of moral observation for Frost, or Hopkins." Nature as the measure, and comfort, whether or not it ought to be, whatever the truth of the matter. All those burdens from earlier years never left Berryman. I have to try to believe that this is more than a matter of chemistry, that he could have turned his back and gone about a different business. In "Dream Song #265" he says "next time it will be nature & Thoreau." Henry admits to loving "the spare, the hit-or-miss, / the mad." Robinson Jeffers would have told Berryman, as he wrote to the American Humanist Association, "most of our time and energy are necessarily spent on human affairs; that can't be prevented, though I think it should be minimized; but for philosophy, which is an endless research of truth, and for contemplation, which can be a sort of worship, I would suggest that the immense beauty of the earth and the outer universe, the divine 'nature of things,' is a more rewarding object. Certainly it is more ennobling. It is a source of strength; the other of distraction." It may be that this goes too far. It may be, in fact, that Jeffers himself so loved and was so concerned with man that, in Hyatt H. Waggoner's words, Jeffers' single real theme was "his desperate effort to teach the heart not to love." I do not mean to oversimplify a very complex matter of balance. I mean to say that during the many years while he was writing *The Dream Songs,* Berryman did not dwell on those things that could have been sources of strength for him.

Many people were much closer to John Berryman than I was. But, as someone said, we can love even a stranger known for only a few moments, and grieve at his death, because the soul does not keep time. I loved / love him, and cherish him, and will always count it among the privileges of my life that I met him. But I realize, also, that I am often afraid of him, that the bad angels also hovered around him, that the God he turned to at the end did not rescue this rare man from his despair. Unless, and I will keep trying to find out, this is exactly what happened.

From Pushing Around the Pantheon

HORTENSE CALISHER

Every art is a church without communicants, presided over by a parish of the respectable. An artist is born kneeling; he fights to stand. A critic, by nature of the judgment seat, is born sitting.

We're hierarchical animals; none of this is new. Why though is the artist as a person as well as a creator, endlessly anatomized, while the psychological make-up of a critic is let go hang? Who has investigated the oedipal pulsings of a Sainte-Beuve? Or the possible anal indelicacies of a Saintsbury? Or the Gestalt of all our critics who wrote a novel once? Nobody hangs *their* laundry out. Or sees them as men and women for a' that, outside the hall of fame like everybody else, beating their little welfare fists against the big bank door.

When the Reform Bill goes through on Olympus, all critics and certainly all biographers, will carry their non-academic *vita* with them at all times, to be checked as freely as the tag on a decanter, before it pours forth. We shan't want to see their medals. What we'll want to know is the state of *their* beds, *their* dreamgoals and psychic pocketbooks, before we listen to them freudenize Twain and stack-sullivanize Keats. What is home to Harold Rosenberg, we'll ask, that Barnett Newman is *this* to him? Where were you, Edmund Gosse, Maurice Bowra, Brander Matthews, *when the lights went out*? And who has collated Arnold Toynbee's "analysis"—a Jungian one, I was told—with his version of history?

Oh, I can see all the arts then, a proper Disneyland, with all the worms turning animatedly to say to the spades "Kindly present a psychiatric background of *your* prejudices. And in print please!" Before you dig *me* up.

Trouble is, would we read it?

Perhaps all artists have to settle for the fact that they don't get justice, but treatment. Sitting men will always see themselves as Jovian. The artist's concept of himself tends to be cruciform—as befits a hanging one. Both will be even further shaped by their situations. The critic spreads bottomwise, into scholarship. An artist's best mobility is above the neck.

Often when he has enough work behind him, he grows a second head on it.

I begin to remember how many artists of the past have had two of them. My prejudice is that we should always carry our critic head a little negligently under the arm, like a collapsible top-hat. In the nineteenth century, the writer-artist sported his less self-consciously; the poets wrote the best literary criticism of the age, and even in the letters of George Eliot (who all her life, according to Gordon S. Haight in his preface to her *Letters*, suffered from "a morbid lack of self-confidence" in her work), we see nevertheless how widely and naturally she expects any writer to range. Europe expected it. There are periods that tolerate this, just as the gardener is allowably the authority on roses, the vintner on wine. Ours is not one of them.

To do this, of course, one must have formidable artists. I think I would always rather read the notebooks of Matisse than the essays of Roger Fry—and a look at Fry's paintings in their room at Kings hasn't disabused me. (Though I would also rather read Hindemith on music than E. M. Forster; an artist has to be in his own art, for this kind of authority.) To have a fan's passion for an art, or even like Fry to help disseminate and explain its new forms, is a kind of hostess function, never to be confused with an artist's data on art's essences.

Literary criticism has yet another confusion at its very heart, in that anyone talking about the medium seriously is in effect using it—and had better have the powers of the artist as well. This often convinces literary critics that they are artists. It convinces me that artists are the best of them. Only the artist can be trusted never to confuse essences with statuses. And every judgment he makes involves him. This is true of the most minor review or conversational flight. *He has no light words.*

The French understand this. To the end that some become exaggerates of it, as the later Sartre becomes the art-spider who must cling to the corpus of Genêt for his energy while his own work in art dwindles, appendage to that suddenly monster second head. (At a certain point in that sort of game, perhaps there is no turning back.) Yet when we say then "But *au fond,* he was always *philosophe,*" something is added. We are subscribing then to the abiding continuum of human thought.

When I was sixteen, Jules Romains seemed to me both boring and mysteriously seductive; I sensed that he was part of some luminous tradition my own hadn't prepared me for. A few years on, Gide bowled me over, above all for his seriousness; for his hairsplittings in the realm of orthodoxy I cared nothing. What was this temper of mind that suited me down to the ground though I might war with its contents? Or feel outside it, as with Simone Weil, whose atmosphere I nevertheless *recognized* to the point of shock—for I was no *religieuse*.

I had been a philosophy student though, happy to deliver a paper on any closed system, from Schopenhauer's *The World As Will and Idea* to a flirt with Kant and Hegel—always holding my breath in wait for that wonderful, acolyte moment when I would see the angel-plan spread out before me, and could hope to believe. Spinoza, as a Jew and hence somehow already in my blood, didn't interest me—perhaps here as elsewhere I always had a taste for Christian boys. Mystics like Jacob Boehme drew me, but uneasily, as half on the road to art, and artists like Blake. In the French attitude what I had found was what the world had long recognized as a perfect agar in which critique could nourish endlessly: the spirit of *rational* inquiry, in a *religious* temperament. It was my air. I too wanted to lay my life on a line.

But did I want that same air for art?

English after all was my language and spirit. Once past Spenser, or midway in Shakespeare, the air turns Protestant. Since Dr. Johnson, a large part of literary talk had been just that—talk, coffee-house commonsensical, with heaven around the corner in Grub Street. Then had come the message of Matthew Arnold's muscular speeches—we must cope—then Ruskin's sentimentality of the chaste, and Pater's watered-down Marcus Aurelius—a whole silly-season of flowers set in a dry sink. Shaw had been a journalist, D.H. Lawrence a bitter heckler; though coping was glorious at times, nothing I saw in English criticism matched the high, tonally fixed seriousness of the French. But the language itself was a fountain to be leaned upon, not formless but forming—always literally more words in it than French, looser, more open to change, yet not as heavy-spawning as German. A fine wool of a language, English, to which cockle-burrs can cling, yet which still has the watercolor vowels and voice-syrups of a Romance tongue. Its writers of the twentieth century have leaned on it like a rationale. And I with them. It suited what we like to think is our lawlessness.

Yet somewhere is a thought-continuum we too yearn for and must have. Nowadays the phrase "He's a renaissance man" is slang. Said not as if we are the forceful owners of a world on the way to knowing everything, but like men who wish that all knowledge once again was one. Or that one man—each—could have a "universal" portion of it. We think of Goethe, the poet-dramatist and novelist of *Elective Affinities* who could also discover the intermaxillary bone in man and quarrel with Newton over their theories of light, as able to do this, aside from his gifts, only because he lived at a time when the intellectual life could be the size of a duke's court, under smaller astronomies than we shall see again. But because knowledge is "larger" now, and no part of the world is sealed to it, must this be the end of seeing the connection of art, philosophy, and yes, science—as real as they ever were in that smaller continuum? Surely the closer interconnection of the physical world is telling us otherwise. In *death* and life.

I begin to see that agnosticism is a pale life unless, like any other religion, it is lived. Because I broke through the egg at the chickhole marked Art, doesn't preclude a temperament as religious as the churched, or an inquiry as rational as—the rational. In my work, it begins to seem to me, I am no longer the "novelist" or "short-story writer" which the American mode likes to have me. Nor even a writer only, though for passports and pickpockets that will do. I am the thing being written at the time. I am *this* one, now.

Going back over one's work, one can see from earliest times certain para-forms emerging. If one is crazy, these are *idées fixes;* if one is sane these are systemic views. A mind is not given but makes itself, out of whatever is at hand and sticking-tape—and is not a private possession, but an offering. Every "essay" I had ever written was in effect a way of telling *what* was offered to *whom.* I had always had to write everything, no matter the subject, as if my life depended on it. Of course—it does.

*   *   *

That year, in a hired hall somewhere, or maybe the Y, three or four writers got together and more or less reported the death of the novel. A lot of people paid to hear. I didn't go, because I already knew about it, but I read the account the next morning. What these sighing Alexanders had said was that "modern times" wasn't good for novel-making. They were right, of course. Modern times never are.

If a writer sees himself too regularly as an inhabitant of this, he may well be in trouble. An Era is such a dull place for a book to be. Once, when I told a "serious" novelist he had a talent for the comic he oughtn't deny, he took it as a put-down. "I want to make a *serious* impact on my times." He and I clearly differed on what comedy was, but still I was awe-struck. He sighted "the times" along the barrel of his .22—bang! Meanwhile I was up to my neck in it—it was having such an impact on me.

Modern times is a bad place for seeing the great metaphors that all art must have. In the mixed media that modernity always inhabits, God is often very possibly dead, but the arts are surely. They are so because they form part of the tangible godhead of that daily life which all men, including artists, are trained to see small. There, in the slim incarnation of our lives as we can see them now, painting is always on its last pop cycle, and music, shorn of the "ancient" melodies, is silent. Even the past is never as rigid as modernity is. For, looking back, we can see without pain that art is fluid, or even celebrate how art has united with document. But for *today,* the arts are always catatonic—fixed. This comes about because the document of our own time affrights us all. And the idea that art must be document, or should be, or *will* be—cuts at the very wrist of the artist, as his hand grips what it can, midstream.

A novel is a kind of enclosure. So of course is a poem, a watercolor, a fugue. But the novel, whether it maps by way of people or dream, or in the very essence of the void, still sets itself up as taking place somewhere within the human stockade. So, in effect it always takes place within that prison. It makes a place for itself there, sometimes cosmic or international, sometimes parochial, in a street or a town or a childhood—or in the great savannahs of a single mind. But always, the novel in some sense will tell us about a place, actual or metaphysical. For the novel, place is the devouring unity. The nature of the novel is to tell us what the nature of some part of the prison is.

"And it was so much easier, wasn't it," you hear people say, "when the enclosures were there for all to see—and almost certain to be strictly regional. When the world had *useful* boundaries, never seeing itself too large or too small—look at Barchester! While look at us—fragmented, moonborne, yet at the same time colonized to the inch, tape-recorded in every known Babelese, and *shhh,* worst of all, *on camera,* down to the very declivities of our newly-to-be-exchanged worlds—or hearts." I think rather that the people of an era never really see themselves as living in those neat amphitheatres which art or history will later assign. Where are we to find again the tidy Barchester of yore? In the reminder that Trollope—a man of many other milieus by the way—gave us it.

In the nineteenth century, a novelist expected to depend on the dignity of a literal setting, often an agreed-upon reality gained from what men already knew of such a habitat—from which starting-place he might then go on. The degree to which he could depart from it into further recesses or heights, would determine the greatness of his work, and this is what keeps great novels accessible. Agreed-upon reality never stays the same. Places disappear. But in time, a great novel sheds its literal place, whatever that may be, for an eternal one.

To that modernity of the moment—us—it is the concept of place itself which has most altered. Will we ourselves be magnificent in all those spaces that are to be—or only ever more cramped back into what we miserably are? In literature, has even the most traditionalist sense of a particular place long been swamped by those other unities, action and time?

What's going to go next? For the world and the novel, what is "place" now?

I guess we see clearest what it no longer is. As late as 1932, there was another English novelist in the tradition of Brontë, Winifred Holtby. Her much-praised *South Riding* could subtitle itself *An English Landscape* and mean it, in the old exhaustive way from manorhouse to councilhall, squire to alderman. Reading it now, one suspects that for many in its own time it was already *déjà vu*. For by then, the concepts of place and place-time had so altered that novelists either were affected, or had already helped to alter them. For all men, the old Aristotelian unities were shaken forevermore— or again. By 1930, Robert Musil had already published *The Man Without Qualities,* where a 1913 Vienna vibrated with all the interpenetrations of a "modern" city, and chapters had headings like "If there is such a thing as a sense of reality . . . ," or "Which remarkably does not get us anywhere." Proust had written. Joyce had given us his Dublin of the mind, and Kafka had given us a paralyzed geography in which man stood on the pinpoint of himself. Some of this had already been done before—some always has. But for the art of the future, and the man—the psyche was to be the recognized "place" now.

So, it's come about that literal place-reality in the novel can no longer impose the same dignity or force. We can neither read nor write about it solely in the old way, without that unalterable flash of *déjà vu*. New enclosures, long since sighted by literature, make this impossible. And these in time become the new convention, as we have it now: "Better to ignore place altogether now. Or make it metaphysical." For of course, a convention is an either-or proposition. It never lets you do both.

And in the American novel, the dilemma has been particularly sharp. For we were still lagging in the pioneer's lively enthusiasm for *real* places, new ones, and for that "American experience" so rooted in them. No one wished to annihilate this, or could. What happened was simpler. Certain places, mostly urban, became proper literary; "modern" novels could take place there without fear or ridicule, or damnwell had to. The rest of the country could go back to pulp, and damnnear did. The West went into the westerns. The South redeemed itself, as the special home of our guilt. The small town disappeared down a trapdoor marked Babbitt. And nobody heard tell anymore of the farm. Not in high places. And so arose a new American literary convention, of unparalleled naiveté.

A "regional" novelist was now a man born in the sticks and doomed to write about it, under rhythmically weathered titles: *Hardscrabble Sky, A Light Sweat Over the Carolinas,* this to let the reader know that the book's prostitutes would come from the fields and there would be no highclass restaurants. Metropolitan novels meanwhile, even if bad were never *re-gional*. The provinces had too much parvenu respect for the city, and the city agreed with them. Across the nation, the whole literary push had been toward the cities—as in Dreiser, whose novels were saved by that fact. Or toward Europe—for experience of which Cather, Anderson and Wescott could be condescended to, and Hemingway praised, for having once again (after Wharton and James) brought Europe back to us. For thirty years, literature rushed east, and many writers sank there, in all the artificialities that a buried nativity can become. But, as with any convention, all writers have been affected by it. For, if "rural" now meant "rube" forever, the city now became the very citadel and symbol of Nowhere.

It has been several other clichés in its time. Once, as in Dos Passos, it was the Great Collage. Before that, the abattoir, and the "teeming poor." Or in a later frivolous era, the Penthouse. For the real American interest is in change, and the city is the place that changes most, and most "modernly." In time, the city has become the best place for an American novel to be, since all psyches of any importance are presumed to be there. At last it has escaped the old dilemma of place altogether, by becoming *the* existential Place. Totally surreal, of course, never parochial; the absolutist novel cannot be both. Personae in the novels of this type wear their eyeballs on stalks and float down nameless avenues, like paranoid balloons. The Action: Unisex in Nighttown. Probable Title: a single symbol, maybe &, or $. And, presto, a new cliché, of sorts. Natives of the city will once again recognize an old one: The City—by an author who comes from somewhere else.

A writer's region is what he makes it, every time. Great novels will not be impeded by the presence of cows there. And the absence of them, or the presence of pavement, has never kept great urban novelists from a kind of rural concentration. Dickens, Musil, Biely, Proust—are all great regionalists of a city kind. London, Vienna, St. Petersburg, Paris all "live" in their pages, through people who if written of elsewhere would not be as they are. Looking back to those eras, the perfumes and stinks, and the ecology, are all clear to us now. The people live in the scenery of those cities, and the city now lives in the people, tangentially, through their eyes and minds, or as in Biely, like a hero itself in the wake of supernumeraries, its streets following like waves the little people it makes flotsam of. Simple. Yet for our times, our own times always, what a balancing! For a novel at best is never a historical or descriptive thesis, but a sub-news or a supra-news of the world, which all but drags the novelist down, or up and out with it. The novel is rescued life.

What a novelist must trust to is that continuity exists somewhere, somehow to be seen, perhaps as a useful terror strikes his heart. Casting ahead, in order to *see* change in the name of intellectual duty, will not help me. Nor will going back—to such as West Egg or Wessex or Yoknapatawpha; these and their kind hang like mosques made for once only, above their own documents. The novel never goes back in that sense, just as it never leaves the documents as they were. After *seeing* an enclosure, which means making one, a writer may then choose to leave it, as a philosopher leaves a fully expressed idea. Or he may elect to spend his writing life there. But except as a reader, another writer will not be able to accompany him.

So, every age is a sighing Alexander—how can there possibly be more than *this*? Yet every decade brings in more documents. Ours asks the literary artist in particular to shiver and to bow before these—forgetting that the "facts" of the past are often very much what art has made of them. Sometimes, one is tempted to say that all art of any kind is an attempt to make the unimaginative imagine—imagination.

And there's no perfect time for it—except now. "Modern times" sees itself as the time of the breaking up of the myths. That may well be its. The age which my own most reminds me of is the medieval—the same brutality and enchantment, the same sense of homunculus peering around the cornice of a history happening far from him—and the same crusade toward a heaven not here. It's chill, lone, and wuthering for some, an overheated faeryland for others, and running with guilty blood for all. An age when change can be caught like quicksilver and held up against the gloss of what we think we remember, where all the gauntlets of starvation and curtailed freedom are still thrown down to us, while sex will be our aphrodisiac and the documents our earthly paradise—who can fail to recognize that description? It is a marvelous time for art.

A Conversation with
Margaret Atwood

This interview took place in early February, 1978, just before Margaret Atwood left for a poetry-reading trip in the United States. The interviewer is Joyce Carol Oates.

INTERVIEWER: Your books of poetry—*The Circle Game* (which was awarded the Governor General's Award in 1966), *The Animals in That Country, The Journals of Susanna Moodie, Procedures for Underground, Power Politics,* and *You Are Happy*—differ a great deal in content, yet there is a remarkable similarity of tone, of rhythm, of "texture." Your earlier poems, for instance "Journey to the Interior" and "The Circle Game" itself, show a mastery of craftsmanship that is rather unusual in first books. From whom did you learn, consciously or unconsciously?

ATWOOD: When I first started writing I was sixteen and in high school, in Toronto, in the fifties, and I knew nothing about either modern poetry or Canadian poetry. So my first influences were Poe and Shelley! When I got to university, I began discovering modern and Canadian poetry, chiefly the latter. I read my way through the library of a faculty member who, being a poet herself, had an extensive collection. I might mention such names as P. K. Page, Margaret Avison, whose *Winter Sun* I reviewed when I was in university, James Reaney, D. G. Jones, and certain poems of Douglas Le Pan. These poets were important to me not only as poets but as examples of the fact that you *could* get a book published. You would have to have known the situation in Canada at the time to realize how important this was to me.

It's kind of you to say that you found my first book accomplished, but by the time it came out, I'd been writing for ten years. Also, *The Circle Game* isn't my real "first book"; there was another one, seven poems long, which appeared in 1961, for which I set the type and designed and printed the cover. I doubt that you would find it quite so unusual!

INTERVIEWER: Do you enjoy reading your poetry, in general?

ATWOOD: A good poetry reading is a delightful and exhilarating experience. A bad one is awful. It depends on the audience, on your mood at the time, on whether you and the audience "like" each other. . . . I guess we've all run into the resident madman and the faculty member who thinks he can put a notch in his gun by being gratuitously rude to you at the little luncheon or whatever thrown in your honor. . . . Mostly I just get colds.

INTERVIEWER: Your sense of the absurd—and of the essential playfulness of the absurd—is one of the elements in your writing that I particularly admire. What inspired your novel *The Edible Woman*—especially that surreal final scene—and *Lady Oracle*?

ATWOOD: *Edible Woman* was written in 1965, before the Women's Liberation Movement had begun. It was still very much the model pattern, in Canada anyway, to take a crummy job and then marry to get away from it. I was writing about an object of consumption (namely, my bright but otherwise ordinary girl) in a consumer society. Appropriately, she works for a market research company. Even in 1969, when the book was finally published, some critics saw the view as essentially "young" or "neurotic." I would mature, they felt, and things (i.e. marriage and kids) would fall into place.

About the cake in the shape of a woman—all I can tell you is that I used to be a very good cake decorator and was often asked to reproduce various objects in pastry and icing. Also, in my walks past pastry stores, I always wondered why people made replicas of things—brides and grooms, for instance, or Mickey Mice—and then ate them. It seems a mysterious thing to do. But for my heroine to make a false image of herself and then consume it was entirely appropriate, given the story—don't you think?

Lady Oracle was written much later—almost ten years later. Again, I'm not sure where it began, but the central character is a writer of Gothic romances partly because I've always wondered what it was about these books that appealed—do so many women think of themselves as menaced on all sides, and of their husbands as potential murderers? And what about that "Mad Wife" left over from *Jane Eyre*? Are these our secret plots?

The hypothesis of the book, insofar as there is one, is: what happens to someone who lives in the "real" world but does it as though this "other" world is the real one? This may be the plight of many more of us than we care to admit.

INTERVIEWER: Your novel *Surfacing* has been related to James Dickey's

Deliverance. I see only a superficial, rather misleading relationship. Could you comment?

ATWOOD: There is a relationship of sorts, but for me it's one of opposites. For the central figure in Dickey's book, as I recall, nature is something wild, untamed, feminine, dangerous and mysterious, that he must struggle with, confront, conquer, overcome. Doing this involves killing. For me, the books cognate with Dickey's are Mailer's *Why We Are in Vietnam*, Faulkner's *Bear*, Hemingway's "Short Happy Life of Francis Macomber," and, if you like, *Moby Dick*, though Ahab was not seen by Melville as having chosen the right path. The books cognate with mine are Canadian and probably unknown in the United States; Howard O'Hagan's *Tay John* is one of them.

INTERVIEWER: "The Man From Mars," which appeared in *Ontario Review* 6, is a delightful story, and drew a great deal of favorable comments from our readers. Were your hapless heroine and indefatigable suitor based on "real" people? And is there any political significance to the title?

ATWOOD: I've found over the years that I can never explain or account for any reader response to my work. It constantly amazes me—and this isn't false modesty—that my work sells as well as it does. I consider it rather quirky and eccentric.

Real people? In a way. The situation was real, the characters are fictional.

The title . . . I'm not sure whether the significance is "political" or not; what it means to me is that we all have a way of dehumanizing anything which is strange or exotic to us. In our arrogance, we take ourselves to be the norm, and measure everyone else against it. The man of course is not from Mars; he is from earth, like everyone else. But there's no way of accounting for the atrocities that people perform on other people except by the "Martian" factor, the failure to see one's victims as fully human.

INTERVIEWER: I believe you're one of the few Canadian writers who is not associated with any university, and I assume this is deliberate.

ATWOOD: Yes, I enjoyed students when I taught in 1967–68, but I could not handle faculty meetings and departmental politics. I don't understand it. I'm not good in those situations. The reason I don't teach is the same reason I don't wait on tables, which I also used to do: right now I don't have to. If I have to do either again, I will. If it's a choice, I'd take teaching, which is less physically exhausting and doesn't put you off your food so much.

INTERVIEWER: You have drawn upon your student days at Harvard quite infrequently in your writing. Did you enjoy your stay there?

ATWOOD: Well . . . Harvard is sort of like anchovies. An acquired taste. But in my case, one that I could never truly acquire, because at that time— early and mid-sixties—they wouldn't let women into Lamont Library, and that was where they kept all the modern poetry and records. So I always felt a little like a sort of wart or wen on the great male academic skin. I felt as if I was there on sufferance. Harvard, you know, didn't hire women to teach in it, so the male professors were all very nice. We ladies were no threat. There was a joke among the woman students that the best way to pass your orals was to stuff a pillow up your dress, because they would all be so terrified of having parturition take place on the Persian rug that they would just ask you your name and give you a pass. One of my female colleagues was almost expelled for dressing like a woman of loose virtue. Actually she was a Latvian Shakespearian scholar with somewhat different ideas of dress than the rest of us tweedy, buttoned types.

So I enjoyed it, yes, in a nervous sort of way. There were some fine lecturers, and Widener Library is wonderful. And little madnesses go on there which seem unlike those of any other place. I often wondered what happened to the man who was rumored to have broken into Houghton Library (Rare Books) in order to expose himself to the Gutenberg Bible. I do have two "Harvard" stories, which are in *Dancing Girls*.

The most important things about the experience for me were: it was the place where I first learned urban fear. (Before I went there, I always walked around at night, didn't bother about locked doors, etc. If you behaved that way in Cambridge you were dead.) And, for various reasons, it was the place where I started thinking seriously about Canada as having a shape and a culture of its own. Partly because I was studying the literature of the American Puritans, which was not notable for its purely literary values—if one can study this in a university, I thought, why not Canadian literature? (you must understand that at that time Canadian literature was simply not taught in high schools and universities in Canada)—and partly because Boston was, in certain ways, so similar, in climate and landscape, to parts of Canada. One began to look for differences.

INTERVIEWER: Did you discover any odd or upsetting attitudes toward Canada while living at Cambridge?

ATWOOD: It's not that anyone in Boston—few in the Graduate School were *from* that area in any case; they came from all over the U.S. and from non-North American countries as well—it's not that the Americans I met had any odd or "upsetting" attitudes towards Canada. They simply didn't have any attitudes at all. They had a vague idea that such a place existed—it was that blank area north of the map where the bad weather came from—but if they thought about it at all they found it boring. They seemed to want to believe that my father was a Mounted Policeman and that we lived in igloos all year round, and I must admit that after a while I took a certain pleasure in encouraging these beliefs. (Recall that this was before the Vietnam crisis, during which many Americans came to regard Canada as the Great Good Place or game refuge to which they might escape.) I met a number of Southerners and got to know some of them; they seemed to resent "the North" in some of the same ways as did the handful of Canadians there, though for different reasons.

INTERVIEWER: Why had you gone to Harvard in the first place?

ATWOOD: Because—to trace it back—Canada had not hired one Jerome H. Buckley back in the Depression when he was looking for work. He had gone to the States and had become a leading Victorianist. The Victorian period was "my period," and I had won a Woodrow Wilson Fellowship, so I went to Harvard to study with Dr. Buckley. There is, you know, a kind of Canadian Mafia at Harvard and elsewhere in the States. Quite a few of the well-known professors at Harvard were closet Canadians. However, they kept their identities secret, for the most part, except when talking with other Canadians. They'd learned by experience that Americans found a revelation of one's Canadian-ness, dropped, for instance, into the middle of a sherry party, about as interesting as the announcement that one had had mashed potatoes for lunch. The beginning of Canadian cultural nationalism was not "Am I really that oppressed?" but "Am I really that boring?" You see, we had never been taught much about our own history or culture—but that's another whole story.

INTERVIEWER: Is there a very distinctive difference between American "literary" responses and Canadian?

ATWOOD: I feel that American literary responses are, quite simply, more literary—at least in the groups of people with whom I'm likely to come in contact. I think the difference is that in the States, there is a "literary" culture and a largely non-literary one, whereas in Canada these overlap a great deal more. I'm saying this only on the basis of who is likely to turn up at a poetry reading. But my experience isn't really wide enough to justify such general statements.

I always enjoy going to the States; it's an escape for me, from my own quite demanding culture. People there are polite to me, as they would be to a visiting foreigner (which I am), and, though interested, disinterested. Americans have such enthusiasms. It's a change from the gloom here, the suspicion. But of course, Canada is where I really live. That's why I can enjoy the States so much for brief periods of time.

INTERVIEWER: What sort of working habits have you?

ATWOOD: My working habits have changed over the years, according to the circumstances of my life. I started writing seriously—though this may seem ludicrous—when I was sixteen and in fourth year high school. At that time I wrote in the evenings when I was supposed to be doing homework, on weekends and occasionally during school hours. After that, I was in university for four years and wrote between classes, after hours, etc.—a haphazard pattern. I didn't have very regular habits as a student, either; I was a procrastinator and still am, so it helps me to set myself deadlines. (This applies only to prose, of course. Poetry does not get written, by me at least, as a matter of will.) During my years as a graduate student, odd-job-holder, university lecturer of the lowest order—up till the age of about twenty-seven or so—I almost had to write at night, and would stay up quite late. I'm not sure how I wrote at all the first year I spent as a "real" university teacher (1967–68, in Montreal). I was very busy and exhausted, and lost a lot of weight. But I seem to have been writing some then, too. I can't remember when I did it.

I became an afternoon writer when I had afternoons. When I was able to write full time, I used to spend the morning procrastinating and worrying, then plunge into the manuscript in a frenzy of anxiety around 3:00 when it looked as though I might not get anything done. Since the birth of my daughter, I've had to cut down on the procrastination. I still try to spend the afternoons writing, though the preliminary period of anxiety is somewhat shorter. I suppose this is a more efficient use of time. The fact is that blank pages inspire me with terror. What will I put on them? Will it be good enough? Will I have to throw it out? And so forth. I suspect most writers are like this.

INTERVIEWER: Do you work on more than one project at a time?

ATWOOD: One project at a time, ideally. I am by nature lazy, sluggish and of low energy. It constantly amazes me that I do anything at all.

INTERVIEWER: How long, approximately, did it take you to write each of your three novels?

ATWOOD: I wrote *Edible Woman* in unused University of British Columbia exam books from April to August of 1965. I revised in the fall. For reasons I won't go into, the publisher lost the manuscript, and I was so naive about the process that I thought it normal for them to take two years to tell me anything about it. The book was finally published in 1969. I had written another unpublished novel before this, and wrote another unpublished, unfinished one after it. Then I wrote *Surfacing*, from about December 1969 to August 1970. There were only minor revisions and some retyping, though the handwritten version was extensively revised. *Lady Oracle* took much longer, partly because I was living a life filled with more interruptions, partly because it changed a lot while I was writing it. It took about two and one-half years, off and on.

INTERVIEWER: I've enjoyed the cartoons of yours I've seen. Is drawing another of your talents . . . ?

ATWOOD: I paint a little and draw, for my own amusement. I've been drawing a political cartoon strip for a Canadian magazine—*This Magazine*—for some years, under the pseudonym of "Bart Gerrard" (it's nice to get hate mail when they don't even know it's *you*) and I have a children's book coming out in Canada, in March, for the smallest age group, written, hand-lettered and illustrated by myself. I hesitate to call this a "talent," since I know I'm not very good; that is, I have to rub out a lot in order to get the heads the same size and I have difficulty drawing owls flying sideways.

INTERVIEWER: You must be disturbed by literary journalists' efforts to categorize you—to package you as "The Reigning Queen of Canadian Literature," or a national prophetess, or even a Medusa. What have your reactions been?

ATWOOD: I dislike the kinds of title you mention; I find "Reigning Queen" a particularly offensive one, implying as it does that literature, as practiced by women anyway, is either a monarchy or a beehive. In any case, there's only room for one "reigning queen," who will presumably be stung to death later on when she can't lay any more eggs. Such titles are insulting to the many fine women writers in this country (Marian Engel, Alice Munro, Margaret Laurence, to name three) and threatening to me. Anyone who takes language seriously would never use such a metaphor without being aware of its sinister range of meanings.

I suppose Canada is hungry for a few visible "stars," having been without any for so long. The danger to the writer is early stellification—one may become a vaporous ball of gas. But only if captivated by one's image. Luckily, my image here, as reflected in the press, has not been very captivating, at least to me. I can do without "Medusa." (It's one of the hazards of naturally curly hair.)

INTERVIEWER: Do you think that reviewers and critics have, on the whole, been "fair" to you? Has there been any sort of backlash, as an inevitable consequence of your "rise to fame"?

ATWOOD: Of course there has been a "backlash"; there always is, but vicious attacks in Canada tend to be much more open and personal than in the United States, partly because of the Celtic, blackly satiric literary tradition and partly because it's much more like a small town. We live in each others' pockets here and the dust and gloom is therefore more intense. There are mixed feelings about small-town boys and girls making good, as you know. On the one hand we're proud of them because they're ours; on the other hand we don't like them getting too big for their boots, so we cut them down whenever possible; on the other hand (Canada, like Kali, has more than two hands), we can't quite believe that one of ours can *really* be any good—surely it's all some kind of hype or fraud; and on yet another hand, the success of one of our members is a reproach to us. If he could do it, why can't we?

There's that; but also, there have been a number of fair-minded, objectively critical pieces which have dealt genuinely with the shape and characteristics of my work and its strengths and weaknesses. Canadian critics are always more close-mouthed than American ones; they seldom go overboard, and they look with great suspicion upon cult figures, especially their own. This has definite advantages. I think American writers are often made dizzy by a sudden rocket-like stellification, then confused when they are just as enthusiastically banished to outer darkness. Canadian writers are (to put it mildly) seldom permitted to get swelled heads.

INTERVIEWER: An entire issue of *The Malahat Review* was devoted to you in Winter 1977. I remember being rather surprised by a photographic essay called "Anima," and wonder what your reactions to it, and to the volume as a whole, were.

ATWOOD: I also was rather surprised. But then, my capacity to be surprised by other people's reactions to me is, I have discovered, infinite. I don't really see myself as a sort of buttock coming out of an egg (or was it the other way around), and as I recall there were quite a few naked ladies with large breasts. But I think the collage sequence was supposed to have been inspired by my work rather than by my finite personal being, which in this climate is usually swathed in wool. Even so???

The truth is that I am not a very glamorous person. Writers aren't, really. All they do is sit around and write, which I suppose is as commendable as sitting around painting your toenails, but will never make it into the fashion magazines. So when I see myself being glamorized or idealized, it makes me squirm somewhat. Of course I'm as vain as most people. I'd rather see a picture of myself looking good than one of myself looking awful. But I've seen so many of both by now, some taken minutes apart. . . . A photo is only a view.

INTERVIEWER: Do you think there are any problems inherent in the fact that so many of the arts are state-supported in Canada? As an American I am impressed with the generosity of the Canadian government, but as a reader and critic I am frequently disturbed by the kinds of publications funded by the Canada Council and the various arts councils. Small presses do not seem to offer much editing advice, with the consequence that books tumble from presses, are "distributed" minimally, and allowed to go out of print almost at once. Without wanting to discourage young writers, I must say that the sheer quantity of hurried and slovenly writing published in Canada is rather demoralizing. (Of course the same thing is rapidly becoming true in the States.) There seems to be no tradition any longer of apprenticeship; student writers are being "published"—or at least printed—and in the long run premature publication will have a deleterious effect on their craft. What is your opinion?—or is this too dangerous an enquiry?

ATWOOD: This is not at all a dangerous enquiry. There are several different questions here, though, and I will try to deal with them one at a time.

The Canadian literary scene has been likened (by myself, in fact), to a group of figures dancing with considerable vigor and some grace on the edge of a precipice. The precipice was always there, though it's become more visible recently. I'm referring of course to the Québec situation and the potential splitting-up of Canada. But the group of figures was not always there—not so long ago there were only a few solitary writers who, in the field of fiction anyway, didn't know each other—and they did not always dance, with or without grace and vigor.

To put it more plainly: When I began writing, in the late fifties and early sixties, there were five or so literary magazines in the entire country. The number of books of poetry that came out in a year—including small press books and privately printed ones—was under twenty. The new Canadian novels published in a year could usually be counted on the fingers of one hand. Canadian literature was not recognized as a legitimate field of study. Canadian books were not taught in schools. The epithet "Canadian writer" was a term of derision, even to Canadian writers. Almost every writer's ambition was to get out of the country to some place "real" in a literary sense, or at least some place where he could get his books published. Canadian writers were not known in their own country, and even when published were rarely bought or reviewed. (Mordecai Richler's first novel sold 3 copies in Canada. The press run of even a respectable book of poetry was considered good at 200. The publishers of *The Circle Game* initially printed 450, and were worried that they had done too many. Even now, Canadian paperbacks account for maybe 3 percent of total paperback sales in Canada, and that includes Harlequin Romances.)

We can't take the publishing industry for granted, as one can in the States. It is *always* tottering on the brink of collapse. We can't take our own existence as writers for granted. True, there has been about a 1,000 percent growth in the publishing industry in the last 20 years, but remember that started from near zero. So what is viewed by an American as "generosity" is seen by us simply as necessity. If the government support that publishers currently receive were to be withdrawn, the industry, by and large, would collapse. The "Canadian Renaissance" in the arts was made possible, in large part, by the Canada Council. None of us like this situation. But none of us want to be back in 1961, either.

Now . . . editing in small presses. As an ex-editor for a small press, Anansi, I have to protest. Editorial time by the bucketful was poured into our books. Our chief editor at that time was Dennis Lee, who is renowned here as an absolutely devoted editor. So it isn't universal. I'd say you get about the same mix as you might in the States: some presses serious about the writing, some existing only to get their members and friends into print. I think you see the bad writing here because more of it makes its way across your desk. You couldn't possibly even *read* all of it that comes out in the States; the sheer volume is so high.

But to me, small presses, good or bad, are a necessity. They're like all those Elizabethan melodramas. Without them, Shakespeare would have had no milieu. They were a place where a writer could, as it were, "try out." Same with "little" magazines. I guess I have a certain belief in the reader, the intelligent reader. I think books will eventually find their own level. This may be overly optimistic.

INTERVIEWER: I am often annoyed by critics' attempts to reduce complex works of art to simple "thematic" statements. Why are Canadian critics in particular so obsessed with statement and theme at the expense of a thoughtful consideration of technique?

ATWOOD: I'm probably one of those critics who has annoyed you, since my only critical work, *Survival: A Thematic Guide to Canadian Literature*, is concerned almost exclusively to demonstrate that there are such things as Canadian themes, which differ either in substance or in emphasis from their counterparts in English and American literature. Would it help if I told you that, even after I had written this book—which caused rather a furor here, almost as if I'd said that the Emperor was naked—many critics resolutely continued to deny that there was any such thing as a "Canadian" literature?

We've tried very hard over the past few decades to demonstrate our own existence, our own right to exist. Usually we ourselves—the writers, that is—don't doubt it; the voices of denial come from elsewhere. But this may explain, a little anyway, the concern with "theme." One can only afford "a thoughtful consideration of technique" when the question of mere existence is no longer a question.

Lies: Notes on Craft

NED ROREM

I

My work is my truth. Insofar as that work is also art it is also your truth. That that art may lie makes it no less true. A symbol posing as the real thing betrays itself, yet the betrayal can't disqualify the symbol's status as symbol.

That painting there's not true to life, it's scarcely true to paint. That tune's not natural, not birdsong, not wind's sough, it's false to outdoors. It sounds like nothing else. It lies.

According to who's listening we all are liars. Artists' fables are worth attending. Lies of art ring true.

Am I incapable of truth because I don't know what it is? Whatever truth may be, it's not the opposite of lie. In art it is that which can be cared about, that which we believe.

Those who say, "Look out, he'll quote you in that diary," are the very ones I never notice. The others, they're safe, they can't win, I don't quote, I misquote.

Lurking behind the exquisite monster, I'm capable of guidance—that is, of guiding him. The matriarch's mother.

Who most loathe the diary are those depicted within. What they most loathe is not precious archness, not opinions stated as facts nor the urbane reflections posing as pastorale pensées, but seeing their life reduced to anecdote, however crass or laudatory: "I was there," they say, "I keep a diary too, I remember what happened, and you're wrong." Of course there's no such thing as *the* truth, there is only *one's* truth, and even that fluxes with each passing hour. Though I disown nothing, I've now come to value discretion, even to claim it among virtues far higher than mere truth. Mere truth. Yet in the old days it never occurred to me that friends would feel hurt by my passing verities.

A book's a book, not real life. Yet when offered for real, as in a diary, a book must be arranged to seem real. From the very arranging an author learns artifices of life itself, artifices which in the telling become more natural than in their earlier stage of mere being. Of mere being.

All true artists are modest but they try not to show it.
No true artists are modest but they pretend to be.
Common to all greatness is the sense of vulnerability, and the keynote of greatness is less genius than patience.

Was Rashomon three versions of a lie, or of a truth? Is any diary less honest inherently than a novel?

Diaries are a sideline, notebooks wherein a person records his problems of work and play. Nearly always, though, they are kept with the intention of being read; so like all art they dissimulate by becoming a sort of code. The diarist doesn't present himself but an idea of himself, and only that idea of himself which he chooses to publicize.

As a literary form the diary is hardly new (it's far older than the novel), except as an indigenous American utterance, public confession not having been our bent until recently. Yet confession risks adopting the features of the very mask that some say novelists hide behind. Our century's best known diarist, André Gide, during the blitzes of World War II blissfully notated adventures with Arab lads in his Biskra retreat. To tell it like it is, is no more a property of diaries than of fiction. Lives are not facts, nor does the present moment exist; an author can necessarily record the present only after the fact. Of itself truth is not persuasive, even less is it art. And who, including the diarist himself, can prove that the character represented is, in this guise, finally, the *real* author? Does Baudelaire's journal disclose more to us of Baudelaire than Genet's novels do of Genet? Could Philip Roth have composed his complaint in another form without its becoming more rather than less of a mask? To fictionalize the real makes it easier to be honest. The realist novel of the thirties became the unrealistic autobiography of the sixties. Still, all real works of art (be they geometric sculptures, children's poetry, or reports on Hanoi) speak to us, by definition, with their creator's voice.

A voice is a voice, unfakeable. No matter what tone we pretend to—or in fact *do*—project, no matter how we try to shade or disguise that voice, no matter what master's words or songs we filch and, like reverse Dybbuks, sing through our own lips, we cannot lie. No one can lie, the body cannot lie, and the wiliest plagiarism is verifiable. What is not verifiable is why those fingerprints are more amusing than these, or why some standard stolen goods take on a wilder luster on a thief's back. Alas, most thefts are of trash and remain trash.

The difference between a journalist and a diarist is that one reports what happened, the other reports a reaction to what happened. Yet both are susceptible to cries of liar. Rightly. Less truthful than a painter, a photographer *is* bias: a camera selects the angle and snaps its subject unaware, especially if the subject is a tree. The tree is a lie, but not the picture of it. If truth is fact, then all art—which only represents fact, and one person's version of that—lies, but by extension speaks true.

Sarah confides she's been glancing through some of my diary notes and hopes, should they ever be published, that I'll delete a reflection about her voice sounding sad on the phone. Now, I'm as responsive to the desires of Sarah as to any living person, but it is a diarist's nature to include precisely what others would choose him to exclude. There lies the danger. Estrangements don't come from what people find gossipy about other people, but from what they find incomplete—and thus untrue—about themselves, for truth means only the whole truth. Indeed, for me to read what others write about myself is to see my life reduced to several lines—sometimes ecstatic, sometimes sarcastic—and to find myself miniaturized, and existing for others who, because they see me just fractionally, see me as peripheral to their own laws. In a diary no mention of a person can be, to that person, the *right* mention, since no mention of anything (even of e = mc²) is all-inclusive and therefore cannot be anything but a lie. Even my own mention of others, or of myself, means to me only what it means during the moment I mention it, since we change pores—natures, *truth*— with each fluid second.

What is comparatively stable is the sadness of Sarah's voice on the phone. If this were all that signified to me I would (at her request) omit mention of it, as wrongly I have omitted whimsies or eccentricities or momentary "perversions," at their request, of others, thereby diluting the blood—the *truth, my* truth, however superficial—of the published diary in the past, because the diary became no longer a biased monologue but a fair exchange. If I mention the sadness of Sarah's voice it's because I am so vulnerable to the sound; in fact my susceptibility is such that, when we met decades ago, I understood that for the remainder of my life another person would never fill her special shoes, and that I could (and largely did) renounce a certain sociability without feeling anything but richer. She is everything, and to write that is to compromise us both far more than any mention of her sad voice. Should she choose that I also delete this paragraph, I shall. Though where then will be my documented verities, fragmented but contradictorily (if only through style) flowing, continual, and in a way necessary because inimitable?

So-called Freudian slips of the tongue would interest me more if they were less precisely just that: mere slips, a foot's accidental excursion into a puddle which is not really too foreign an environment for a foot. Sound-alikes are too predictably the result of fatigue or embarrassment, or the human penchant for rhyme, for building on a given: mercy for merry, sorrow queen for sour cream, sew me to a sheet for show me to a seat, maybe money for honey. To call your present lover by the name of a previous lover is not even so rare. Give me someone who unexpectedly says butterfly instead of oatmeal, who says ambergris for confidential, yes for when, peach for swan, or who, at twenty and for the first time ever, calls his father mother.

Full time and willy nilly do I pursue two careers without ever knowing for sure if their mutual infringement is harmful or fruitful. To spill out verbs instead of notes should disquiet me. Yet this prose is a sieve: What oozes through is rarefied, becomes distilled and turns to "abstract" sound on staves. Whatever clogs the meshes I scrape out and smear undiluted onto diary paper.

How can I know if my prose and music interfere with each other. Without the prose would the music be better or just thicker? Without the music would there be a subject for the prose?

Only as a composer am I qualified to soliloquize, since my life is no longer amorous, garrulous, or drunk, and since I've no more friends— certainly no new ones (who would they be? and what could they give me that I couldn't find in their works?—except maybe a taxi ride to the hospital in moments of need, moments, however, growing paradoxically fewer as one gets feebler). Killing time. Now that I am allowed to speak, have I any more to say?

A diary—a public diary—is no more spontaneously composed than a symphony. Yes, themes may come all of a piece from the impulsive and recalcitrant muse, but they are set in gold alone, or sewn together, and forever revised before they are published. That the expressive (the artistic, if you will) process can be untampered-with is fallacy. Abandon takes rehearsal. Sometimes a song, a paragraph (like this one) emerges effortlessly. However it springs forth, art must seem seamless.

The hero of my diary is a fictional man upon whom I've worked hard but who has little to do with me—including the me penning this sentence, who is also the hero of my diary.

II

Music's the grandest lie. Music's not Truth, but a representation of one aspect of fact which, in turn, is but one aspect of truth. Even possibly truth has no needed tie to fact. In which case, yes, truth approaches music (or vice versa) but only in that generalized, befuddled, Polonius-Browning equation of truth & beauty.

Friends never complain that they have been misrepresented in my music. Have they, indeed, been represented? Even the composer cannot say.

Persuasiveness of harmony. Harmony fixes mood more than do tune or rhythm. Thus it's Chopin, or 1930's Swing, with the rapid shifting of regular secondary sevenths, that most moves me. . . . To no poet am I drawn more than to Goodman, to no painter more than to Vuillard, to no male or female visages more than to Belmondo's or Monica Vitti's. No pastry's more tempting than warm pear tarts, no sonic formula more than Bach's sequences, no ambience more than a verdant cloister, and no time of day more than twilight if I'm not alone. No danger thwarts more than the past, no fragrance exalts more than winter chestnuts (though I loathe any odor of body, perfumed or natural, even of youth which once I praised).

Beauty outlasts youth. Beauty's tougher than. Sex increasingly repels— the smell of it. To grow old is to climb higher and higher through branches which become scarcer, brittler. Almost alone up there one does see clearly far and wide and behind and beneath. But the seeing contains no understanding, nor is there much to look at, nothing to compel the gaze.

Someday formulate an answer to the oft-asked but fair question, "Does your mood effect your composition?" (The question's as fertile as: What makes a good poem for music? Depends on kind of music, requirements of singer, etc.) The answer is: I don't know—it's for an outsider to judge. Definitions of happy and sad music change with the generations, and a composer at his happiest might pen his saddest refrains. Does he compose according to how he feels today, to how he feels in general, or in delayed reaction to how he felt last year or as a child? He composes less according to momentary states than to the needs of the piece which takes on a life of its own once underway. Personal mood depends on flow of time, but when a composer is composing, his woes and joys are suspended and time jells.

People need formulas. They ask, "When do you work?", hoping to learn that composers put pen to paper each morning at seven and go on till tea. Now, by the time they put pen to paper the composing is done; this is the inscription of the act, not the act itself.

Never say, "I'm working well" to anyone, it brings bad luck. The nightmare—or rather, nightmare's sibling—which composers know too well: insomnia forcing them to jot notes all night, notes which next morning seem trivial.

The sorry postponement of writing it down, writing it down . . . because when written down it might not be good enough. Such intellectual trepidation is, if you will, uncreative—and I say "intellectual" advisedly: the intelligence of certain composers impedes them from simply making it up as it goes along. Rule of thumb: compose first, worry later. Or: speak before you think and write it down afterwards. Actually all composers think before they speak. The speaking is the writing down.

Which came first, the punishment or the crime? Was the Inquisition concocted to legitimize the pleasures of torture? Are cruel acts, committed in the name of the Lord or for the good of the people, ever honestly meant for the good of the people or in the name of the Lord? Which came first, lawbreaker or law? In music, of course, rules came after the fact, to substantiate—to justify, *excuse*—what composers made up as they went along. Let a piece flow out, then think up reasons for the flow. Yet what teacher could thus counsel a student, though precisely the reverse is straitjacketing: fearing the flow because of reasons coming before the flow?

Composers' secrets? Some love to tell secrets of the way a piece is made. It shouldn't be how, but how well. Describe form, and form is all a hearer hears. Then see that fugue of Bach, crystalline, with friendly head or heads intermittently popping forth from the tangles. Tangles? No, tails continually attached. Friends in tangled tails, crystalline, which need not be sliced like Medusa's curls or the Gordian knot, for at the end the tails grow heads again, codas, stretti, logical hoorays.

I am never *not* working, yet I never catch myself in the act. At the end of each year I've somehow produced around an hour of music, and that hour is not a few sheets of pencilled whole notes, but hundreds of pages of inked orchestration. Work is the process of composing—making it up as it goes along, which is the only precise description for the process since Homer. The action is at once so disparate and so compact that the actor is unaware, which is doubtless why I "never find myself," etc. I don't consider as work the post-compositional drudgery (often pleasant) of copying, instrumentation, rehearsal, letter-writing, or dealing with publishers, though all this is time consuming. Nor do I consider as work the compiling of my books which is the assembling of top-of-the-head prewritten fragments. I do consider as work the answering of this question—"When do you work?"—since it concerns, like musical composition, the placement of notion into order. As to when, and is it daily, I notate when I have a commissioned deadline and don't when I don't: the goal is functional, and its approach makes me scribble eight or ten hours a day. Between commissions months are eaten up looking at soap operas.

It's been decades since I've worked with the youthful Need To Express Myself, though what I do express today is better wrought and aims higher than yesterday although it might not ring truer. Our gifts are not gifts but paid for terribly. Work is not play. The crunching responsibility forces many to throw in the sponge at the height of glory. Would they have persisted even that long without encouragement?

I am able to postpone indefinitely the notation of a composition on the senseless rationale that, once written, it can never *become* written. With equal reason, I cannot complete a composition without feeling, well, there's one more piece chalked up before I die.

My musical memory is visual. Should the muse approach incongruously—on the subway, in a steambath—and find me without a notebook, I will quickly picture in my mind the five strands of a staff, snatch from the air the inspiring notes glittering like bats, glue them to the staff, take a snapshot with an imaginary camera and, reaching home, develop the film on actual paper. The result is usually worthwhile, more so than similar transactions in dreams which next morning turn out to be trash. The music of night is unworked-for, untrue; true music, transmittable music, true ease, is difficult.

Often when composing large non-vocal works I am geared less to musical format, such as a sonata, than to visual pattern or literary plot. (Sonatas have plots too, but plots without stories.) I have always associated music with words and images, and feel most at home when writing songs, choruses, operas—pieces with the impurity of an extramusical requirement. I need a propelling sight the way a dressmaker needs a dummy. But sometimes when the work is completed, to cover my traces I throw out the dummy and offer the music as an "abstraction." (The reverse process would be that of a choreographer who imposes his story upon a symphony.)

Glamour, temperament, etc.—the supposed attributes of a star—are luxury items, qualities reserved for intermissions. No true artist—no Auden, say, or Callas—brings his "difficult" side to the scene of work except as priority to speed up matters; a demanding artist, if he's an artist, is right in his demands. A nonprofessional is one who brings glamour to rehearsals.

"What do you consider your most important education?"

"Self-taught."

"But we've read you had a Master's from Juilliard."

"So I have. I'd quite forgotten."

For a degree at Juilliard one must take nonmusical courses. Having passed the entrance exams with flying colors I was not required to attend musical classes except in piano and composition. What I therefore recall most clearly of that illustrious school in 1946–48 are studies in Sociology, American History, Physical Education and, yes, Hygiene (which taught that the human diet needs copper as well as iron, copper being obtained both through apricots and through milk stored in brass vats). Also two semesters of World Literature which, if nothing else, did inspire some musical output including songs on texts both sacred and profane, notably *Four Madrigals* to Sappho fragments.

What genius! one hears of the soloist during an intermission. Why genius? He doesn't invent the music, nor does he, as people say, bring it to life. Music exists always, unrendered yet breathing, even on Grecian urns. The soloist is a vessel (an urn) through which preexisting music passes. Now a vessel may be of Steuben glass or a tin can, but a vessel is not the cause of its contents. Genius is a word I don't use. If I did, I would not, surely, apply it to an interpreter. To a composer? Well, vessel is not my word either, but Stravinsky's. Questioned as to the creative process which brought one of his masterpieces into being, he replied, "I am merely the vessel through which *Le Sacre* flowed."

Laziness is due not to too few but to too many notions, all fully realized. They aren't waiting to be born, but to be notated, and oh the drudgery, because they exist, almost complete—at least theoretically—there on the staves of the brain. The hours spent writing them down could be better spent thinking them up. Or so I reason, and get sick.

"When do you find time to compose?" people ask, assuming that to compose is a transitive verb, the action of placing notes on paper (or worse, of rambling over the keys). Time for that action is comparatively minimal: anyone finds time for any action that means anything to him. When do I do anything else? might be a better question, since in some way each breath drawn, awake or asleep, is musical; at parties, the A & P, a turkish bath, in the Métro, reading *Lear*, I'm never not composing, will it or no. Euterpe's a healthy succubus. The action? That's merely the final boring chore.

Being a computer, I lack imagination and cannot guess at meanings, so I must *learn* languages. I have no intuition and cannot recognize music unless I already know it, so I must memorize each example of a repertory. I have no ear and cannot think up colors or tunes, so to compose music I mimic the great (like the voiceless Chaplin who sings beautifully only when imitating Caruso). I am literal minded and thus without humor, so I must employ a programmed intelligence which shows me what is truly witty.

III

People sometimes ask why I don't set myself to music. I set words to music I feel can take a change. As a composer of songs I don't seek to improve words so much as to reemphasize them—to alter their dimension. Music can't heighten the meaning of words, only change their meaning (unless to heighten be a form of change). Occasionally the words benefit from the change; but although they might not inherently *need* this change, I must feel that they need it.

Now, to write words with intention of setting them would be to write words I intended by definition to change. Only a bad text could emerge from so inhibiting a task. Nor could I musicalize words I had written at another time and for their own sake, since those words would not exist if I had been able (at that other time) to express their sense in music. As for composing words and music simultaneously, that is a game for precocious children, and presupposes a third party beneath the skin of the composer-poet: the performer. Balladeers are triple personalities dealing in short forms (or repetitious narratives). The mere dual personality, or nonperforming composer-writer, usually deals in large librettos which he writes as he goes along. Menotti, Blitzstein, Tippett, Nono.

There is already a presumption in a composer who sets a poet to music. To direct this presumption toward his own prose would be presumptuosissimo.

Practicing and learning are unrelated practices. Learning's highest intensity is in the first minutes of deciphering (or even in the first hearing) of a new piece. Once learned, the only reason for practicing is not so that the piece will get better, but so that it won't get worse. Once learned, pieces don't get better with practice, though they can get different, and sometimes stale. (I don't swallow Casals' claim that he found newness in Bach each day of his life. With everything new we find, we lose something old.) Practicing is so that, even if your performance is at its worst, it will be up to your own minimum standards.

JH is not garrulous, he speaks when there's something to say. I talk all the time, for there's never much that needs saying. Yet the exercise stimulates, and "communication" for me comes by restating what *is*. Art is redundant. JH is really more of a Quaker than I.

Can silence be an art? A fine art? Silence, of course, is the very leavening that makes music breathe and rise, but silence by itself is just silence, not an art.

"Who hath wrote so much as the Quakers?" asked Francis Bugg.

"He that doth not write whilst he is alive, can't speak when he is dead," answered John Bellers in the seventeenth century.

Silence as craft, however, is cultivated by Quakers, not to mention Trappists.

God knows I've never believed that experience had anything to do with what we call creativity, for artists don't need knowledge, they need artistry. (You don't have to know what makes babies to make babies.) Each new word an infant learns withdraws him further from what we call nature. The wiser our books become the less knowledge (knowledge?) we control of sensual things; yet it's too late to learn from, or even play with, the deer and the antelope as though they were like us, and music—with its poor, canny, dislocated imitations—is all there remains for humans.

What I avidly believe for years and finally freeze into words (as I freeze this phrase here) I can no longer believe avidly. Like composing a piece. Once it's composed I obviously no longer need to compose it—it's a truth I don't now crave. Such sloughing off of a truth leaves me hollow and fearful of death before I latch on to another truth to fertilize and forsake. For there are many truths, but alas, no One Truth. Except maybe memory, a receding street, a solacing blank.

When We Dead Awaken: Writing as Re-Vision (1971)

ADRIENNE RICH

The Modern Language Association is both marketplace and funeral parlor for the professional study of Western literature in North America. Like all gatherings of the professions, it has been and remains a "procession of the sons of educated men" (Virginia Woolf): a congeries of old-boys' networks, academicians rehearsing their numb canons in sessions dedicated to the literature of white males, junior scholars under the lash of "publish or perish" delivering papers in the bizarrely lit drawing-rooms of immense hotels: a ritual competition veering between cynicism and desperation.

However, in the interstices of these gentlemanly rites (or, in Mary Daly's words, on the boundaries of this patriarchal space[1]), some feminist scholars, teachers, and graduate students, joined by feminist writers, editors, and publishers, have for a decade been creating more subversive occasions, challenging the sacredness of the gentlemanly canon, sharing the rediscovery of buried works by women, asking women's questions, bringing literary history and criticism back to life in both senses. The Commission on the Status of Women in the Profession was formed in 1969, and held its first public event in 1970. In 1971 the Commission asked Ellen Peck Killoh, Tillie Olsen, Elaine Reuben, and myself, with Elaine Hedges as moderator, to talk on "The Woman Writer in the Twentieth Century." The essay that follows was written for that forum, and later published, along with the other papers from the forum and workshops, in an issue of College English *edited by Elaine Hedges ("Women Writing and Teaching," vol. 34, no. 1, October 1972.) With a few revisions, mainly updating, it was reprinted in* American Poets *in 1976, edited by William Heyen (New York: Bobbs-Merrill, 1976). That later text is the one published here.*

The challenge flung by feminists at the accepted literary canon, at the methods of teaching it, and at the biased and astigmatic view of male "literary scholarship," has not diminished in the decade since the first Women's Forum; it has become broadened and intensified more recently by the challenges of black and lesbian feminists pointing out that feminist literary criticism itself has overlooked or held back from examining the work of black women and lesbians. The dynamic between a political vision and the demand for a fresh vision of literature is clear: without a growing feminist movement, the inroads of feminist scholarship could not have been made; without the sharpening of a black feminist consciousness, black women's writings would have been left in limbo between misogynist black male critics and white feminists still struggling to unearth a white women's tradition; without an articulate lesbian/feminist movement, lesbian writ-

ing would still be lying in that closet where many of us used to sit reading forbidden books "in a bad light."

Much, much more is yet to be done; and university curricula have of course changed very little as a result of all this. What is changing is the availability of knowledge, of vital texts, the visible effects on women's lives of seeing, hearing our wordless or negated experience affirmed and pursued further in language.

Ibsen's *When We Dead Awaken* is a play about the use that the male artist and thinker—in the process of creating culture as we know it—has made of women, in his life and in his work; and about a woman's slow struggling awakening to the use to which her life has been put. Bernard Shaw wrote in 1900 of this play:

> [Ibsen] shows us that no degradation ever devized or permitted is as disastrous as this degradation; that through it women can die into luxuries for men and yet can kill them; that men and women are becoming conscious of this; and that what remains to be seen as perhaps the most interesting of all imminent social developments is what will happen "when we dead awaken." [2]

It's exhilarating to be alive in a time of awakening consciousness; it can also be confusing, disorienting, and painful. This awakening of dead or sleeping consciousness has already affected the lives of millions of women, even whose who don't know it yet. It is also affecting the lives of men, even those who deny its claims upon them. The argument will go on whether an oppressive economic class system is responsible for the oppressive nature of male/female relations, or whether, in fact, patriarchy—the domination of males—is the original model of oppression on which all others are based. But in the last few years the women's movement has drawn inescapable and illuminating connections between our sexual lives and our political institutions. The sleepwalkers are coming awake, and for the first time this awakening has a collective reality; it is no longer such a lonely thing to open one's eyes.

Re-vision—the act of looking back, of seeing with fresh eyes, of entering an old text from a new critical direction—is for women more than a chapter in cultural history: it is an act of survival. Until we can understand the assumptions in which we are drenched we cannot know ourselves. And this drive to self-knowledge, for women, is more than a search for identity: it is part of our refusal of the self-destructiveness of male-dominated society. A radical critique of literature, feminist in its impulse, would take the work first of all as a clue to how we live, how we have been living, how we have been led to imagine ourselves, how our language has trapped as well

as liberated us, how the very act of naming has been till now a male pre
rogative, and how we can begin to see and name—and therefore live—
afresh. A change in the concept of sexual identity is essential if we are not
going to see the old political order reassert itself in every new revolution.
We need to know the writing of the past, and know it differently than we
have ever known it; not to pass on a tradition but to break its hold over us.

For writers, and at this moment for women writers in particular, there is
the challenge and promise of a whole new psychic geography to be explored. But there is also a difficult and dangerous walking on the ice, as we
try to find language and images for a consciousness we are just coming
into, and with little in the past to support us. I want to talk about some
aspects of this difficulty and this danger.

Jane Harrison, the great classical anthropologist, wrote in 1914 in a
letter to her friend Gilbert Murray:

> By the by, about "Women," it has bothered me often—why do women never
> want to write poetry about Man as a sex—why is Woman a dream and a terror
> to man and not the other way around? . . . Is it mere convention and propriety,
> or something deeper? [3]

I think Jane Harrison's question cuts deep into the myth-making tradition, the romantic tradition; deep into what women and men have been to
each other; and deep into the psyche of the woman writer. Thinking about
that question, I began thinking of the work of two twentieth-century
women poets, Sylvia Plath and Diane Wakoski. It strikes me that in the
work of both Man appears as, if not a dream, a fascination and a terror;
and that the source of the fascination and the terror is, simply, Man's
power—to dominate, tyrannize, choose, or reject the woman. The cha-
risma of Man seems to come purely from his power over her and his control of the world by force, not from anything fertile or life-giving in him.
And, in the work of both these poets, it is finally the woman's sense of
herself—embattled, possessed—that gives the poetry its dynamic charge,
its rhythms of struggle, need, will, and female energy. Until recently this
female anger and this furious awareness of the Man's power over her were
not available materials to the female poet, who tended to write of Love as
the source of her suffering, and to view that victimization by Love as an
almost inevitable fate. Or, like Marianne Moore and Elizabeth Bishop, she
kept sexuality at a measured and chiseled distance in her poems.

One answer to Jane Harrison's question has to be that historically men
and women have played very different parts in each others' lives. Where
woman has been a luxury for man, and has served as the painter's model

and the poet's muse, but also as comforter, nurse, cook, bearer of his seed, secretarial assistant, and copyist of manuscripts, man has played a quite different role for the female artist. Henry James repeats an incident which the writer Prosper Mérimée described, of how, while he was living with George Sand,

> he once opened his eyes, in the raw winter dawn, to see his companion, in a dressing-gown, on her knees before the domestic hearth, a candlestick beside her and a red *madras* round her head, making bravely, with her own hands the fire that was to enable her to sit down betimes to urgent pen and paper. The story represents him as having felt that the spectacle chilled his ardor and tried his taste; her appearance was unfortunate, her occupation an inconsequence, and her industry a reproof—the result of all which was a lively irritation and an early rupture.[4]

The specter of this kind of male judgment, along with the misnaming and thwarting of her needs by a culture controlled by males, has created problems for the woman writer: problems of contact with herself, problems of language and style, problems of energy and survival.

In rereading Virginia Woolf's *A Room of One's Own* for the first time in some years, I was astonished at the sense of effort, of pains taken, of dogged tentativeness, in the tone of that essay. And I recognized that tone. I had heard it often enough, in myself and in other women. It is the tone of a woman almost in touch with her anger, who is determined not to appear angry, who is *willing* herself to be calm, detached, and even charming in a roomful of men where things have been said which are attacks on her very integrity. Virginia Woolf is addressing an audience of women, but she is acutely conscious—as she always was—of being overheard by men: by Morgan and Lytton and Maynard Keynes and for that matter by her father, Leslie Stephen.[5] She drew the language out into an exacerbated thread in her determination to have her own sensibility yet protect it from those masculine presences. Only at rare moments in that essay do you hear the passion in her voice; she was trying to sound as cool as Jane Austen, as Olympian as Shakespeare, because that is the way the men of the culture thought a writer should sound.

No male writer has written primarily or even largely for women, or with the sense of women's criticism as a consideration when he chooses his materials, his theme, his language. But to a lesser or greater extent, every woman writer has written for men even when, like Virginia Woolf, she was supposed to be addressing women. If we have come to the point when this balance might begin to change, when women can stop being haunted, not only by "convention and propriety" but by internalized fears of being and saying themselves, then it is an extraordinary moment for the woman writer—and reader.

I have hesitated to do what I am going to do now, which is to use myself as an illustration. For one thing, it's a lot easier and less dangerous to talk about other women writers. But there is something else. Like Virginia Woolf, I am aware of the women who are not with us here because they are washing the dishes and looking after the children. Nearly fifty years after she spoke, that fact remains largely unchanged. And I am thinking also of women whom she left out of the picture altogether—women who are washing other people's dishes and caring for other people's children, not to mention women who went on the streets last night in order to feed their children. We seem to be special women here, we have liked to think of ourselves as special, and we have known that men would tolerate, even romanticize us as special, as long as our words and actions didn't threaten their privilege of tolerating or rejecting us and our work according to *their* ideas of what a special woman ought to be. An important insight of the radical women's movement has been how divisive and how ultimately destructive is this myth of the special woman, who is also the token woman. Every one of us here in this room has had great luck—we are teachers, writers, academicians; our own gifts could not have been enough, for we all know women whose gifts are buried or aborted. Our struggles can have meaning and our privileges—however precarious under patriarchy—can be justified only if they can help to change the lives of women whose gifts—and whose very being—continue to be thwarted and silenced.

My own luck was being born white and middle-class into a house full of books, with a father who encouraged me to read and write. So for about twenty years I wrote for a particular man, who criticized and praised me and made me feel I was indeed "special." The obverse side of this, of course, was that I tried for a long time to please him, or rather, not to displease him. And then of course there were other men—writers, teachers—the Man, who was not a terror or a dream but a literary master and a master in other ways less easy to acknowledge. And there were all those poems about women, written by men: it seemed to be a given that men wrote poems and women frequently inhabited them. These women were almost always beautiful, but threatened with the loss of beauty, the loss of youth—the fate worse than death. Or they were beautiful and died young, like Lucy and Lenore. Or the woman was like Maud Gonne, cruel and disastrously mistaken, and the poem reproached her because she had refused to become a luxury for the poet.

A lot is being said today about the influence that the myths and images of women have on all of us who are products of culture. I think it has been a peculiar confusion to the girl or woman who tries to write because she is peculiarly susceptible to language. She goes to poetry or fiction looking for *her* way of being in the world, since she too has been putting words and images together; she is looking eagerly for guides, maps, possibilities; and over and over in the "words' masculine persuasive force" of literature she comes up against something that negates everything she is about: she meets the image of Woman in books written by men. She finds a terror and a dream, she finds a beautiful pale face, she finds La Belle Dame Sans Merci, she finds Juliet or Tess or Salomé, but precisely what she does not find is that absorbed, drudging, puzzled, sometimes inspired creature, herself, who sits at a desk trying to put words together.

So what does she do? What did I do? I read the older women poets with their peculiar keenness and ambivalence: Sappho, Christina Rossetti, Emily Dickinson, Elinor Wylie, Edna Millay, H. D. I discovered that the woman poet most admired at the time (by men) was Marianne Moore, who was maidenly, elegant, intellectual, discreet. But even in reading these women I was looking in them for the same things I had found in the poetry of men, because I wanted women poets to be the equals of men, and to be equal was still confused with sounding the same.

I know that my style was formed first by male poets: by the men I was reading as an undergraduate—Frost, Dylan Thomas, Donne, Auden, MacNiece, Stevens, Yeats. What I chiefly learned from them was craft.[6] But poems are like dreams: in them you put what you don't know you know. Looking back at poems I wrote before I was twenty-one, I'm startled because beneath the conscious craft are glimpses of the split I even then experienced between the girl who wrote poems, who defined herself in writing poems, and the girl who was to define herself by her relationships with men. "Aunt Jennifer's Tigers" (1951), written while I was a student, looks with deliberate detachment at this split.[7]

> Aunt Jennifer's tigers stride across a screen,
> Bright topaz denizens of a world of green.
> They do not fear the men beneath the tree;
> They pace in sleek chivalric certainty.
>
> Aunt Jennifer's fingers fluttering through her wool
> Find even the ivory needle hard to pull.
> The massive weight of Uncle's wedding band
> Sits heavily upon Aunt Jennifer's hand.
>
> When Aunt is dead, her terrified hands will lie
> Still ringed with ordeals she was mastered by.
> The tigers in the panel that she made
> Will go on striding, proud and unafraid.

In writing this poem, composed and apparently cool as it is, I thought I was creating a portrait of an imaginary woman. But this woman suffers from the opposition of her imagination, worked out in tapestry, and her life-style, "ringed with ordeals she was mastered by." It was important to me that Aunt Jennifer was a person as distinct from myself as possible—distanced by the formalism of the poem, by its objective, observant tone—even by putting the woman in a different generation.

In those years formalism was part of the strategy—like asbestos gloves, it allowed me to handle materials I couldn't pick up barehanded. A later strategy was to use the persona of a man, as I did in "The Loser" (1958):

A man thinks of the woman he once loved: first, after her
wedding, and then nearly a decade later.

I
I kissed you, bride and lost, and went
home from that bourgeois sacrament,
your cheek still tasting cold upon
my lips that gave you benison
with all the swagger that they knew—
as losers somehow learn to do.

Your wedding made my eyes ache; soon
the world would be worse off for one
more golden apple dropped to ground
without the least protesting sound,
and you would windfall lie, and we
forget your shimmer on the tree.

Beauty is always wasted: if
not Mignon's song sung to the deaf,
at all events to the unmoved.
A face like yours cannot be loved
long or seriously enough.
Almost, we seem to hold it off.

II
Well, you are tougher than I thought.
Now when the wash with ice hangs taut
this morning of St. Valentine,
I see you strip the squeaking line,
your body weighed against the load,
and all my groans can do no good.

Because you are still beautiful,
though squared and stiffened by the pull
of what nine windy years have done.
You have three daughters, lost a son.

I see all your intelligence
flung into that unwearied stance.

My envy is of no avail.
I turn my head and wish him well
who chafed your beauty into use
and lives forever in a house
lit by the friction of your mind.
You stagger in against the wind.

I finished college, published my first book by a fluke, as it seemed to me, and broke off a love affair. I took a job, lived alone, went on writing, fell in love. I was young, full of energy, and the book seemed to mean that others agreed I was a poet. Because I was also determined to prove that as a woman poet I could also have what was then defined as a "full" woman's life, I plunged in my early twenties into marriage and had three children before I was thirty. There was nothing overt in the environment to warn me: these were the fifties, and in reaction to the earlier wave of feminism, middle-class women were making careers of domestic perfection, working to send their husbands through professional schools, then retiring to raise large families. People were moving out to the suburbs, technology was going to be the answer to everything, even sex; the family was in its glory. Life was extremely private; women were isolated from each other by the loyalties of marriage. I have a sense that women didn't talk to each other much in the fifties—not about their secret emptinesses, their frustrations. I went on trying to write; my second book and first child appeared in the same month. But by the time that book came out I was already dissatisfied with those poems, which seemed to me mere exercises for poems I hadn't written. The book was praised, however, for its "gracefulness"; I had a marriage and a child. If there were doubts, if there were periods of null depression or active despairing, these could only mean that I was ungrateful, insatiable, perhaps a monster.

About the time my third child was born, I felt that I had either to consider myself a failed woman and a failed poet, or to try to find some synthesis by which to understand what was happening to me. What frightened me most was the sense of drift, of being pulled along on a current which called itself my destiny, but in which I seemed to be losing touch with whoever I had been, with the girl who had experienced her own will and energy almost ecstatically at times, walking around a city or riding a train at night or typing in a student room. In a poem about my grandmother I wrote (of myself): "A young girl, though sleeping, is certified dead" ("Halfway"). I was writing very little, partly from fatigue, that female fatigue of suppressed anger and loss of contact with my own being;

partly from the discontinuity of female life with its attention to small chores, errands, work that others constantly undo, small children's constant needs. What I did write was unconvincing to me; my anger and frustration were hard to acknowledge in or out of poems because in fact I cared a great deal about my husband and my children. Trying to look back and understand that time I have tried to analyze the real nature of the conflict. Most, if not all, human lives are full of fantasy—passive daydreaming which need not be acted on. But to write poetry or fiction, or even to think well, is not to fantasize, or to put fantasies on paper. For a poem to coalesce, for a character or an action to take shape, there has to be an imaginative transformation of reality which is in no way passive. And a certain freedom of the mind is needed—freedom to press on, to enter the currents of your thought like a glider pilot, knowing that your motion can be sustained, that the buoyancy of your attention will not be suddenly snatched away. Moreover, if the imagination is to transcend and transform experience it has to question, to challenge, to conceive of alternatives, perhaps to the very life you are living at that moment. You have to be free to play around with the notion that day might be night, love might be hate; nothing can be too sacred for the imagination to turn into its opposite or to call experimentally by another name. For writing is re-naming. Now, to be maternally with small children all day in the old way, to be with a man in the old way of marriage, requires a holding-back, a putting-aside of that imaginative activity, and demands instead a kind of conservatism. I want to make it clear that I am *not* saying that in order to write well, or think well, it is necessary to become unavailable to others, or to become a devouring ego. This has been the myth of the masculine artist and thinker; and I do not accept it. But to be a female human being trying to fulfill traditional female functions in a traditional way *is* in direct conflict with the subversive function of the imagination. The word *traditional* is important here. There must be ways, and we will be finding out more and more about them, in which the energy of creation and the energy of relation can be united. But in those years I always felt the conflict as a failure of love in myself. I had thought I was choosing a full life: the life available to most men, in which sexuality, work, and parenthood could coexist. But I felt, at twenty-nine, guilt toward the people closest to me, and guilty toward my own being.

I wanted, then, more than anything, the one thing of which there was never enough: time to think, time to write. The fifties and early sixties were years of rapid revelations: the sit-ins and marches in the South, the Bay of Pigs, the early antiwar movement, raised large questions—questions for which the masculine world of the academy around me seemed to have expert and fluent answers. But I needed to think for myself—about pacifism and dissent and violence, about poetry and society, and about my own relationship to all these things. For about ten years I was reading in fierce snatches, scribbling in notebooks, writing poetry in fragments; I was looking desperately for clues, because if there were no clues then I thought I might be insane. I wrote in a notebook about this time:

> Paralyzed by the sense that there exists a mesh of relationships—e.g., between my anger at the children, my sensual life, pacifism, sex (I mean sex in its broadest significance, not merely sexual desire)—an interconnectedness which, if I could see it, make it valid, would give me back myself, make it possible to function lucidly and passionately. Yet I grope in and out among these dark webs.

I think I began at this point to feel that politics was not something "out there" but something "in here" and of the essence of my condition.

In the late fifties I was able to write, for the first time, directly about experiencing myself as a woman. The poem was jotted in fragments during children's naps, brief hours in a library, or at 3:00 A.M. after rising with a wakeful child. I despaired of doing any continuous work at this time. Yet I began to feel that my fragments and scraps had a common consciousness and a common theme, one which I would have been very unwilling to put on paper at an earlier time because I had been taught that poetry should be "universal," which meant, of course, nonfemale. Until then I had tried very much *not* to identify myself as a female poet. Over two years I wrote a ten-part poem called "Snapshots of a Daughter-in-Law" (1958-1960), in a longer looser mode than I'd ever trusted myself with before. It was an extraordinary relief to write that poem. It strikes me now as too literary, too dependent on allusion; I hadn't found the courage yet to do without authorities, or even to use the pronoun "I"—the woman in the poem is always "she." One section of it, No. 2, concerns a woman who thinks she is going mad; she is haunted by voices telling her to resist and rebel, voices which she can hear but not obey.

> 2.
> Banging the coffee-pot into the sink
> she hears the angels chiding, and looks out
> past the raked gardens to the sloppy sky.
> Only a week since They said: *Have no patience.*
>
> The next time it was: *Be insatiable.*
> Then: *Save yourself; others you cannot save.*
> Sometimes she's let the tapstream scald her arm,
> a match burn to her thumbnail,

or held her hand above the kettle's snout
right in the woolly steam. They are probably angels,
since nothing hurts her anymore, except
each morning's grit blowing into her eyes.

The poem "Orion," written five years later, is a poem of reconnection
with a part of myself I had felt I was losing—the active principle, the
energetic imagination, the "half-brother" whom I projected, as I had for
many years, into the constellation Orion. It's no accident that the words
"cold and egotistical" appear in this poem, and are applied to myself.

Far back when I went zig-zagging
through tamarack pastures
you were my genius, you
my cast-iron Viking, my helmed
lion-heart king in prison.
Years later now you're young

my fierce half-brother, staring
down from that simplified west
your breast open, your belt dragged down
by an oldfashioned thing, a sword
the last bravado you won't give over
though it weighs you down as you stride

and the stars in it are dim
and maybe have stopped burning.
But you burn, and I know it;
as I throw back my head to take you in
an old transfusion happens again:
divine astronomy is nothing to it.

Indoors I bruise and blunder,
break faith, leave ill enough
alone, a dead child born in the dark.
Night cracks up over the chimney,
pieces of time, frozen geodes
come showering down in the grate.

A man reaches behind my eyes
and finds them empty
a woman's head turns away
from my head in the mirror
children are dying my death
and eating crumbs of my life.

Pity is not your forte.
Calmly you ache up there
pinned aloft in your crow's next,

> my speechless pirate!
> You take it all for granted
> and when I look you back
>
> it's with a starlike eye
> shooting its cold and egotistical spear
> where it can do least damage.
> Breathe deep! No hurt, no pardon
> out here in the cold with you
> you with your back to the wall.

The choice still seemed to be between "love"—womanly, maternal love, altruistic love—a love defined and ruled by the weight of an entire culture; and egotism—a force directed by men into creation, achievement, ambition, often at the expense of others, but justifiably so. For weren't they men, and wasn't that their destiny as womanly, selfless love was ours? We know now that the alternatives are false ones—that the word "love" is itself in need of re-vision.

There is a companion poem to "Orion," written three years later, in which at last the woman in the poem and the woman writing the poem become the same person. It is called "Planetarium," and it was written after a visit to a real planetarium, where I read an account of the work of Caroline Herschel, the astronomer, who worked with her brother William, but whose name remained obscure, as his did not.

> *Thinking of Caroline Herschel, 1750–1848, astronomer, sister of William; and others*
>
> A woman in the shape of a monster
> a monster in the shape of a woman
> the skies are full of them
>
> a woman   "in the snow
> among the Clocks and instruments
> or measuring the ground with poles"
>
> in her 98 years to discover
> 8 comets
>
> she whom the moon ruled
> like us
> levitating into the night sky
> riding the polished lenses
>
> Galaxies of women, there
> doing penance for impetuousness
> ribs chilled
> in those spaces   of the mind

An eye,
    "virile, precise and absolutely certain"
    from the mad webs of Uranisborg
                      encountering the NOVA

every impulse of light exploding
from the core
as life flies out of us

       Tycho whispering at last
       "Let me not seem to have lived in vain"

What we see, we see
and seeing is changing

the light that shrivels a mountain
and leaves a man alive

Heartbeat of the pulsar
heart sweating through my body

The radio impulse
pouring in from Taurus

       I am bombarded yet   I stand

I have been standing all my life in the
direct path of a battery of signals
the most accurately transmitted most
untranslateable language in the universe
I am a galactic cloud so deep   so invo-
luted that a light wave could take 15
years to travel through me   And has
taken   I am an instrument in the shape
of a woman trying to translate pulsations
into images   for the relief of the body
and the reconstruction of the mind.

In closing I want to tell you about a dream I had last summer. I dreamed I was asked to read my poetry at a mass women's meeting, but when I began to read, what came out were the lyrics of a blues song. I share this dream with you because it seemed to me to say something about the problems and the future of the woman writer, and probably of women in general. The awakening of consciousness is not like the crossing of a frontier—one step and you are in another country. Much of woman's poetry has been of the nature of the blues song: a cry of pain, of victimization, or a lyric of seduction.[8] And today, much poetry by women—and prose for that matter—is charged with anger. I think we need to go through that anger, and we will betray our own reality if we try, as Virginia Woolf was trying, for an objectivity, a detachment, that would make us sound more like Jane Austen or Shakespeare. We know more than Jane Austen or Shakespeare knew: more than Jane Austen because our lives are more complex, more than Shakespeare because we know more about the lives of women—Jane Austen and Virginia Woolf included.

Both the victimization and the anger experienced by women are real, and have real sources, everywhere in the environment, built into society, language, the structures of thought. They will go on being tapped and explored by poets, among others. We can neither deny them, nor will we rest there. A new generation of women poets is already working out of the psychic energy released when women begin to move out towards what the feminist philosopher Mary Daly has described as the "new space" on the boundaries of patriarchy.[9] Women are speaking to and of women in these poems, out of a newly released courage to name, to love each other, to share risk and grief and celebration.

To the eye of a feminist, the work of Western male poets now writing reveals a deep, fatalistic pessimism as to the possibilities of change, whether societal or personal, along with a familiar and threadbare use of women (and nature) as redemptive on the one hand, threatening on the other; and a new tide of phallocentric sadism and overt woman-hating which matches the sexual brutality of recent films. "Political" poetry by men remains stranded amid the struggles for power among male groups; in condemning U.S. imperialism or the Chilean junta the poet can claim to speak for the oppressed while remaining, as male, part of a system of sexual oppression. The enemy is always outside the self, the struggle somewhere else. The mood of isolation, self-pity, and self-imitation that pervades "nonpolitical" poetry suggests that a profound change in masculine consciousness will have to precede any new male poetic—or other—inspiration. The creative energy of patriarchy is fast running out; what remains is its self-generating energy for destruction. As women, we have our work cut out for us.

NOTES

1. Mary Daly, *Beyond God the Father: Towards a Philosophy of Women's Liberation* (Boston: Beacon, 1973), pp. 40-41.
2. G. B. Shaw, *The Quintessence of Ibsenism* (New York: Hill & Wang, 1922), p. 139.
3. J. G. Stewart, *Jane Ellen Harrison: A Portrait from Letters* (London: Merlin, 1959), p. 140.
4. Henry James, "Notes on Novelists," in *Selected Literary Criticism of Henry James,* Morris Shapira, ed. (London: Heinemann, 1963), pp. 157-58.

5. A. R., 1978: This intuition of mine was corroborated when, early in 1978, I read the correspondence between Woolf and Dame Ethel Smyth (Henry W. and Albert A. Berg Collection, The New York Public Library, Astor, Lenox and Tilden Foundations); in a letter dated June 8, 1933, Woolf speaks of having kept her own personality out of *A Room of One's Own* lest she not be taken seriously: " . . . how personal, so will they say, rubbing their hands with glee, women always are; *I even hear them as I write.*" (Italics mine.)

6. A. R., 1978: Yet I spent months, at sixteen, memorizing and writing imitations of Millay's sonnets; and in notebooks of that period I find what are obviously attempts to imitate Dickinson's metrics and verbal compression. I knew H. D. only through anthologized lyrics; her epic poetry was not then available to me.

7. A.R., 1978: Texts of poetry quoted herein can be found in A. R., *Poems Selected and New: 1950-1974* (New York: Norton, 1975).

8. A. R., 1978: When I dreamed that dream, was I wholly ignorant of the tradition of Bessie Smith and other women's blues lyrics which transcended victimization to sing of resistance and independence?

9. See note No. 1.

An Interview with Howard Nemerov

The following interview was conducted on January 23, 1979 on the morning after the poet's talk and reading at Iowa State University. The interviewers are Neal Bowers and Charles L. P. Silet.

NEMEROV: Do you want me to provide answers first?

INTERVIEWER: That might be a better way.

NEMEROV: I've got a good answer.

INTERVIEWER: Okay.

NEMEROV: Yes, theoretically, but in practice it comes up so seldom as to be negligible.

INTERVIEWER: Can you tell us a little bit about how you go about composing poetry? For example, do you write every day? How much do you depend upon inspiration? Do you have a form in mind before you start writing or does that develop as you write the poem?

NEMEROV: There are several questions in there. I do not write every day. In fact, except for correspondence, which is fairly extensive, I may not write for a couple of years. And, of course, you worry about that, and worrying about it is part of the process itself. I've got a notion you have to get depressed before something happens. On the other hand, after twenty books it is harder to get depressed than after two. You know, so if you didn't write anything . . . so what? I would like to do it but the world is full enough of literature; probably my little mite would not be missed if I didn't do any more. When it is there it's wonderful and it's easy, and when it's not there it's impossible. And I don't know what makes it be there. Unlike many friends who write, I do my best, such as it is, very fast.

Ninety-five percent of the *Western Approaches* was written in four months—again, after two years of . . . "I can't write." You would think that if you wanted to be a professional and make a business out of it that with, you know, what even my nastiest reviewers allow to be virtuoso technique, I could turn the poetry crank seven lines every morning and come out with far too much at the end of the year, but it doesn't work that way at all. When it's not there I tend to whistle on my walks. Horrible little tunes I can't get rid of go through my head—things I wouldn't want to listen to. When it's there things start saying themselves in my head, usually in blank verse, but that's my fault, sometimes in rhyme. And the little things in two and four lines make themselves up and I can remember long enough to get to the desk and put them down. The other things, you get the beginning of something, a notion, a line, a line-and-a-half, and it's always—not always, I never thought about it in earlier years—but latterly, it's always remarkable to me that one thing should follow another. It's the most remarkable feature of thought, and nobody seems to study it; perhaps people do and I just don't know about it. As to the form things take, well, those little epigrams, gnomes, they tell you "I'm not going to be the *Iliad*." I sent one to Kenneth Burke who said, "You know, if you do something this short, you have to rhyme it." I said, "Kenneth, you're right." I up and ripped the whole thing apart and rhymed it, six lines; I thought that was a great achievement. That little couplet of Pope's on the collar of the dog he gave to the Prince of Wales: "I am his highness' dog at Kew. / Pray tell me, sir, whose dog are you?" That wouldn't be anything without the rhyme, would it? In the longer things there is a slight tendency for my laziness to turn them into blank verse, but sometimes things clearly say, "I'm a sestina" or "I want to be rhymed and quatrained." If I know it's going to go like maybe two pages, I tend to write it in blank verse. I'm always worried I might not find a rhyme for the last two lines or something. But rhyme is a marvelous thing all the same. It makes you think of things you would not be forced to think of—wouldn't have had a chance to think of—otherwise.

INTERVIEWER: What do you see as the relationship between your fiction and your poetry? Is there an overlap? Are they part of the same process?

NEMEROV: I would have said earlier, when I did more fiction, that I tried to make them as different as possible. No poetic prose when you're writing a novel, or at least try to stay away from it.

INTERVIEWER: Do you write novels in the same sort of burst of energy as you write your poetry?

NEMEROV: Well, I didn't write enough to be able to generalize about it. For a story or a chapter I think I tried to get it all done in one day because you can never be certain that the idea will still be there the next morning. In novels, the first one I wrote took me three years during the summers, and the second one I wrote in fifty-eight days, and the third one in twenty-eight days. Then I said to my wife, "The next one I will write on Labor Day." It didn't work.

INTERVIEWER: Some critics speak of a progression in your work from a somewhat more academic style reminiscent of Eliot or Pound to a much more conversational, relaxed style. Do you see such a progression in your poetry?

NEMEROV: It may be true. You know, writing of poetry is just one of the specialized forms of what happens when you grow up or grow older. Of course, you live life forward and think about it backwards. You might spend a lot of time in embarrassment about the silly, trivial things you did when young, that you didn't know you were doing silly, trivial things when you were old too. You know, there is a beautiful place in Proust where the painter Elstir talks to Marcel about this. Marcel has just discovered that this great master must have been the silly young man who was referred to at parties, and Elstir, instead of turning away and refusing ever to see him again, sets him down and gives him a little talk about growing up and about how it's only nonentities who have nothing to be ashamed of in their past, how you have to overcome what you were before, and it's only, he says, in this way that something a little above the common life of the atelier is achieved.

INTERVIEWER: Do you consider yourself to be a poet of reflections—in the Wordsworthian sense? And, if so, do you feel this necessarily implies an absence of emotion?

NEMEROV: Yes, I might be a pretty cold fellow in some ways, except I know I'm a weepy slob. But I don't see that the two are incompatible. We mostly have both capacities at once. In younger days, my colleagues and friends from *Furioso* magazine used to tell me solemnly that I was a meditative poet, and in those days meditative poetry was a very dirty word in that you were not dramatic like John Donne—"Busy old fool, unruly Sunne," he says just before he starts meditating on the subject. Those terms all collapse as soon as you look at them, like a world full of traffic lights with no cars. Yes, I've got a touch of the Wordsworthian or what Keats called the egotistical sublime, but only a touch, I think. And some of my poems are obviously dramatic in the sense that somebody not myself is talking in a particular situation. That's about as dramatic as I get. I never did quite feel at home in that idea that the dramatic is always conveyed to me as some opera singer making huge gestures and stamping his foot petulantly on the stage.

INTERVIEWER: You have been a teacher for a long time.

NEMEROV: Yes, longer than Jesus lived.

INTERVIEWER: Does being a teacher influence your poetry?

NEMEROV: I'm quite sure it must. As a very nice review in the *Times Literary Supplement* said about a poem of mine called "The Pond," "it is like Frost but it's more sophisticated than Frost, and also it's a teacher's poem." The reviewer didn't go on to explain, but I could sort of see. You know, if you're brought up under the New Criticism of Eliot and Empson there are certain things you probably do as a matter of course without realizing that they are matters of convention. There is one particular convention that I'm sure I don't do as much as I did when I began, cute little puns and stuff, but I'm sure I still do it some.

INTERVIEWER: What do you think about the position of someone like Robert Bly, for example, who deliberately keeps himself away from a position in a university because he thinks a poet should not earn his living by teaching but should, somehow, divorce himself from that kind of a pursuit?

NEMEROV: As John Ransom said about a similar question, "It's a free country isn't it?" I mean, you know, is it for me to criticize how Robert Bly runs his life?

INTERVIEWER: Several critics have pointed out, for lack of a better word, the pessimistic side of your poetry. Do you consider yourself basically pessimistic?

NEMEROV: That's a hard one, isn't it? The optimist thinking the glass is half full and the pessimist thinking it's half empty. You see, pessimism has gone out of fashion. I notice that in reviews they treat me much nicer than they ever used to. But there is this notion that he's too bitter to be a really great American poet. Whereas, I was brought up under this great tradition of things like *The Waste Land* and *Ash Wednesday*, where you'd better be bitter because that's what poetry was. And even if Dante ends up in paradise with the sight of God himself, he doesn't sound exactly what you would call happy about the situation on earth.

INTERVIEWER: Can you elaborate on a comment that you've made in several different places (and I think this is a direct quote), "The serious and the funny are one"?

NEMEROV: How about *King Lear*, which I would rate (as I tell my students, this is enthusiasm, not theory) as one of the few great human achievements. What about when Gloucester thinks he is jumping off the cliff and falls flat on his face on the stage? That may be my only example, but it's quite an example to get by. That is, many people have recorded the feeling that they want to laugh at a funeral and that they mustn't, you know. Because whether something is serious or funny, solemn or unsinging, is but an expression of our predicament, where for every soulful sacred notion we have there is some wonderful bodily analogy to it. So if you are seated among the angels it is still on your butt. I know I do have a tendency to be funny in what people say are serious places. I remember Randall Jarrell saying I spoiled a perfectly good poem by saying something cute right in the middle of it. I only just say I don't think so. These things are matters of opinion.

INTERVIEWER: Do you see this bonding of the funny and the serious as producing a fundamental tension in your poetry?

NEMEROV: I suppose so. There have to be always at least two voices. You wouldn't want to be all one nervous system or you'd fly to pieces, or be all the other nervous systems or you'd shrivel up. Nietzsche was very strong on all this business that everything that is ironic, joyous and evasive belongs to life. Everything absolute belongs to death. I have more and more come to take the view that little Howard Nemerov is not the fellow who is responsible for deciding these mighty matters. People are so inclined, especially in writing, to behave apocalyptically—"Depart from me. Thou my elect." Five minutes later the situation has changed. Like one of those pictures of Bruegel's, it's hard to decide which lot is headed for heaven and which lot is headed for hell.

INTERVIEWER: Is humor a way of handling that darker side?

NEMEROV: Humor is a remedy against lust. It's very often been said to be a way of dealing with that. It's like dirty jokes, which provide some kind of release to something. Many subversive tendencies are probably not directly connected with sex as such but connected with our wonder about whether we live in the body or whether we are the body. So, something Innocent III said, only a little piece, "De Miseria Humanae Conditionis." Wit is essentially ascetic against the flesh.

INTERVIEWER: What about the relationship between your criticism and your poetry, and then the criticism of others of your poetry?

NEMEROV: That's two questions, isn't it? As to the first, I think I quoted in there something Leonardo said about "He is a bad master whose work outruns his criticism." Well, there's some sense to that. I've learned that the real criterion, in which I have learned to trust somewhat, is not verification but falsification. That is, you can never prove of a theory that there is no fact in the known or unknown universe that contradicts. Or what you do once you've got your theory is to try to disprove it as hard as you can. As for people's criticism of my poems, you do get inured to that. Also, you're never going to like public contumely followed by private apologies, but you damn well get used to it—guys writing sneaky little letters saying, "I didn't really mean to destroy your book." Well, they didn't destroy my book. I think I've come not to worry about it. I had a beautifully salutary experience—some chap who said he was writing a bibliography of me. I thought he meant twelve pages of titles, but no, he'd collected reviews and swatches of reviews for thirty years called *The Critical Reception of HN*. It's very funny to look back on those things, the lady writing on a book, a novel of mine, I forget which one, who said, "It's good, but finally, is it good enough?" That's the kind of a sentence you might have heard at a Harvard cocktail party in 1940. And I thought, "Well, that's criticism in the highest and unanswerablest degree." Then I had the answer; I said, "Well, lady, it depends on what you're gonna use it for."

INTERVIEWER: Do you learn from critics? Are there critics, which you have respect for and who are judicious in their treatment of your work, that you'd pick up something from?

NEMEROV: Yes. I think that's true. These are serious people. They are not reviewers as a rule, like Mary Kinzie, in *Parnassus*, fifty-seven pages, by God, about me! I thought some of that was pretty illuminating, and some of that I even didn't know. And there's another critic, Julia Randall, who is a splendid poet herself; well, she wrote in *Hollins Critic* a dozen pages on what I was about. Stanley Hyman told me one day he was going to take a few months off and write a piece about my poetry that would show me so much I would never write again, but maybe I was lucky. He never got around to it.

INTERVIEWER: Do you ever change anything? Do you ever question what you've done as a result of somebody else's criticism?

NEMEROV: I don't think so. After all, those things are by definition written about things that are published already. I tell you, Mary Kinzie wrote me a letter about some twenty new poems I sent to her, which caused me to agree that I should simply suppress four or five of them—that they're just not up to it. I think perhaps one reckonable result of receiving prizes, getting to be a slight bump on the horizon, is that you do think about next time. Maybe you ought not to put in every little remark you make; maybe you'd better wait. I hope to wait another five years before the next book. It may come earlier than that.

INTERVIEWER: Is criticism easier to take when you're younger?

NEMEROV: Well, I think when you're younger you get most use out of criticism by your fellows, not your teachers. They will say things to you that the teacher would gentle down a bit. Then you get to a point; I remember Stanley Hyman saying to me, "Howard, I couldn't tell you about your poetry. I might not like something in it but I figure he's grown-up; it's his business; he knows what he's doing and he wants to do it that way."

INTERVIEWER: Do you enjoy talking shop with your fellow poets?

NEMEROV: I don't think we do, mostly, talk shop. Lowell told me once that he circulated his poems to fellow poets for advice and criticism, and I was shocked. Yesterday afternoon was the only time I've ever done it and it was partly because I didn't know what else to do—give a lecture. That's why I told the audience yesterday, "I'm not going to take any of your advice; I'm just trying to pass the time."

INTERVIEWER: Some critics seem to think that you're getting mellower as you get older, becoming more accepting of the limitations of life and being less angry. Do you feel that's correct, and if so why?

NEMEROV: Well, you're looking at the complacent, smug old slob instead of the nasty, mean young slob. It's true, when I was reading the proofs of my *Collected Poems*, I kept thinking about the first two books, "What did that young fellow think he was doing?" And I said, of course, he was trying to be bitter like Eliot and Pound and the other fellows. A lot depends on what time you come into the world, like the early Yeats, looking around. People spend volumes and hours of class time worrying what those early poems mean. But he's an eighteen-year-old fellow come from Ireland. He's trying to find a way of doing something that isn't either Browning or Swinburne. He avoided Browning pretty well, but he doesn't avoid Swinburne too well. That's too bad; we don't come into the world fully formed, but there it is, back to that lecture that Elstir gives to Marcel. That's the way it is. What Keats said, this is "the vale of Soul-making," with the stress on making.

INTERVIEWER: Is that just a gradual realization, you think, that most people come to?

NEMEROV: Well, there's a gradual realization, in plain, literal terms, of what the world is. You may continue to have high ideals, but you know they are high ideals. A favorite exercise of mine is trying to imagine that you were born, say, in the time of Pope. For one thing, the first imagination is that you would have been Pope. How do you know you wouldn't have been one of the dunces? And second, if you were born in any time, it would be a time of the usual apocalyptic expectations. John Donne, Thomas Browne after him, believed that there wasn't much point in doing much because the world had pretty much run its course. Pessimism of the darkest sort informed their thoughts about everything but the resurrection. But nobody recognizes it as that now because we read them with eyes conditioned to the idea that the universe has a very considerable future and that discovery is proceeding at such an incredible exponential rate of acceleration that, who knows, the place will be transformed tomorrow with results both wonderful and terrible. We're supposed to be learning not to expect that the future will be some kind of steady prolongation of the past. You know the fashionable example of the very respectable physicists around 1890-1900, who said, "Well, we really do know the universe pretty well; there are some details to fill in but we know pretty much how it works in large." They didn't know relativity and quantum theory were coming in the future. You know, not just little finagles but absolute change in the way people thought.

INTERVIEWER: Are you disturbed by science and technology?

NEMEROV: I'm fascinated by it. Talking with Stanley Elkin about it—he said, "Science is marvelous; I wish I'd gotten more of it." And I said, "Me too, it's such fascinating stuff." And he said, "It's not fascinating, it's true." And there is a point there.

INTERVIEWER: So you don't see that traditional division between science and art?

NEMEROV: No, the two cultures, I agreed with a physicist once, the two cultures are really the monsters who do the work and the nice guys who talk about it.

INTERVIEWER: The monsters being . . . ?"

NEMEROV: People like Einstein, Freud. Geez, if I knew enough I'd want to write a book about the rise and decline of that Freudian business, which transformed the world about as much as Edison did. People were worrying about the Marxist revolution when the Freudian one was going on inside them the whole time, making the world again incalculably different from what it had been. I'd like, if I could write one more book, to write about the nature of theory and fashions in theory. I shall never know enough because I can't read in a scholarly manner consecutively, and I rarely take enough notes or keep them in order if I do. But what a wonderful subject for somebody, to write about fashion in thought, about the rise and fall of the most powerful and influential theories. Much more interesting than the rise and fall of even the British Empire. How people can be taught to teach and think this way for a generation, to make enormous conquests and it all looks like knowledge, finally we've got it, now it's solid, and if some small voice speaks up and says Plato said only geometry was solid, only mathematics because it's entirely self-contained and has no relation to the world, he would be snowed under and told, "You don't know; we've got it, kid. All this before was just theory, but now this is structuralism," or whatever it's being called this decade. You know, I am reminded of what an awful lot of garbage we all talk. Sometimes it is conspicuous because it pretends to affect the real world, to be a scheme of government, of methodizing knowledge, and so forth, but what we talk in our classrooms, I would say, is probably not fundamentally so different.

INTERVIEWER: Don't you think we grasp sometimes, though, with a certainty, the theory that ties all the loose ends together?

NEMEROV: Well, remember that when you're young, if you get into this stuff at all, you're an intellectual. I think that's the only way people do get into teaching, writing, and so forth; they want to know. My favorite book, from eighteen on, probably still is, is *The Magic Mountain,* because while it is a fiction it also teaches much which, incidentally, is probably no longer true. But you are compelled to learn as you get older. Again, this exercise of thinking of yourself as having been born in an earlier time and having long since died without having seen the end of the world after all. But, you know that you're going to be as ignorant on your death-bed as you were in the crib. Well, it may or may not be a happy thought, but it's one I think is a salutary thing once in a while. It needn't stop you from making all the effort to do what you can. But you see, the most enormous effect of literature upon the world is to make people believe, including ourselves, that the world is a story. But so far it's a bedtime story where all the children fall asleep before the end. And probably it will be the same for us, even supposing a shattering series of nuclear explosions in Russia and our country; the rest of the world would say oof and go on about its business. Our apocalypticians are so fond of proclaiming that the end is coming that they scarcely seem to notice how many great things have ended, cities destroyed, great regimes gone down in dust and rubble, the end of ways of thinking. This world is always weaving itself over the ruins. It's sort of like a fountain that flowers in its fall; it's always going on. That doesn't mean that it will always go on, only that we have no reason to suppose otherwise.

INTERVIEWER: So then the whole world is a series of construction/ destruction.

NEMEROV: Well, now that we've put it so bluntly it seems to be one of the oldest ideas in the world. Hindu mythology is full of it. Most other mythologies appear to have some derivation from it.

INTERVIEWER: Was it Freud who said that the only certain thing is uncertainty?

NEMEROV: How could it have taken Freud to think of that? It sounds like something the PTA might have got up. I'm sure he said something like it. But it is remarkable, when you read the greatest sayings of the great philosophers, how ordinary they come to seem sometime. There is so much a matter of glamour and fashion, and of course style, in the way of putting things. "Style is the ultimate morality of mind." Makes you feel about ten foot tall to say it, but it doesn't mean anything identifiable.

INTERVIEWER: Somewhere you have said that style is that fire which consumes what it illuminates.

NEMEROV: Well, something very like that.

INTERVIEWER: Would you say that's one of those ornate witticisms?

NEMEROV: Well, yes, but I'm not pretending to be an informative philosopher. I think I've always admired statements which were in the last degree uninformative and tautological. The greatest saying in the world is found in Edwin Arlington Robinson's Arthurian poems, in *Merlin:* "And that was as it was." Ah, absolute! Well, when they say things like that, that's what snows you about poetry. Imagine inventing a cliché, inventing your own platitude. Now that's what it's about. You've got to have a bit of natural knowledge first, but that's what it comes to. That's the way it is. It's over, kid. Wonderful sayings, we don't use them for information, we use them for some nonsense we call wisdom.

INTERVIEWER: Do you think your poetry is getting simpler; I don't mean to say simpleminded.

NEMEROV: I would accept simpleminded. The object, now that I'm nearing my sixtieth year I can say this, the object is to get dumber not smarter. That's another thing *King Lear* has to say. Eyes are made for weeping, not seeing. The Chinese, Taoists have a similar saying, "The student of knowledge learning more every day, the student of Tao forgetting more every day." That's not so much a recommendation as a statement of fact. I certainly forget more all the time.

INTERVIEWER: Have you been consciously working the poetry to touch a broader audience?

NEMEROV: Oh, no. I've never thought about that. I'm not a salesman, not a preacher (I hope I'm not a preacher). If people want to read what I write, it's there; it's offered for sale in the usual manner. But about poetry and its turning into truth, you know I was saying to Howard Moss that lines you admired when you were twenty, that sounded like beautiful poesy, turned into the most commonplace statements of fact without losing any of their beauty at all. And I saw also the literal truth of that supposedly feeble-minded Platonic doctrine of archetypes, that the idea comes first. And it's easy enough to jeer at it if you use his example, the idea of a chair or table or the good. But it is absolutely the indestructible basis of everything human that we've done with the world. You don't throw a lot of stuff in the corner and expect it to turn into a television set. No, you've got to have the idea of a television set first. You've got to dream about flying for five hundred years before anything comes of it: five different kinds of after-shave in the forward cabin of an American Airlines jet. Of course, you lose something when the dream turns into fact, but it's all done on this Platonic basis. The only place where you might question is to ask whether God did in fact found the world on the same basis by having the idea of it first. But for everything that has made the human world rise up out of the natural one, the theory of archetypes, which is still, I believe, believed by most people on the earth, is absolutely sound. There is a logos and it's up here. Well, end of sermon.

INTERVIEWER: Well, we could draw you toward a conclusion here by asking you what you're currently working on. You say you don't plan to publish another book for five years.

NEMEROV: Well, it's not a plan. I do, as I've said, write in bursts. It comes in a great rush, and I attend to business with considerable constancy while it's happening. And when it's not there, just no voice speaks, then there's not much good sitting at the desk, so you might as well study, learn a little something, read. I'm afraid most of my access to the world is from reading. At my age, I'm not expected to have radically new experiences except of the disastrous kind. Stanley Elkin said to me, "Howard, do you expect any pleasant surprises?" It's a good question. Well, yes I do. There are still lots of pleasant surprises. So, it's not a plan not to publish for another five years.

INTERVIEWER: Well, what do you see yourself doing in the future?

NEMEROV: I hope to win more battles in the losing war.

The Parable of the Cave or: In Praise of Watercolors

MARY GORDON

Once, I was told a story by a famous writer. "I will tell you what women writers are like," he said. The year was 1971. The women's movement had made men nervous; it had made a lot of women write. "Women writers are like a female bear who goes into a cave to hibernate. The male bear shoves a pine cone up her ass, because he knows if she shits all winter, she'll stink up the cave. In the spring, the pressure of all that built-up shit makes her expel the pine cone, and she shits a winter's worth all over the walls of the cave."

That's what women writers are like, said the famous writer.

He told the story with such geniality; he looked as if he were giving me a wonderful gift. I felt I ought to smile; everyone knows there's no bore like a feminist with no sense of humor. I did not write for two months after that. It was the only time in my life I have suffered from writer's block. I should not have smiled. But he was a famous writer and spoke with geniality. And in truth, I did not have the courage for clear rage. There is no seduction like that of being thought a good girl.

Theodore Roethke said that women poets were "stamping a tiny foot against God." I have been told by male but not by female critics that my work was "exquisite," "lovely," "like a watercolor." They, of course, were painting in oils. They were doing the important work. Watercolors are cheap and plentiful; oils are costly: their base must be bought. And the idea is that oil paintings will endure. But what will they endure against? Fire? Flood? Bombs? Earthquake? Their endurance is another illusion: one more foolish bet against nature, or against natural vulnerabilities, one more scheme, like fallout shelters, one more gesture of illusory safety.

There are people in the world who derive no small pleasure from the game of "major" and "minor." They think that no major work can be painted in watercolors. They think, too, that Hemingway writing about boys in the woods is major; Mansfield writing about girls in the house is minor. Exquisite, they will hasten to insist, but minor. These people join up with other bad specters, and I have to work to banish them. Let us pretend these specters are two men, two famous poets, saying, "Your experience is an embarrassment; your experience is insignificant."

I wanted to be a good girl, so I tried to find out whose experience was not embarrassing. The prototype for a writer who was not embarrassing was Henry James. And you see, the two specters said, proffering hope, he wrote about social relationships, but his distance gave them grandeur.

Distance, then, was what I was to strive for. Distance from the body, from the heart, but most of all, distance from the self as writer. I could never understand exactly what they meant or how to do it; it was like trying to follow the directions on a home permanent in 1959.

If Henry James has the refined experience, Conrad had the significant one. The important moral issues were his: men pitted against nature in moments of extremity. There are no important women in Conrad's novels, except for *Victory*, which, the critics tell us, is a romance and an exception. Despite the example of Conrad, it was all right for the young men I knew, according to my specters, to write about the hymens they had broken, the diner waitresses they had seduced. Those experiences were significant. But we were not to write about our broken hearts, about the married men we loved disastrously, about our mothers or our children. Men could write about their fears of dying by exposure in the forest; we could not write about our fears of being suffocated in the kitchen. Our desire to write about these experiences only revealed our shallowness; it was suggested we would, in time, get over it. And write about what? Perhaps we would stop writing.

And so, the specters whispered to me, if you want to write well, if you want us to take you seriously, you must be distant, you must be extreme.

I suppose the specters were not entirely wrong. Some of the literature that has been written since the inception of the women's movement is lacking in style and moral proportion. But so is the work of Mailer, Miller, Burroughs, Ginsberg. Their lack of style and proportion may be called offensive, but not embarrassing. They may be referred to as off the mark, but they will not be called trivial.

And above all I did not wish to be *trivial*; I did not wish to be embarrassing. But I did not want to write like Conrad, and I did not want to write like Henry James. The writers I wanted to imitate were all women: Charlotte Brontë, Woolf, Mansfield, Bowen, Lessing, Olsen. I discovered that what I loved in writing was not distance but radical closeness; not the violence of the bizarre but the complexity of the quotidian.

I lost my fear of being trivial, but not my fear of being an embarrassment. And so, I wrote my first novel in the third person. No one would
publish it. Then a famous woman writer asked why I had written a first-
person novel in the third person. She is a woman of abiding common
sense, and so I blushed to tell her: "I wanted to sound serious. I didn't
want to be embarrassing."

Only her wisdom made me write the novel I meant to. I can say it now:
I will probably never read Conrad again; what he writes about simply does
not interest me. Henry James I will love always, but it is not for his distance that I love him. The notion that style and detachment are necessary
blood brothers is crude and bigoted. It is an intellectual embarrassment.

And I can say it now: I would rather own a Mary Cassatt watercolor
than a Velasquez oil.

Here is the good side of being a woman writer: the company of other
women writers, dead and living. My writer friends, all women, help me
banish the dark specters. So does Katherine Mansfield; so does Christina
Rossetti. I feel their closeness to the heart of things; I feel their aptness and
their bravery.

I think it is lonelier to be a man writer than a woman writer now, because I do not think that men are as good at being friends to one another
as women are. Perhaps, since they have not thought they needed each
other's protection, as women have known we have needed each other's,
they have not learned the knack of helpful, rich concern which centers on a
friend's work. They may be worried, since they see themselves as hewers of
wood and slayers of animals, about production, about the kind of achievement that sees its success only in terms of another's failure. They may not
be as kind to one another; they may not know how. These are the specters
that men now must banish. Our specters may be easier to chase. For the
moment. They were not always so.

To this tale there should be an appendix, an explanation. Why was I so
susceptible to the bad advice of men? What made me so ready to listen?
Where did I acquire my genius for obedience?

I had a charming father. In many crucial ways, he was innocent of sex-
ism, although he may have substituted narcissism in its place. He wanted
me to be like him. He was a writer, an unsuccessful writer, and my mother
worked as a secretary to support us. Nevertheless he was a writer; he could
think of himself as nothing else. He wanted me to be a writer too. I may
have been born to be one, which made things easier. He died when I was
seven. But even in those years we had together I learned well that I was his
child, not my mother's. His mind was exalted, my mother's common. That

she could earn the money to support us was only proof of the ordinariness of her nature, an ordinariness to which I was in no way heir. So I was taught to read at three, taught French at six, and taught to despise the world of women, the domestic. I was a docile child. I brought my father great joy, and I learned the pleasures of being a good girl.

And I earned, as a good girl, no mean rewards. Our egos are born delicate. Bestowing pleasure upon a beloved father is much easier than discovering the joys of solitary achievements. It was easy for me to please my father; and this ease bred in me a desire to please men—a desire for the rewards of a good girl. They are by no means inconsiderable: safety and approval, the warm, incomparable atmosphere created when one pleases a man who has vowed, in his turn, to keep the wolf from the door.

But who is the wolf?

He is strangers. He is the risk of one's own judgments, one's own work.

I have learned in time that I am at least as much my mother's daughter as my father's. Had I been only my mother's daughter it is very possible that I would never have written: I may not have had the confidence required to embark upon a career so valueless in the eyes of the common-sense world. I did what my father wanted; I became a writer. I grew used to giving him the credit. But now I see that I am the *kind* of writer I am because I am my mother's daughter. My father's tastes ran to the metaphysical. My mother taught me to listen to conversations at the dinner table; she taught me to remember jokes.

My subject as a writer has far more to do with family happiness than with the music of the spheres. I don't know what the nature of the universe is, but I have a good ear. What it hears best are daily rhythms, for that is what I value, what I would wish, as a writer, to preserve.

My father would have thought this a stubborn predilection for the minor. My mother knows better.

Love Across the Lines

REYNOLDS PRICE

For nearly two centuries now a love, almost Wagnerian in intensity, has grown between two kinds of English and American literature. Vast and enduring and often unrequited as it's proved to be, it is little noticed and hardly discussed. The lovers are novelists and poets. The epic and dramatic poets of the ancient world appear, from our perspective at least, to have been content in their roomy, narrative-lyric forms. There were no long prose fictions by Homer, Aeschylus, Sophocles, Euripides, Vergil—or by Dante, Shakespeare, or Milton. And there are none by Dryden, Pope, Wordsworth, Coleridge, Byron, Shelley, Keats, Tennyson, or Browning. If we consider writers in English who are mainly regarded in the recent and relatively unGreek sense of writers of verse, then the first important poet to produce a long prose fiction would seem to be Sir Philip Sidney. But he has no immediate heirs (unless we choose to argue over the amphibious but chiefly prosy Samuel Johnson and Oliver Goldsmith). On the continent, to be sure, Goethe won his fame and profoundly affected the life-expectancy of nineteenth-century German adolescents with *The Sorrows of Young Werther* and in *Wilhelm Meister* achieved a rich combination of prose and verse which has too seldom been emulated. Victor Hugo succeeded enormously with *The Hunchback of Notre Dame* and *Les Misérables*. In English however the next poet to excel in prose is Sir Walter Scott, who is now read for his prose fiction—as is, in America at least, Edgar Allen Poe. With curiosities and grotesqueries along the way—such as Walt Whitman's temperance novel, *Franklin Evans;* George Eliot's long poem, *The Spanish Gypsy;* and such honorable versatilities as the poems of Emily Brontë, Robert Louis Stevenson, Rudyard Kipling, Stephen Crane, Gertrude Stein, James Joyce, and D. H. Lawrence—we arrive in Thomas Hardy at the first writer in English to achieve substantial and equal distinction in long fiction and verse. And rather quickly we come to our second, and so far as I know, only other truly ambidextrous poet-novelist/novelist-poet of large productivity and equal distinction—Robert

Penn Warren. (The fact that they both earned first notice as novelists is of interest, for I cannot think of an example of the reverse—a writer first widely admired as a poet who then proceeded to extensive excellence in fiction—and I cannot think why.)

Some lesser achievements are famous—the poems of Hemingway and Faulkner, of interest to cultists, have recently been reprinted. Buried forever perhaps are whole volumes of poems by William Dean Howells, Willa Cather, and Theodore Dreiser (though some of Howells' poems bear comparison with his best fiction and though Dreiser's volume—*Moods, Cadenced and Declaimed,* which followed his successful *An American Tragedy* by a single year but sold only 922 copies—should probably be retained in print, *pro bono publico,* by the National Endowment for the Arts as a species of warning to heedless poachers across the genre-lines). Among American and British contemporaries such poets as Stephen Spender, Dylan Thomas, Randall Jarrell, Howard Nemerov, James Dickey, James Merrill, Sylvia Plath, Maxine Kumin, Galway Kinnell, and D. M. Thomas have published good long fiction; and novelists of the quality of John Updike, Joyce Carol Oates, and Larry Woiwode have published quantities of serious verse.

The lists could continue well into the night and might provide occasional amazements—what for instance of the great plastic artists like Michelangelo who've managed brilliant poems in an idle moment?—but the lists only postpone an obvious and necessary question: why, for the past hundred years, say, has there been this ever-increasing trespass across the boundaries of form; this oceanic if unrewarded yearning of poets for prose, novelists for verse?

A first answer would note that the boundary between verse and prose in English and other Western languages did not become rigidly fixed until well after the development of the novel as the popular receptacle and purveyor of narrative—extended imitations of interesting human action (conflict and resolution) presented in the order in which sane human witnesses perceive the world outside themselves: that is, chronological order; the order of ruthless clock-time. In most Western countries, the gradual triumph of the novel began in the mid-eighteenth century but was not complete until the late nineteenth, when the maturing of the form itself coincided with (and no doubt encouraged) the rise of mass literacy. Thus Tennyson and Browning are the last major English poets to write long verse narratives. In America the impulse survived a little longer in Edwin Arlington Robinson and Robert Frost; but by the 1930's the wall between extended narrative and verse had been raised and pretty thoroughly secured (a rewarding comparison could be made with the famous effect of the invention of photography upon painting—a similar abandonment of mimetic narrative content and a consequent inversion of attention and vision). In short, those writers who by gift and training were inclined to the production of verse abandoned as indefensible vast provinces over which they had long and fruitfully roamed. Those invaders or benign colonists who inherited by vigor and default the ancient treasures of epic, drama, romance, and tale were required to surrender the ancient containers and vehicles of those treasures—metrical line, paragraph, and stanza with all their still-uncomprehended and uninvestigated subliminal powers to enchant, seduce, and conquer; perhaps even to *control* for brief periods. Once those drastic mutual surrenders were made, however; once the border walls were in place (and the border guards—more of them later), the yearning could begin, the fraternization and the often furtive mergings.

A second answer would ignore the effect of the novel on poetry (and of the powerful influence of movies over both) and would remark simply that verbal craftsmen share with other humans and beasts an impatience with forms, restrictions, shortages of material imposed upon their lives. Is it more peculiar that Dreiser wrote quantities of poems than that Michelangelo made, as his only work while in the employ of Piero de Medici, one single snowman in the Florentine winter of 1494? Probably not, though I can easily guess which oddity most of us would rather know. And anyone can sympathize with either man's impatience with the tyranny of forms and materials, the brute and unpredictable power which all our conscious and unconscious choices have to shape each subsequent moment of our lives. But surely no one who has not chosen a particular *literary* form as the container of his curiosity and knowledge can know the degree to which the form itself—the sonnet, the free-verse paragraph, the epic, the realistic novel, the prose tale—will not merely receive an artist's questions and convey him to the Ultima Thule of an answer but will simultaneously shape, alter, distort, disfigure, clarify, even beautify both question and answer. It is so obvious as perhaps to bear mentioning that *King Lear* could not be a novel or even a long narrative poem; that Shakespeare's discoveries in the interior of human folly, cruelty, and devotion are to an extent beyond calculation forced upon him by his initial commission—a stage-drama of manageable length written generally in lines of five-stress rising rhythm, interspersed with passages of a prose which (though it appears to obey looser laws) is also marching under iron discipline: the discipline of the form of the play, the form of the *idea* as it is conceived, born, and matured by the physical form of act, scene, verse, prose and by the presumed pressure on Shakespeare to write both quickly and lucratively for a commercial enterprise. It is equally obvious, and made even more so by several screen adaptations, that *Anna Karenina* could not be a play or a poem. The immense prowl of Tolstoy's immense and glacial attention over an entire civilization at a particular moment of poise-before-collapse could only have been contained by the elastic and pawky realistic novel, the shaggy monster which Henry James so inaccurately deplored when he spoke of Tolstoy and Dostoevsky as "fluid puddings," devoid of composition, economy, and architecture—a form, not at all incidentally, which required more than four years of Tolstoy's time. That discovery then of the constricting and liberating power of particular forms is among the most enduring impulses which send novelists and poets outside their accustomed forms into new and strange country—promising, forbidding, and often treacherous.

A third important distinction between contemporary novelists and poets, and a force in their mutual attraction, is memorably stated in Howard Moss's illuminating introduction to an anthology of short stories by poets. The collection is called *The Poet's Story;* and among other acute observations, Moss says, "The mirror is the totem of the poet, who looks *at* and *into* himself, who creates himself, as it were. And I would say the window belongs to the fiction writer, who looks *out* and *around,* and is a product of the world." The generalization can stand a little adjustment of course, but at heart it's unassailable. Robert Penn Warren's *Brother to Dragons*, despite the incorporation of the character RPW into the poem, is surely a long poem whose totem is the window. So are the many related poems of Robert Lowell's *History*. But with the decline of verse narrative, verse drama, and with the virtual disappearance of the religious lyric (the song to and about God), contemporary poets are fairly strictly committed to self-contemplation—even the multitudinous neo-surrealists, whose relatively brief poems are inescapably charts of their own preoccupations. And the general abandonment of strict poetic forms, in America at least, has perhaps deepened the poet's solipsistic entrapment—the old complexities of meter and rhyme being, arguably, skills which lured the craftsman out of his cave of mirrors into a world of similarly employed workers, a large guild of journeymen fabricating gold watches set to tell the same time. Any novel of course is also a function of its author's preoccupations, and one of the obsessive aims of the experimental American prose writers of the 1960's and 70's was the prose domestication of the verse surrealist's luxuriant access to memorable image and to revealing disjunctions in time and human nature. If their often gaudy and always academic efforts found few readers—and indeed assisted the serious novel in its drift toward the reader-desertion so lamented by poets—it's worth remembering how si-

lently and steadily great novelists from Defoe to Malamud have smuggled
the tools of verse into their prose: metaphor, heightened speech, interior
monologue, and (far more often than is noticed) meter itself. So the novelist at his window, scarily aimed at the world of others, and the poet at his
seldom flattering or consoling mirror have naturally yearned to swap
views.

Before moving on to what I think is the strongest of the attractions
between the genres, let me glance at a weaker though very real one. The
contemporary poet, with his sales in the hundreds or low thousands, envies the novelist his book clubs and paperbacks, his *Today* show interviews,
his presumed larger audience (an audience which, when scrutinized, often
proves small and which may soon vanish altogether, given the present
lemming-rush by publishers to drown in an artificially heated marsh of
ephemera). The novelist envies the poet his ancient and still assiduously
maintained priestly robes and wand, his evident but inexplicable access to
the gods of language; his tiny but fervent band of disciples, summonable
at any American crossroads at the mere announcement of a poetry reading.
The novelist also envies, I think the strong odor of smoke and blood that
hovers above American poets—a continuous effluvium from the ceaseless
poetry wars: the Redskins vs. the Palefaces, in whatever get-ups they fight
this season. If there was in American fiction a similar aesthetic division in
the 60's and early 70's between the realistic novel and the commercially
doomed experimental, it produced few memorable skirmishes—perhaps
only Gore Vidal's massive napalming of the experimentalists. But any novelist craving a touch of real aesthetic frostbite has only to write a handful of
poems, then dare to read them to a room containing a minimum of one
licensed American poet. Any craven need for an alley-fight can be quickly
satisfied by the novelist's daring to *publish* the poems. I'm open to correc-
tion, but it seems to me that poets' novels are met with actual tolerance
from novelists. My own four years' service on the literature grants-panel of
the National Endowment for the Arts gave me constant occasion to wonder why, when compared with the brawling and backbiting of poets, most
novelists seem positively somnolent if not beatific. Perhaps poets envy that
tranquility—professional at least, if not personal. And is the tranquility a
simple result of the novelist's access to larger audiences and more money?
(We're speaking of course of relative, and pitiably small, figures—a few
hundred vs. a few thousand generally. In any culture at any time there is
apparently a mystically fixed number of earnest readers for serious verse or
fiction, not quite as small a number as the thirty-six Just Men of rabbinical
tradition but stunningly low; and any trade-paper's news that a novel of
Saul Bellow's or a volume of Frost's poems has sold a hundred thousand

copies is not to be interpreted as an indication that the gross number of serious readers is increasing. An informal canvass of ten of those buyers will silence your hopes.)

If that last-mentioned attraction between poets and novelists—an attraction of commerce and psychic violence—seems less than noble, let me attempt to suggest how it produces and even disguises the most potent attraction of all. The essence of this long rivalry between genres (I'm omitting entirely those dramatists who write novels or verse, those painters who have so often written well, those journalists who serenade every window in the House of Art). Look first at a sonnet by W. H. Auden. It's called "The Novelist" and I'll quote it in its earliest published form, not in Auden's late and damaging revision.

> Encased in talent like a uniform,
> The rank of every poet is well known;
> They can amaze us like a thunderstorm,
> Or die so young, or live for years alone.
>
> They can dash forward like hussars: but he
> Must struggle out of his boyish gift and learn
> How to be plain and awkward, how to be
> One after whom none think it worth to turn.
>
> For, to achieve his lightest wish, he must
> Become the whole of boredom, subject to
> Vulgar complaints like love, among the Just
>
> Be just, among the Filthy filthy too,
> And in his own weak person, if he can,
> Must suffer dully all the wrongs of Man.

Sweet words—to a novelist, even one who like me recalls that the older Auden appeared to read no fiction more ambitious than detective thrillers. Sweet and no doubt too simple, however interestingly it agrees with Scott Fitzgerald's observation that in every good novelist there is something of the peasant. (Is the corollary to that that in every good poet there is something of the baron?—the lord of the manor, subject to outbursts of largess and rage?) To stick with Auden's simplification for a moment though, if we think of modern poets as hussars (cutlasses drawn, hurtling on fevered steeds through hails of grapeshot toward larger ordnance and certain death), then we may think of the more prevalent kind of novelist (that is, the clock-time realist) as footsoldiers or maybe even mess sergeants, cooks, and bottlewashers.

However coarse such distinctions, they do finally chart the lines of the strongest magnetic force that draws poets proseward and novelists to verse. My own simplification is this. The novelist envies the poet's intensity of emotion, language, consequent rhythm, and kinetic effect; the poet envies the novelist his stamina, his endless enlistment, his helpless commitment to the long haul—the slowly drawn but finally enormous net of fish, the ripe fields of standing grain in late summer light. What each in fact envies in the other is his particular command of time—the literal chronological realities of his form: the lyric poem's command of the moment, the novel's command of human generations.

Howard Moss makes another interesting division which is relevant at this point—". . . time is different for the novelist and the poet. The fiction writer is dominated by the clock and the poet by the metronome. They are just dissimilar enough—metronomes can be sped up, slowed down, or stopped—to provide a fertile field of transaction." My own suggestion is two-fold and so obvious as to be generally ignored. With uncharacteristic exceptions like Joyce's *Ulysses,* novels concern themselves with stretches of time which, by human clocks, are relatively long—weeks, months, years. Most novels literally portray the passage of a good deal of time: time is their subject but also their predicate and object. The traditional novel (and the one still most popular with readers) is lengthy—five hundred pages and upward, say. Lady Murasaki, Richardson, Stendhal, Dickens, Tolstoy, Dostoevsky, George Eliot, Proust, Roger Martin du Gard—all actually depict, by various chronologically consecutive methods, the flow of time through particular persons; and the length of their depictions becomes in turn a slow stream of time running through us, the readers. Only a postgraduate student of Speed Reading can consume the majority of classic novels quickly, and most of us suspect that consumption is not synonymous with assimilation. Like most of you, I've spent whole summers with *War and Peace;* winters with *Bleak House,* a calendar year doing Proust like a job (tedious but well-paid with grand office-parties). And many contemporary novelists continue that traditional request for substantial stretches of the reader's actual life, novelists from a broad spectrum of schools—from Anthony Powell, Eudora Welty, and Saul Bellow through John Barth and Thomas Pynchon. But of the already-canonized great twentieth-century poems, how many demand—for a single earnest reading—more than an hour of a sane reader's life? (I discriminate here between reading and scholarship. A perusal of the author's notes to *The Wasteland* and the academic barnacles upon its hull and that of *The Four Quartets* can take a long decade. The same might almost be said of Pound's *Cantos,* William Carlos Williams' *Paterson,* Hart Crane's *The Bridge,* David Jones's *In Parenthesis,* Wallace Stevens' *Notes Toward a Supreme Fiction,* Charles Olson's *Maximus* poems—though in those cases, the process of canonization is still being argued.) Among living poets, an increasing number have attempted relatively long poems or cycles—Anthony Hecht, James Merrill, John Ashbery, Galway Kinnell, Ed Dorn, Geoffrey Hill, and Ted Hughes—but a rollcall of widely admired twentieth-century poets from Yeats through Robert Lowell and, say, Philip Levine is its own illustration of my point: that modern poets, with curious diffidence, have requested or required relatively small portions of our clock-time. That the diffidence is new, odd, and sacrificial is indicated by an earlier muster— *The Iliad, The Odyssey, De Rerum Natura, The Aeneid, The Metamorphoses, The Divine Comedy, Paradise Lost, The Hind and the Panther, The Dunciad, The Prelude, Hyperion, Prometheus Unbound, Idylls of the King, The Ring and the Book.* And lest they be thought of as isolated continents amid rafts of small lyric islands, we could spend an all but endless night reciting the names of their failed long companions—a number of them by honorable poets.

However critical then that difference in the clock-demand of contemporary verse and prose, it is still not the essence of the final attraction between the genres. (My generation may have been the last to memorize poems—I had an uncle who could recite perfectly Walter Scott's *Lady of the Lake*—but the memorability of traditional brief verse forms went a long way toward eliminating the difference. Over nearly thirty years now, I have frequently recited to myself poems as short as Emily Dickinson's "Success Is Counted Sweetest" or as long as Milton's "Lycidas," but I cannot recall one entire sentence from any great novel.)

The essence again, lies in each genre's peculiar grasp on time. The novel, like the drama, is helplessly and gloriously dependent upon scene—present action, however portrayed (even the most radical experiments, even novels of irregular chronology and unreliable narration cannot stray for long from scenes-in-the-present: characters observed in motion and, whether observed with the actual eye or the eye of memory, observed *now* and conveyed thus to the reader). Even a philosophical novelist like Proust or Mann must stage frequent scenes; and the chief problem that their pages present to the common reader is impatience, the often-protracted wait for *scenes*—impatience which easily becomes boredom and anger. The contemporary poem however, with its liberation or expulsion from scenic narrative, has chosen or been compelled to ally itself with the traditional metaphysical monologue, the sacred or secular sermon. Not that numerous poets haven't continued to produce the occasional scenic poem—or the quickly sketched scene which becomes the text of the homily—but any broad reading will confirm the alliance. Poetry has indeed selected the mirror or the telescope (another kind of mirror) as its totem. The novel remains on its knees at the window (though, since the window is glazed, it will inevitably interpose glimpses of the novelist between the reader and the world). Mirrors offer us a perpetual present—our faces aging instant by discrete instant, as long as we can bear to watch them. Windows also reveal a present, but their partial transparency is capable of producing at least the illusion of merger with external objects in slow or rapid flux. Mirrors are therefore, as Auden again says, "lonely"—and as most other poets might say "bored." Windows are—what?—well, if not lonely or often bored, then certainly fixed in place (in the novelist's eyes) and rather more humble than they can steadily enjoy being: humble in their servitude to chronology and appearance, peasants in harness from dawn till dark. By nature then they long for one another; who else have they? Any small-town decorator knows how the mirror in a room loves the window—accepts its constant messages of light and motion, both holds and returns them: a satisfying love. But they cannot really *become* one another (despite a clean window's dim reflectiveness).

Is it also the nature and fate of narrative prose and metaphysical lyric verse to love as mirrors and windows and human beings love?—as solitudes fixed to opposite walls? The history of literature before our own century says a long and thunderous No. The vast displays of Hardy and Warren reverberate the claim more recently. Are the present mutual solitudes and yearnings only another grim result of American obsession with expertise?—limited workmen at limited tasks in limited space? Or, to recall Virginia Woolf, did human nature really change early in our century? Did the human mind really begin a mass migration inward, into the perilous refuge of its own lone self? Contemporary verse says a clear if rueful Yes. So does a great deal of contemporary fiction. But so surely do the swollen and vaunting heroes of Homer, the baffled Choruses of Aeschylus, the desolate lyrics of Sappho. Is the job of the literary craftsman in twentieth-century America really so complex as to require the set of stalls into which the craftsmen have sorted themselves?—with, as I've said at all this length, frequent trespass in the night. Is a perfect lyric narrative of Emily Dickinson's the perfect motto for the question?

> I died for Beauty—but was scarce
> Adjusted in the Tomb
> When One who died for Truth, was lain
> In an adjoining Room—
>
> He questioned softly "Why I failed"?
> "For Beauty," I replied—
> "And I—for Truth—Themself are One—
> We Brethren, are", He said—

And so, as Kinsmen, met a Night—
We talked between the Rooms—
Until the Moss had reached our lips—
And covered up—our names—

The questions posed by the voices of the poem, though whispered, are hardly idle. Neither are my own, which come down at last to a single question—can the narrative-lyric impulse, perhaps the oldest and unquestionably the strongest of literary impulses, recover in the hands of numerous willing but fractured craftsmen the sane and sanguine unity of earlier, even recent, times? I've glanced here at valiant and incessant tries by many. If few of them have achieved precise aim and brought down the whole breathing brilliant prey—well, surely few arrows achieve *their* mark; but driven archers still roam the woods.

"A Trap to Catch Little Birds With"
An Interview with John Hawkes

This interview was recorded in the Muhlenberg Room of the Muhlenberg College Library on Saturday afternoon, April 10, 1976, during the Hawkes Symposium. The interviewers are Anthony C. Santore and Michael Pocalyko.

INTERVIEWER: Let's start with some of our reasons for doing this. One is that people who write about your work would like to know more about you. And secondly, there hasn't been a published interview with you since the triad has been completed.

HAWKES: I did do one—about a fifteen-page piece with excerpts from the books scattered through it—quite nice; but on the other hand, there are two of you here so you'll probably have different questions.

INTERVIEWER: Well, our whole approach is to try to understand you as a person.

HAWKES: I don't understand myself.

INTERVIEWER: Let's give you an example: You really enjoy being John Hawkes. We'd like to know why. We'd like to know what you enjoy about being John Hawkes—John Hawkes as a person, John Hawkes as an author, John Hawkes as a man who has written . . .

HAWKES: I'm not feeling very self-confident right now.

INTERVIEWER: Maybe not, but you do enjoy being yourself. That's very obvious. You are a unique person and you care about yourself. So what really makes John Hawkes different? What do you enjoy about being John Hawkes?

HAWKES: About being myself?

INTERVIEWER: Yes.

HAWKES: Well, you see, usually I'm not aware of being myself.

INTERVIEWER: Well, who are you aware of being, then?

HAWKES: I'm not aware of being anybody. I mean I'm simply aware of my mundane tasks, my terrible anxieties. You know, I always have overwhelming anxieties. But I do have an unusual capacity for compassion; and I think I have an almost profound relationship to the less fortunate, the deviant, the maimed, the criminal, the outcast, and so on. I think that I am a fear-ridden sensualist. I love good white wine and flowers and idyllic landscapes.

INTERVIEWER: You do so much with landscapes. What kind of landscapes do you like? Do you like craggy alps? Do you like plains?

HAWKES: No, not craggy alps. I really don't like plains either. Although I was moved by a visit in Kansas. I stayed at the University of Kansas. It was the kind of place that had a rather glorious desolation; the rolling country was magnificent. But I prefer the sea, the Mediterranean climate, or a semi-tropical climate. I love Greece; I love France; I loved the Caribbean when we were there. I like orchids growing on pine trees. We were living out at Stanford one year where roses were growing all over a cyprus tree. I remember the profusion of roses; I remember the flowers.

INTERVIEWER: Is there anything else you enjoy about being John Hawkes?

HAWKES: I enjoy my work. I enjoy my family. I enjoy my life. These are all very vague terms—it is very hard to make them more specific. I think even though I am a person of so much uncertainty and anxiety who is rather poorly read, untrained, and so on, I am also oddly self-confident. I have a way of being enormously persuasive. I believe Albert Guerard said I can persuade anyone to do anything—and I have exercised those persuasive powers in places like faculty meetings. I've been involved in changing things at Brown.

I'm a person of bad dreams and good work. I dream bad dreams every night and I try to do good work every day. And I am someone who achieves almost immediate rapport with students. It's not that I'm interested in trying to usurp the role of University chaplain or psychiatrist, but the fact of the matter is that I do relate very directly, swiftly, and immediately to people; we come to know each other almost momentarily in the most intimate way.

People do look to me for—I don't know what you would call it—a kind of ultimate sensibility. I'm not at all adverse to giving people advice. I advise people even though I don't know them, telling them precisely what they ought to do. I do that too much even in my own household, so that I have a nickname for myself—"boj"—Bad Old Jack. I tell my own family what to do, so that they can't set the table without my telling them to change the angle of the forks a little. In the home, I become somewhat irascible at times, sort of an eccentric.

INTERVIEWER: What about the public, Jack? It came through very clearly that you are different when you are reading to the public than you are in ordinary conversation. Are you aware that you are different when you are John Hawkes, the novelist, as opposed to when you are Jack Hawkes in the real world?

HAWKES: Right now you can see that I am not sure who I am. I'm trying to find out. I'm trying to feel my way into some kind of existence. I think it is perfectly true that what I actually give to my readers is a figure of authority, clear authority. Although I'm terrified to give the readings and I often don't really like doing it . . .

INTERVIEWER: But you feed so well off the audience.

HAWKES: Yes, well, I guess in most readings, once they're under way, I tend to be all right. But I've been to some readings where it hasn't been that way, where the audience has not responded, where my mouth has remained dry forever, and it was really an excruciating experience. But on the other hand, I know there is a point where I develop a form of detachment that is the right kind of distance—a certain security where I can hear the sound of my voice change.

I am often that way as a teacher, even when I'm most relaxed and drinking wine in a class—or beer—or both at the same time; I'm likely to be both aggressive and open. I was never a good student, and am still trying in a sense to make up for the failures of my past. I know I have a special kind of presence and a special kind of bearing or intensity. I'm a person who thinks he is right most of the time.

INTERVIEWER: You're an Emersonian whether you will admit it or not.

HAWKES: Is that right? I don't even know what an Emersonian is.

INTERVIEWER: You're self-reliant and you know it. Emerson said something to that effect: "If you would be a man speak what you think today in words as hard as cannonballs, and tomorrow speak what tomorrow thinks in hard words again, though it contradict everything you said today."

HAWKES: And yet, the funny thing is that wherever I go, I'm comforted by people. There are always several people who gather around me protectively, who want to take care of me, who want to amuse me, who want to be sure that I have a good time. So I must be vulnerable.

INTERVIEWER: Well no, it is not so much vulnerability, but attractiveness. You are an attractive person.

HAWKES: It has taken me over forty years to figure out that I'm not simply a scrawny, asthmatic child crouching in a corner somewhere.

INTERVIEWER: Let's say there was a year when you could do nothing but read, and you wanted to pick up on some things that you'd never had a chance to read. What would those things be?

HAWKES: Last year I had such a year. I was writing, but I also had a lot of time to read. I read some things from the complete works of de Sade, translated by my old classmate Austryn Wainhouse. I read Camus's *The Fall*. I read Michel Leiris's *Manhood* (that book was suggested to me by Sophie). I read the Ford Madox Ford tetralogy *Parade's End* with a sinking heart. It is painful to read such a long ambitious fictional work which falls so short of *The Good Soldier,* written fifteen years before. Yet I still read it with pleasure. I would read more of Barth, although I think I've read pretty much of Barth. What a lousy answer. You don't . . .

INTERVIEWER: We'll take it out.
How about another aspect of what you enjoy about yourself? For example, what do you enjoy about being "the novelist"? Is it in the creation of an idea? Is it in the working out of a novel—which you have described as "agonizing"? Is it in seeing the finished product work on people?

HAWKES: I have a shelf on top of one of our bookcases at home that has my books—the first hardbound copy of each of my books that I have received (I believe ten of them in all). Each one of them is significant to me; they have become totemic. I wrote my name in them and put them away. I have these ten books with all the other editions and translations and other versions of the books all in one place. And every once in a while, I look at them, especially the first ten, with a real sense of pleasure. I want to touch them. I do touch them. Sometimes I smell them. I like the smell—they are no longer fresh, some of them being very old. I used to think of them as my tombstones, but that was when I was in an earlier stage of the male midlife crisis, I guess. I don't think of them as tombstones any more.

I try to imagine what it would be like to get all of that imagined experience going all at once. It gives me a thrill to think of them that way—as a kind of totality of life that wouldn't have existed if I hadn't written them.

INTERVIEWER: In that moment you enjoy the pleasure of being John Hawkes. We can appreciate that.

HAWKES: Well, you see, generally I am not aware of being John Hawkes, the writer.

INTERVIEWER: You are though.

HAWKES: I based my whole life on the premise that I didn't want to be burdened with one role.

INTERVIEWER: You aren't burdened with one role, you're burdened with a dozen, and the one role that all of us who read you do know is that of "the novelist."

HAWKES: The consciousness of being a "novelist" has increased only recently. Generally speaking, I go through my days not conscious of being a "novelist."

I'm conscious of the totemic things we have in the house, the things I care about. Sheep bells brought back from Greece by my son. A boat made by my son. A model boat he made in Greece. Or a paper sent to me by my son on a birthday. An etching done by my daughter. Sophie and I live in a small, modest house which is a respository of tangible concrete things, like a conch shell, sea sand, some peacock feathers, a lot of sea shells (Sophie collects sea shells), and a trap to catch little birds with—a beautiful thing that somebody gave us in France. It looks like an anchor, and the top part of it twirls, and it has little pieces of colored glass. You tie a string around it, wind it up like a top, drive it into the ground, hide in the bush, pull the string—it whirls, and the bright colors really . . .

INTERVIEWER: Do you know what you're describing?

HAWKES: What?

INTERVIEWER: Your novels. You are describing your novels.

HAWKES: The point is, I don't have a tremendous constant sense of identity as a novelist. I simply don't make all my gestures in that context. I'm sure some people do. I suspect that there are certain people whose identities are so incredibly dependent on that outside support of knowing "I am a writer." You know—pick up the phone and call this agent, get that telegram from this reviewer, and so on. I am not interested in the role or the burden of the personality of a "writer." I am simply myself and usually not very conscious of having been a writer.

At this Symposium, when I hear quotations from my work, I hardly recognize them. I say, "My God, aren't they extraordinary—what amazing pieces of writing."

And then every once in a while I think I really am an important writer, a significant writer. It is just that the United States as a whole doesn't exactly know it yet. But they probably will one of these days.

INTERVIEWER: No question of that. So many of the best writers are so far ahead that it takes a while for readers to develop a taste for their work. When that happens, the writer finds himself "at the top." And that is happening to you.

Don't you think that because you don't put on that "writer with a capital W" image it has helped you very much—especially in the last three novels—in conveying that sense of "cruel detachment" you've worked so hard to develop?

HAWKES: Of course, I had the cruel detachment from the very beginning. I think the lack of a writing persona is valuable only to me personally. I don't have to be concerned with whether or not I'm a writer. I know that I am a writer. I don't need to worry about it and I don't need to have it constantly called to my attention from outside sources.

On the other hand, there are certainly times when I feel a considerable amount of bitterness, such as when *Travesty*, for example, is not being reviewed nationally in the large public media. I don't see *Time* or *Newsweek* rushing out to review it; in fact, they undoubtedly will not review it. There is probably a strange conspiracy, conscious or not, to keep my work from getting really public attention. And every once in a while, I feel a lot of bitterness about it; I suppose that my feeling is some way related to what's been said of me as a writer. Although I think I am quite invulnerable as a writer.

INTERVIEWER: There is another interesting question that we really can't ask. You don't have to get away from novel writing to do other things—you get away from other things to write novels, which is both exciting and healthy. So, let's say you are intensely in the middle of writing a novel: what do you do to distract yourself?

HAWKES: Take walks, drink wine—I don't really distract myself.

INTERVIEWER: Any sports that really excite you?

HAWKES: No. I love horseback riding, but I'm not really able to pursue that sport now. It costs too much money, and where we are, there are no horses. I suspect that one of the reasons that I want to go to England year after next is to be in a country where there is at least the possibility of a horse. I don't have distractions. When I was an adolescent, I was a fairly good fencer. But I don't have a single hobby—I don't believe in them. I suppose I should have some kind of hobby.

INTERVIEWER: How about swimming? It's in your novels. Do you swim?

HAWKES: No. I cannot swim. I can float. One of the characters—I think it was in a story that Bob Steiner was reading from this morning—talked about himself as being a great floater. Well, I can float; that's about all. I really can't swim. I had asthma when I was a child and was a bit under-weight and skinny and scrawny and not athletic and I hated gymnasiums and any form of sport—fearful of physical harm—and we traveled around a great deal. I was born in Stamford, Connecticut, and lived there about eight years, then lived in New York for maybe a year and a half where I went to some kind of church school or church-affiliated school. Then we went to Juneau, Alaska, where it was too cold and there was no place to swim.

My life has been one of odd isolation, with separation from a lot of the rituals and experiences that would comprise "normal" living. By the time I was eight years old in Connecticut, I had developed a real passion for horses. Perhaps only little girls are supposed to love horses, but I loved horses when I was a child and still do.

INTERVIEWER: Do you think that what you just told us reflects on your being attracted to what you call "weak" or "vulnerable" characters—not only in your own work, but in the work of others?

HAWKES: Yes. My mother had to learn to give me injections for my asthma—I remember she used to practice on an orange to give me the injections which I didn't like at all. I think that my early asthmatic years probably did contribute to my attraction for the weak or the less fortunate.

INTERVIEWER: You have identified yourself with influences by a number of people whom we've already heard about . . .

HAWKES: Jay Laughlin, Albert Guerard . . .

INTERVIEWER: How about some artists you have known? Writers . . .

HAWKES: Well, there are three writers that I care a great deal about. I met Flannery O'Connor for about half an hour once and corresponded with her for about six years until she died. Since then, that correspondence and she have meant a great deal to me. I know Bernard Malamud, who has been thoroughly supportive of me and a very good friend. And John Barth is very sustaining; he is an extraordinary man. I think of him as a comic Melville—simply an extraordinary human being who would never say anything so banal about me . . .

INTERVIEWER: Probably some others would have some banal things to say . . .

HAWKES: . . . but Barth is a truly great writer who has such a beautiful intelligence and, of course, a tremendous strength.

INTERVIEWER: Do you have a favorite Barth novel?

HAWKES: Yes. *The Sot-Weed Factor*, which is certainly one of the greatest American novels. I like *The Floating Opera* immensely. And I love the story "Night Sea Journey." It seems amazing that a writer like Barth, whose vision is so gargantuan, was able to write a single short story that mirrored the entirety of his works, with the whole psychic dimension of suicide and the imagination.

INTERVIEWER: There are several writers—Melville, for example—who wrote the same novel over and over again, with different characters in a different setting, but with the same themes. Do you feel that there is anything of yours that comes close to being an "ideal statement"? Is there in fact an "ideal statement"?

HAWKES: I find it difficult to think in terms of ideal statements. Barth has a totally recognizable voice just as Faulkner had. These voices are audible in almost everything they have written. There is a certain unchangingness, if you like, in Barth's work. The man is always trying to risk something new, and he risks an enormous amount each time he writes. If Barth is publishing a new novel, we have expectations about it. But suppose someone had said to you, "Hawkes has a new novel called *Travesty*." What could you have anticipated? You really would not have had any sense at all of what to expect. You couldn't have predicted that it was necessarily going to be a first-person novel. With Barth, you know it is going to be first-person. It has to be. You anticipate the dry wit and the convolutions of a Barthian work. I pride myself on the fact that no one could anticipate one work of mine from the previous one, yet I like to think that I too have a certain consistency of thematic preoccupation—and with language.

INTERVIEWER: That is exactly what we were talking about. Although we can't predict what the next novel is going to be like, after we see it, it fits. So there is a certain . . .

HAWKES: There is a certain continuity, sure.

INTERVIEWER: Then let's get back to the earlier question—is there any one work that you feel gets closest to being the essential work of John Hawkes?

HAWKES: It is terribly hard to say. The title that leaps to mind is *The Cannibal*, which seems to have earned a kind of historical position and permanence. Since the moment of its appearance twenty-five years ago, it has certainly seemed to be a classic—at least a small classic of sorts. Now, *Second Skin* is one of the most continuously lyrical pieces I've written; and I love *The Blood Oranges*. But I think that *Travesty* is probably the purest fiction I've written, and probably the most powerful. And yet, *Travesty* is a comment on *The Cannibal*, not just a completion of the triad of *The Blood Oranges* and *Death, Sleep & the Traveler*. I think it reflects back on my entire writing life so far.

INTERVIEWER: Do you think in that sense Fred Busch might be correct, that you have been learning from the earlier John Hawkes?

HAWKES: No, I honestly don't believe that thesis. I have gained self-confidence, it is true, and to some extent I have parodied myself; but I can't say that I've "learned" from myself. Maybe I can't answer that question. I don't know why I am reluctant to admit that I'm learning from myself. I have a language and I have a vision and I believe they are growing and changing.

INTERVIEWER: Not so much learning from yourself as extending yourself?

HAWKES: I'm an artist—someone who "wroughts" things.

INTERVIEWER: So language and vision together make the essential core of your work.

HAWKES: Sure. What I'm interested in is language and vision. Someone told me that in a recent lecture Barth said that he didn't know what I meant by the word "vision." I suppose "vision" is an ambiguous word, but the only kind of novel that interests me is a visionary novel. Visionary fiction is a unique world, separate and different from the world we live in despite surface semblances. Visionary fiction is a fish bowl in which the clarity of the bowl is unique and you see the stream of fish, the gleam of fins—it is a fish bowl different from any other.

INTERVIEWER: And the purest expression of that is *Travesty*.

HAWKES: I think so.

INTERVIEWER: Do you have any pets?

HAWKES: We used to have three cats, but I managed to get them all exterminated.

INTERVIEWER: Did they talk?

HAWKES: They did not talk.

INTERVIEWER: How about dogs?

HAWKES: We used to have a bird. Sophie and I had a bird—a little parakeet—before we had children. We taught him to talk.

INTERVIEWER: John Hawkes dogs are amazing—when we do the movie version of *The Beetle Leg* they will play a very prominent part. Jim Hoffman said this morning that he cannot understand why *The Lime Twig* has not been made into a movie; Bob Scholes cannot understand why *The Owl* hasn't been made into a movie; and we can't understand why *The Beetle Leg* wasn't either. What about movies? Have you ever considered screenplays?

HAWKES: I'm not interested in writing screenplays.

INTERVIEWER: Have you considered having someone else do it?

HAWKES: *The Lime Twig* has been under option almost from the time of its publication, but there is no way they can make the film without money or connections. Recently, someone wrote what I think is an excellent script for *The Lime Twig;* he worked with a group of film editors in New York, but they were not able to find the producer, or a person with money, or a person with the ability to make the film. It just never worked out. But I don't know much about the film-making business.

INTERVIEWER: How about photography? It's important in the triad.

HAWKES: I know nothing about photography. I'm sure it is a highly specialized and complicated world—as is the theater. The theater is very problematical; film is even worse.

I think that *The Blood Oranges* would make a fantastic film. And I think *Travesty* will make a great film. I met a man at Temple University who thinks that *Death, Sleep & the Traveler* would be a very special film. He even knows the man who he thinks ought to make it.

Of course, a lot of books would make good films, but the ones I'd really like to see on film are *The Blood Oranges* and *Travesty;* but the screenplay for *Travesty* would have to be written.

INTERVIEWER: It's been written.

HAWKES: *Travesty?* There's no dialogue.

INTERVIEWER: The whole book is dialogue—what more do you need? Sane direction, close-up here, pan out there, shots of moving scenery, a monologue. It would probably be best if the faces of the other two characters were never seen.

HAWKES: Really?

INTERVIEWER: Absolutely. Shoot nearly the whole thing from the back—shoot only the back of Henri's head and the back of Chantal's head. Of course, flashbacks would be shot normally, but when we're in that car, we see either the sharp face of the narrator or the backs of the others' heads. The dialogue is written—without the change of a word.
   Do you have a favorite film?

HAWKES: *La Dolce Vita* is probably the film I liked most. I liked *Diabolique*. And although I was rather horrified the first time I saw it, I am impressed by Fellini's *Satyricon*. *Last Tango in Paris* is one of my favorites.

INTERVIEWER: What about *The Day of the Locust?*

HAWKES: I haven't seen it yet.

INTERVIEWER: Are you interested in talking about the publication of your books? Your relationship with New Directions? How your books sell?

HAWKES: New Directions is a unique publisher; it's very small and very intimate—and Jay Laughlin has been a friend for twenty-five years. Fred Martin and Peter Glassgold are friends also, along with all the other New Directions people. I love their company. It's all very harmonious and intimate and small—not at all like a large commercial publisher. I have a lot to say about what the books look like, the format, the design, cover illustrations . . .

INTERVIEWER: Photographs on the back?

HAWKES: Photographs on the back.

INTERVIEWER: They say a lot about you.

Is there one book that sold more than you thought, or less than you thought?

HAWKES: Over all, *The Lime Twig* has sold the most.

INTERVIEWER: Is there someone you would like to interview? And what questions would you ask?

HAWKES: Interview someone? No, I wouldn't want to interview anyone. I'd like to meet them, but—good Lord, do you think when Barth and I met we asked each other questions?

INTERVIEWER: No, that's not what we mean. You see, a lot of people read interviews carefully because they believe they have learned a lot about your work from interviews you've already done. As proof of that, we'd be willing to bet that virtually every scholar who spoke about your work during this Symposium has referred to an interview.

HAWKES: Is that so?

INTERVIEWER: Yes.

HAWKES: If I could interview someone, it would be Barth, Flannery O'Connor, Nathanael West, Melville, or Malamud.

INTERVIEWER: Keep the premise going. What kinds of questions would you ask? Would you ask personal questions? Would you ask about their literature—how they write?

HAWKES: That's the point. Now the metaphor breaks down, because I can't imagine what one would ask. In the case of most of these people, what you are interested in is the discrepancy between the man and the writer.

INTERVIEWER: Our whole purpose is to reconcile that.

HAWKES: It's hard to do.

INTERVIEWER: Well, that is our whole purpose.
    The thing is, you did it unconsciously. Take your crystalline glass, your trap to catch little birds with, and your fish bowl, and . . .

HAWKES: Corny metaphor, that fish bowl. You know yourself that before this interview, we've talked together and you never asked any questions. I'm just a friend. We've known each other only as people.

INTERVIEWER: We can accept that, but how can people who know you and care about you write criticism of your work if you separate yourself from them? This is not for our tape, but in all sincerity, you are a most likeable person. You've made this conference for the last two days really a pleasure . . .

HAWKES: Leave that on the tape.

INTERVIEWER: . . . but we can separate that out for the purpose of this interview, as we ask you questions that will make sense to someone who wants to get a better handle on your fiction and a better understanding of what is important to you.

HAWKES: Let me ask you this: if you knew that I was going to answer you in really exciting, original, powerful terms, what are some of the questions you would ask? What is it about me as a writer that you'd like to know?

INTERVIEWER: We did ask what you enjoy about being John Hawkes. That was a curve ball. But O.K., here's one: what effect does criticism from both reviewers and literary critics have on you? Not on your work, but on you. Does it ever infuriate you?

HAWKES: Sure.

INTERVIEWER: Do you ever learn from them?

HAWKES: I don't know whether I learn from them or not, but I have been enormously infuriated and I have been enormously pleased. It is as simple as that. A really talented, sensitive, and appreciative review gives me a thrill. And yet when my work does get public acclaim or appreciation, I suffer a kind of grief reaction.

INTERVIEWER: Your works are not like little pieces of wrought iron sculpture that you toss off and forget about?

HAWKES: Certainly not. They are permanent. They are one of my life's permanent acquisitions.

INTERVIEWER: Do you ever deliberately play games in the later works with the critics who have found things in your early novels? Dropping hints, seeds? Sinclair Lewis did it, and Nemerov and Nabokov have been known to do it, for instance.

HAWKES: No.

INTERVIEWER: What about the owl in *Travesty*?

HAWKES: No.

INTERVIEWER: Do you have any notions on sanity—what it means? Your work deals with people who are not necessarily sane in the eyes of everyone who perceives them. Is sanity important in your works?

HAWKES: Yes, of course sanity is important. But basic harmony, serenity, and a rational equilibrium can be achieved only out of a workshop of the irrational. And that is all I can say about it. I am more respectful of, more related to, the irrational than to the concept of sanity.

I am trying to be sane in an insane world, but the world that's insane thinks it's sane. Although ninety per cent of America is really the insane world, it is the apparent norm. The other ten per cent are the unusual, the peculiar, the eccentric, the outcast—and these are the people who are providing us with the true norms of sanity.

INTERVIEWER: Do you feel at all willing to talk about suicide in your novels? Americans do not like to talk about death, and they especially do not like to talk about suicide. It's amusing. Perhaps what happened when George Sanders said "I'm bored" and ended it made sense.

HAWKES: I would rather that he got un-bored.

INTERVIEWER: That may be the better solution.

HAWKES: I really feel very strongly about suicide. If you were talking with Barth, you would probably get a more open-minded response. I have very conventional views about suicide.

Suicide is one of the worst acts I can think of—not only from the point of view of the person who is so hopelessly driven that he is compelled to take his own life, but for the wreckage he leaves behind. I had one very good friend who committed suicide, and I have never gotten over it. You simply cannot ever replace that human being. He exists as a kind of ghost in the head—you are always aware of him. His death occurred in 1961 or 1962 and energized *Second Skin.* I hadn't planned to write about suicide. I was going to write about a man who loves his daughter who was going crazy. Then all of a sudden my friend shot himself and changed the novel.

We probably all have suicidal impulses and there have been moments in my life when I've been obsessively concerned with suicide. But this is not the real thing: it is adolescent suicide which most people experience.

INTERVIEWER: There are many forms of symbolic suicide, such as the person who puts a stereo headset on, closes his eyes, and removes himself from the world—a delightful symbolic suicide. These are healthy forms of suicide; even thinking about them is healthy, because they turn life off for a moment and refresh you.

HAWKES: But being involved in the tremendous ambivalence of an actual suicide is a very different thing. The discrepancy between the person and the person within the person who absolutely longs for the sleep of death while being afraid to die or suffer the pain and mystery of dying, can be excruciating. Suicidal people are extremely difficult, so uncannily clever, disturbed, perturbed, and usually so gifted—or can be—that you get involved in extremely complex situations which I wouldn't avoid.

If I could enact my anti-suicide law and have it enforced safely, I certainly would do it. I am utterly opposed to suicide. It is a form of emotional disturbance or mental illness in all but a few cases. Generally speaking, the object is to prevent suicide.

INTERVIEWER: And how does that whole idea relate to the works that you have written which contain suicide?

HAWKES: I don't know.

INTERVIEWER: For example, *Second Skin* is a statement about Skipper's continuing life . . .

HAWKES: In a sense, it is.

INTERVIEWER: . . . and its affirmation is in the birth of Catalina Kate's baby.

HAWKES: That is true, but throughout the writing of *Second Skin,* I kept contemplating whether or not Skipper should actually commit suicide. It was Sophie who insisted that he is too great a character, too extraordinary a figure to commit suicide. So he cannot. By the very end of the novel, in the last paragraph, there is a point in which his life and death are poised. It's as if he had died in the last paragraph, except that he's still alive. His voice merges with Sonny's, so that the two voices become one. Still there is a death-like knell in that final paragraph. I think you are right. *Second Skin* is certainly an effort to cope with the concept of suicide and to try to pose the life drive in opposition to suicide.

The irony is that I'm not appalled yet by the privileged man's murder/suicide in *Travesty*. This is because I think of it as so purely a work of art that he assumes responsibility rather than commits an outrage against life itself.

INTERVIEWER: People often misinterpret Hugh's death in *The Blood Oranges* as a suicide by hanging. In a sense, the novel can work that way. But obviously there are forces in the novel working for his survival—in Cyril—even though his accidental death is interpreted as suicide.

How can there be an "accidental" suicide?

HAWKES: At the University of Iowa, as part of a class I was visiting, a woman told me what I could have done to make it clearer. The point about Hugh is that sexuality didn't matter essentially for him. Although Fiona loves him and he finally does capitulate and allow himself to be seduced by her (a kind of goddess), his first love is for his peasant nudes. Not even for the nudes, but for the photographic images of those nudes. You remember how the narrator of *Travesty* says that when he was a child he was drawn to two kinds of magazines: magazines that contained photographs of violence, and pornographic magazines. Well, that mentality runs through a lot of what I've written. In a sense it is emblematic of the authorial consciousness in what I've written. At any rate, all the while Hugh is involved with Fiona, he nonetheless daily performs *coupe courte*. He goes through a pseudo-hanging in order to give himself the ultimate sexual release—which is described in de Sade's *Justine*—while he is looking at a photograph that he himself has taken. It seems to me that Hugh is the imperfect or failed artist. My point was that he was never able to escape from his solipsism despite his extraordinary love for Fiona, but one day made a mistake while practicing *coupe courte*. Part of the reason, part of the pleasure of pseudohanging is the risk of death. But Hugh didn't mean to hang himself. He was simply trying to have a superb private ejaculation. Now the reason that you can't tell that from the novel is that we have only

Cyril's word for it; but as my student pointed out, I could have given Hugh something like a little bench to stand on for his ritual. If that object had not been far from his feet, we would then know that he died by accident, because someone who intends to commit suicide by hanging will kick the object—the bench—far out of reach so as to be absolutely certain to die. One little detail would have changed the entire interpretation of his death.

INTERVIEWER: Suppose we pointed out that in *Second Skin*, the suicides are not condoned, but condemned; that you move further along in *The Blood Oranges* to what we are calling an "accidental" suicide; and that you move still further in *Travesty* to a suicide that is deliberately planned. How do you explain that progression?

HAWKES: It isn't that I don't want to explain it. I can't. I'm not really sure.

INTERVIEWER: Is there not a change in your attitude?

HAWKES: No, not toward suicide. I feel very violently opposed to it. Artistically, there is no change in attitude; I think suicide is just as awful as I've ever thought it. In *Travesty*, murder and suicide are instruments that are deliberately being used thematically. They are the substance out of which something is created—something having to do with the imagination itself.

INTERVIEWER: Is there anything else other than suicide that you particularly abhor but have used in your novels?

HAWKES: Do you have any ideas in mind?

INTERVIEWER: The dead baby in *The Beetle Leg* or the fetus in the jar in *Second Skin*. These are terrifying images that often contribute to a misunderstanding of your work.

HAWKES: I feel ultimate compassion toward the dead fetus and am personally repelled by it. Yet as a writer of fiction, I would want to be able to pick it up. The moment in *The Beetle Leg* when Luke Lampson fishes the fetal baby out of the flood and tenderly holds it, then puts it back into the flood, is an analogue for what I think the artist ought to be able to do. We should feel a strong attachment to human life even in its most frightening form. There is something about the fetus with its unformedness, its total tremendous potential, and its connection to lower life forms, that makes it terribly, terribly frightening. Also, you can think of fetuses as little penises; and if you have any kind of sexual insecurity, you can then reinforce your fears of fetuses all the more. I confess that I have a powerful abhorrence of the fetus, but am powerfully drawn to it as well.

INTERVIEWER: What the artist ought to be able to do. There is a statement made by your privileged man in *Travesty* that is intriguing because you are skirting it. He says that "imagined life is more exhilarating than remembered life." This is so important that he repeats it.

HAWKES: Yes.

INTERVIEWER: To what extent is "imagined life" exhilarating?

HAWKES: Well, the novelist is testimony to that fact.

INTERVIEWER: That seems obvious.

HAWKES: It's such a vast subject matter that I can't really . . .

INTERVIEWER: Then we'll open Pandora's box and close it immediately.

HAWKES: That's like "Why do you write?" or "What is the real purpose of writing?"

INTERVIEWER: Or "What about sex, Mr. Hawkes?"

HAWKES: Yes, something like that.

INTERVIEWER: Or "What about poetry?" You have mentioned a strong affinity for Keats. Are there any other poets, not necessarily well known or even contemporaries, whom you feel really strongly about?

HAWKES: Eliot. I did feel very strongly about Eliot, but not as I do about Keats. Perhaps because I can remember "Nightingale" and "Urn" a little more easily than Eliot.
    Last year when visiting the south of France, the area around our house was inundated with nightingales. They would sing all night long—until then, I had never heard a nightingale sing. I had seen one in Greece six or eight years before—a lovely little russet-colored creature. Keats simply

gives voice to that something that comes from nothing. It is such a power-ful model, in a way—what language and vision. Notice his essentials—what work it must have taken to make sentences out of what are really ugly little fragments.

I've never read either the poetry or the essays of Wallace Stevens, but people tell me my feelings about the imagination are very similar to his.

INTERVIEWER: What about Edwin Honig?

HAWKES: Honig is a poet who has an original voice which has not yet been responded to. He is a comic, bitter, lyrical writer. He is a good poet and someone whom I care enormously about. His poem "Island Storm" really did relate very strongly to my novel *Second Skin*. Honig is an old friend to whom I owe a great deal—I went to Brown University because of him.

INTERVIEWER: The whole subject of poetry is interesting because a lot of people see you as a poet, using Emerson's distinction of the poet as "the sayer, the namer . . . sent into the world to the end of expression . . ." And considering that, we'd all like to know what is in your future.

HAWKES: I really don't know.

INTERVIEWER: Do you have an urge to write more poetry?

HAWKES: Never.

INTERVIEWER: Do you have an urge to write biography?

HAWKES: Never.

INTERVIEWER: To write more criticism?

HAWKES: No, definitely none of those—no poetry, no biography, no criticism, no non-fiction; only fiction. I don't even write letters any-more—I am about forty letters behind in my correspondence. I don't want to write anything except fiction. I've written really a rather small amount of fiction, and I'd like to write more. I feel that I haven't done justice to my potential yet. As long as I'm living, I will be casting about, trying to find something to write.

Still Just Writing

ANNE TYLER

While I was painting the downstairs hall I thought of a novel to write. Really I just thought of a character; he more or less wandered into my mind, wearing a beard and a broad-brimmed leather hat. I figured that if I sat down and organized this character on paper, a novel would grow up around him. But it was March and the children's spring vacation began the next day, so I waited.

After spring vacation the children went back to school, but the dog got worms. It was a little complicated at the vet's and I lost a day. By then it was Thursday; Friday is the only day I can buy the groceries, pick up new cedar chips for the gerbils, scrub the bathrooms. I waited till Monday. Still, that left me four good weeks in April to block out the novel.

By May I was ready to start actually writing, but I had to do it in patches. There was the follow-up treatment at the vet, and then a half-day spent trailing the dog with a specimen tin so the lab could be sure the treatment had really worked. There were visits from the washing machine repairman and the Davey tree man, not to mention briefer interruptions by the meter reader, five Jehovah's Witnesses, and two Mormons. People telephoned wanting to sell me permanent light bulbs and waterproof basements. An Iranian cousin of my husband's had a baby; then the cousin's uncle died; then the cousin's mother decided to go home to Iran and needed to know where to buy a black American coat before she left. There *are* no black American coats; don't Americans wear mourning? I told her no, but I checked around at all the department stores anyway because she didn't speak English. Then I wrote chapters one and two. I had planned to work till three-thirty every day, but it was a month of early quittings: once for the children's dental appointment, once for the cat's rabies shot, once for our older daughter's orthopedist, and twice for her gymnastic meets. Sitting on the bleachers in the school gymnasium, I told myself I could always use this in a novel someplace, but I couldn't really picture writing a novel about twenty little girls in leotards trying to walk the length of a wooden beam without falling off. By the time I'd written chapter three, it was Memorial Day and the children were home again.

I knew I shouldn't expect anything from June. School was finished then and camp hadn't yet begun. I put the novel away. I closed down my mind and planted some herbs and played cribbage with the children. Then on the 25th, we drove one child to a sleep-away camp in Virginia and entered the other in a day camp, and I was ready to start work again. First I had to take my car in for repairs and the mechanics lost it, but I didn't get diverted. I sat in the garage on a folding chair while they hunted my car all one afternoon, and I hummed a calming tune and tried to remember what I'd planned to do next in my novel. Or even what the novel was about, for that matter. My character wandered in again in his beard and his broad-brimmed hat. He looked a little pale and knuckly, like someone scrabbling at a cliff edge so as not to fall away entirely.

I had high hopes for July, but it began with a four-day weekend, and on Monday night we had a long-distance call from our daughter's camp in Virginia. She was seriously ill in a Charlottesville hospital. We left our youngest with friends and drove three hours in a torrent of rain. We found our daughter frightened and crying, and another child (the only other child I knew in all of Virginia) equally frightened and crying down in the emergency room with possible appendicitis, so I spent that night alternating between a chair in the pediatric wing and a chair in the emergency room. By morning, it had begun to seem that our daughter's illness was typhoid fever. We loaded her into the car and took her back to Baltimore, where her doctor put her on drugs and prescribed a long bed-rest. She lay in bed six days, looking wrteched and calling for fluids and cold cloths. On the seventh day she got up her same old healthy self, and the illness was declared to be not typhoid fever after all but a simple virus, and we shipped her back to Virginia on the evening train. The next day I was free to start writing again but sat, instead, on the couch in my study, staring blankly at the wall.

I could draw some conclusions here about the effect that being a woman/wife/mother has upon my writing, except that I am married to a writer who is also a man/husband/father. He published his first novel while he was a medical student in Iran; then he came to America to finish his training. His writing fell by the wayside, for a long while. You can't be on call in the emergency room for twenty hours and write a novel during the other four. Now he's a child psychiatrist, full-time, and he writes his novels in the odd moments here and there—when he's not preparing a lecture, when he's not on the phone with a patient, when he's not attending classes at the psychoanalytic institute. He writes in Persian, still, in those black-

and-white speckled composition books. Sometimes one of the children will interrupt him in English and he will answer in Persian, and they'll say, "What?" and he'll look up blankly, and it seems a sheet has to fall from in front of his eyes before he remembers where he is and switches to English. Often, I wonder what he would be doing now if he didn't have a family to support. He cares deeply about his writing and he's very good at it, but every morning at five-thirty he gets up and puts on a suit and tie and drives in the dark to the hospital. Both of us, in different ways, seem to be hewing our creative time in small, hard chips from our living time.

Occasionally, I take a day off. I go to a friend's house for lunch, or weed the garden, or rearrange the linen closet. I notice that at the end of one of these days, when my husband asks me what I've been doing, I tend to exaggerate any hardships I may have encountered. ("A pickup nearly sideswiped me on Greenspring Avenue. I stood in line an hour just trying to buy the children some flip-flops.") It seems sinful to have lounged around so. Also, it seems sinful that I have more choice than my husband as to whether or not to undertake any given piece of work. I can refuse to do an article if it doesn't appeal to me, refuse to change a short story, refuse to hurry a book any faster than it wants to go—all luxuries. My husband, on the other hand, is forced to rise and go off to that hospital every blessed weekday of his life. *His* luxury is that no one expects him to drop all else for two weeks when a child has chicken pox. The only person who has no luxuries at all, it seems to me, is the woman writer who is the sole support of her children. I often think about how she must manage. I think that if I were in that position, I'd have to find a job involving manual labor. I have spent so long erecting partitions around the part of me that writes—learning how to close the door on it when ordinary life intervenes, how to close the door on ordinary life when it's time to start writing again—that I'm not sure I could fit the two parts of me back together now.

Before we had children I worked in a library. It was a boring job, but I tend to like doing boring things. I would sit on a stool alphabetizing Russian catalogue cards and listening to the other librarians talking around me. It made me think of my adolescence, which was spent listening to the tobacco stringers while I handed tobacco. At night I'd go home from the library and write. I never wrote what the librarians said, exactly, but having those voices in my ears all day helped me summon up my own characters' voices. Then our first baby came along—an insomniac. I quit work and stayed home all day with her and walked her all night. Even if I had found the time to write, I wouldn't have had the insides. I felt drained; too much care and feeling were being drawn out of me. And the only voices I heard now were by appointment—people who came to dinner, or invited us to dinner, and who therefore felt they had to make deliberate conversation. That's one thing writers never have, and I still miss it: the easy-going, on-again-off-again, gossipy murmurs of people working alongside each other all day.

I enjoyed tending infants (though I've much preferred the later ages), but it was hard to be solely, continually in their company and not to be able to write. And I couldn't think of any alternative. I know it must be possible to have a child raised beautifully by a housekeeper, but every such child I've run into has seemed dulled and doesn't use words well. So I figured I'd better stick it out. As it happened, it wasn't that long—five years, from the time our first daughter was born till our second started nursery school and left me with my mornings free. But while I was going through it I thought it would be a lot longer. I couldn't imagine any end to it. I felt that everything I wanted to write was somehow coagulating in my veins and making me fidgety and slow. Then after a while I didn't have anything to write anyhow, but I still had the fidgets. I felt useless, no matter how many diapers I washed or strollers I pushed. The only way I could explain my life to myself was to imagine that I was living in a very small commune. I had spent my childhood in a commune, or what would nowadays be called a commune, and I was used to the idea of division of labor. What we had here, I told myself, was a perfectly sensible arrange-ment: one member was the liaison with the outside world, bringing in money; another was the caretaker, reading the Little Bear books to the children and repairing the electrical switches. This second member might have less physical freedom, but she had much more freedom to arrange her own work schedule. I must have sat down a dozen times a week and very carefully, consciously thought it all through. Often, I was merely trying to convince myself that I really did pull my own weight.

This Iranian cousin who just had the baby: she sits home now and cries a lot. She was working on her master's degree and is used to being out in the world more. "Never mind," I tell her, "you'll soon be out again. This stage doesn't last long."

"How long?" she asks.

"Oh . . . three years, if you just have the one."

"Three years!"

I can see she's appalled. Her baby is beautiful, very dark and Persian; and what's more, he sleeps—something I've rarely seen a baby do. What I'm trying to say to her (but of course, she'll agree without really hearing me) is that he's worth it. It seems to me that since I've had children, I've grown richer and deeper. They may have slowed down my writing for a while, but when I did write, I had more of a self to speak from. After all, who else in the world do you *have* to love, no matter what? Who else can you absolutely not give up on? My life seems more intricate. Also more dangerous.

After the children started school, I put up the partitions in my mind. I would rush around in the morning braiding their hair, packing their lunches; then the second they were gone I would grow quiet and climb the stairs to my study. Sometimes a child would come home early and I would feel a little tug between the two parts of me; I'd be absent-minded and short-tempered. Then gradually I learned to make the transition more easily. It feels like a sort of string that I tell myself to loosen. When the children come home, I drop the string and close the study door and that's the end of it. It doesn't always work perfectly, of course. There are times when it doesn't work at all: if a child is sick, for instance, I can't possibly drop the children's end of the string, and I've learned not to try. It's easier just to stop writing for a while. Or if they're home but otherwise occupied, I no longer attempt to sneak off to my study to finish that one last page; I know that instantly, as if by magic, assorted little people will be pounding on my door requiring Band-Aids, tetanus shots, and a complete summation of the facts of life.

Last spring, I bought a midget tape recorder to make notes on. I'd noticed that my best ideas came while I was running the vacuum cleaner, but I was always losing them. I thought this little recorder would help. I carried it around in my shirt pocket. But I was ignoring the partitions, is what it was; I was letting one half of my life intrude upon the other. A child would be talking about her day at school and suddenly I'd whip out the tape recorder and tell it, "Get Morgan out of that cocktail party; he's not the type to drink." "Huh?" the child would say. Both halves began to seem ludicrous, unsynchronized. I took the recorder back to Radio Shack.

A few years ago, my parents went to the Gaza Strip to work for the American Friends Service Committee. It was a lifelong dream of my father's to do something with the AFSC as soon as all his children were grown, and he'd been actively preparing for it for years. But almost as soon as they got there, my mother fell ill with a mysterious fever that neither the Arab nor the Israeli hospitals could diagnose. My parents had to come home for her treatment, and since they'd sublet their house in North Carolina, they had to live with us. For four months, they stayed here—but only on a week-to-week basis, not knowing when they were going back, or whether they were going back at all, or how serious my mother's illness was. It was hard for her, of course, but it should have been especially hard in another way for my father, who had simply to hang in suspended animation for four months while my mother was whisked in and out of hospitals. However, I believe he was as pleased with life as he always is. He whistled Mozart and puttered around insulating our windows. He went on long walks collecting firewood. He strolled over to the meetinghouse and gave a talk on the plight of the Arab refugees. "Now that we seem to have a little time," he told my mother, "why not visit the boys?" and during one of her outpatient periods he took her on a gigantic cross-country trip to see all my brothers and any other relatives they happened upon. Then my mother decided she ought to go to a faith healer. (She wouldn't usually do such a thing, but she was desperate.) "Oh. Okay," my father said, and he took her to a faith healer, whistling all the way. And when the faith healer didn't work, my mother said, "I think this is psychosomatic. Let's go back to Gaza." My father said, "Okay," and reserved two seats on the next plane over. The children and I went to see them the following summer: my mother's fever was utterly gone, and my father drove us down the Strip, weaving a little Renault among the tents and camels, cheerfully whistling Mozart.

I hold this entire, rambling set of events in my head at all times, and remind myself of it almost daily. It seems to me that the way my father lives (infinitely adapting, and looking around him with a smile to say, "Oh! So *this* is where I am!") is also the way to slip gracefully through a choppy life of writing novels, plastering the dining room ceiling, and presiding at slumber parties. I have learned, bit by bit, to accept a school snow-closing as an unexpected holiday, an excuse to play seventeen rounds of Parcheesi instead of typing up a short story. When there's a midweek visitation of uncles from Iran (hordes of great, bald, yellow men calling for their glasses of tea, sleeping on guest beds, couches, two armchairs pushed together, and discarded crib mattresses), I have decided that I might as well listen to what they have to say, and work on my novel tomorrow instead. I smile at the uncles out of a kind of clear, swept space inside me. What this takes, of course, is a sense of limitless time, but I'm getting that. My life is beginning to seem unusually long. And there's a danger to it: I could wind up as passive as a piece of wood on a wave. But I try to walk a middle line.

I was standing in the schoolyard waiting for a child when another mother came up to me. "Have you found work yet?" she asked. "Or are you still just writing?"

Now, how am I supposed to answer that?

I could take offense, come to think of it. Maybe the reason I didn't is that I halfway share her attitude. They're *paying* me for this? For just writing down untruthful stories? I'd better look around for more permanent employment. For I do consider writing to be a finite job. I expect that any day now, I will have said all I have to say; I'll have used up all my characters, and then I'll be free to get on with my real life. When I make a note of new ideas on index cards, I imagine I'm clearing out my head, and that soon it will be empty and spacious. I file the cards in a little blue box, and I can picture myself using the final card one day—ah! through at last!—and throwing the blue box away. I'm like a dentist who continually fights tooth decay, working toward the time when he's conquered it altogether and done himself out of a job. But my head keeps loading up again; the little blue box stays crowded and messy. Even when I feel I have no ideas at all, and can't possibly start the next chapter, I have a sense of something still bottled in me, trying to get out.

People have always seemed funny and strange to me, and touching in unexpected ways. I can't shake off a sort of mist of irony that hangs over whatever I see. Probably that's what I'm trying to put across when I write; I may believe that I'm the one person who holds this view of things. And I'm always hurt when a reader says that I choose only bizarre or eccentric people to write about. It's not a matter of choice; it just seems to me that even the most ordinary person, in real life, will turn out to have something unusual at his center. I like to think that I might meet up with one of my past characters at the very next street corner. The odd thing is, sometimes I have. And if I were remotely religious, I'd believe that a little gathering of my characters would be waiting for me in heaven when I died. "*Then* what happened?" I'd ask them. "How have things worked out, since the last time I saw you?"

I think I was born with the impression that what happened in books was much more reasonable, and interesting, and *real,* in some ways, than what happened in life. I hated childhood, and spent it sitting behind a book waiting for adulthood to arrive. When I ran out of books I made up my own. At night, when I couldn't sleep, I made up stories in the dark. Most of my plots involved girls going west in covered wagons. I was truly furious that I'd been born too late to go west in a covered wagon.

I know a poet who says that in order to be a writer, you have to have had rheumatic fever in your childhood. I've never had rheumatic fever, but I believe that any kind of setting-apart situation will do as well. In my case, it was emerging from that commune—really an experimental Quaker community in the wilderness—and trying to fit into the outside world. I was eleven. I had never used a telephone and could strike a match on the soles of my bare feet. All the children in my new school looked very peculiar to me, and I certainly must have looked peculiar to them. I am still surprised, to this day, to find myself where I am. My life is so streamlined and full of modern conveniences. How did I get here? I have given up hope, by now, of ever losing my sense of distance; in fact, I seem to have come to cherish it. Neither I nor any of my brothers can stand being out among a crowd of people for any length of time at all.

I spent my adolescence planning to be an artist, not a writer. After all, books had to be about major events, and none had ever happened to me. All I knew were tobacco workers, stringing the leaves I handed them and talking up a storm. Then I found a book of Eudora Welty's short stories in the high school library. She was writing about Edna Earle, who was so slow-witted she could sit all day just pondering how the tail of the *C* got through the loop of the *L* on the Coca-Cola sign. Why, I knew Edna Earle. You mean you could *write* about such people? I have always meant to send Eudora Welty a thank-you note, but I imagine she would find it a little strange.

I wanted to go to Swarthmore College, but my parents suggested Duke instead, where I had a full scholarship, because my three brothers were coming along right behind me and it was more important for boys to get a good education than for girls. That was the first and last time that my being female was ever a serious issue. I still don't think it was just, but I can't say it ruined my life. After all, Duke had Reynolds Price, who turned out to be the only person I ever knew who could actually teach writing. It all worked out, in the end.

I believe that for many writers, the hardest time is that dead spot after college (where they're wonder-children, made much of) and before their first published work. Luckily, I didn't notice that part; I was so vague about what I wanted to do that I could hardly chafe at not yet doing it. I went to graduate school in Russian studies; I scrubbed decks on a boat in Maine; I got a job ordering books from the Soviet Union. Writing was something that crept in around the edges. For a while I lived in New York, where I became addicted to riding any kind of train or subway, and while I rode I often felt I was nothing but an enormous eye, taking things in and turning them over and sorting them out. But who would I tell them to, once I'd sorted them? I have never had more than three or four close friends, at any period of my life; and anyway, I don't talk well. I am the kind of person who wakes up at four in the morning and suddenly thinks of what she should have said yesterday at lunch. For me, writing something down was the only road out.

You would think, since I waited so long and so hopefully for adulthood, that it would prove to be a disappointment. Actually, I figure it was worth the wait. I like everything about it but the paperwork—the income tax and protesting the Sears bill and renewing the Triple-A membership. I always did count on having a husband and children, and here they are. I'm surprised to find myself a writer but have fitted it in fairly well, I think. The only real trouble that writing has ever brought me is an occasional sense of being invaded by the outside world. Why do people imagine that writers, having chosen the most private of professions, should be any good at performing in public, or should have the slightest desire to tell their secrets to interviewers from ladies' magazines? I feel I am only holding myself together by being extremely firm and decisive about what I will do and what I will not do. I will write my books and raise the children. Anything else just fritters me away. I know this makes me seem narrow, but in fact, I *am* narrow. I like routine and rituals and I hate leaving home; I have a sense of digging my heels in. I refuse to drive on freeways. I dread our annual vacation. Yet I'm continually prepared for travel: it is physically impossible for me to buy any necessity without buying a travel-sized version as well. I have a little toilet kit, with soap and a nightgown, forever packed and ready to go. How do you explain that?

As the outside world grows less dependable, I keep buttressing my inside world, where people go on meaning well and surprising other people with little touches of grace. There are days when I sink into my novel like a pool and emerge feeling blank and bemused and used up. Then I drift over to the schoolyard, and there's this mother wondering if I'm doing anything halfway useful yet. Am I working? Have I found a job? No, I tell her.

I'm still just writing.

Assays

DAVE SMITH

What can be said about the subjects of poetry? Only, I suppose, that everything has a potential beauty which poetry seeks. But some subjects appear more likely to yield significant results than others. Or is this merely fear of being trivial? Isn't it possible a great poetry might arise from a sequence about fenceposts as well as in a sequence involving a black-face mummer and a variety of historical personages? Why does one grow weary of poems about one's father, one's mother, one's sexual disappointments, one's admiration of certain painters? Is it a distinctly modern characteristic that poets seem not to choose large subjects around which poems are then composed, as a novelist might choose to dramatize a war, a family chronicle, or a philosophy? No subject is, in and of itself, the same thing to all readers. No subject is inherently beautiful or meaningful or expressive. Ordinary phenomena are not necessarily interesting or beautiful—but that is where interest and beauty begin, where the poet establishes the appropriate context for revelation. The thing itself is only itself, scarcely art, until art alters it. It is in the measure of this alteration that the artist's skill and limitations may be found, his skill or limitations as a visionary—not as a craftsman. Poe's remarks about the death of a beautiful woman being the most propitious subject for poetry seem a little slippery but it is apparently the case that some subjects, like certain soils, are on the whole more fertile than others. Nevertheless there are no great poets whose greatness resides primarily in their choice of subject. Still I think it can be said that the image poet is handicapped by the severity of his subject as well as by the choice of form. In this, like the minimalist attitude which is widespread among contemporary poets, the imagist is remarkable not for what he does but for what he is prohibited from doing: he fails to embrace the fullest opportunities of his art.

Art begins in the ordinary, the physical, the material. If the poet is to lift his subject to the value of art he must first recognize the uses and the limitations of both his subject and his tools—his formal skills. Art does nothing on its own. The artist creates and uses art, as a jeweler deploys his stones, toward a context of suggestion. There is no poem entirely without narrative direction, be it epic or couplet; moreover, narrative direction always implies an authorial statement. This statement may be as oblique as Casey Stengel's soliloquies or it may be explicit as a philosophical proposition. Every poem comments on human experience: that is the poem's function. Any organization of words shaped by a man is, by definition, a statement. Statements do not occur in the natural world. Poems do not occur organically as do lemons, worms, or uranium. Human deliberation which leads to a shaping of words, the mere intent to order, is the first step toward any poem's meaning. Meaning, however, is a great deal more than the terse paraphrase of plot and result. For example, the Anglo-Saxon poem "The Wanderer" is about the loneliness of a man who will never see his homeland, his comrades, or any reward for having accomplished valorous deeds. My summary is no more the poem's meaning than it is the poem, for it carries nothing of the feeling that is the poem. Feeling cannot exist apart from the context of generational events and the poem's voice than it could exist apart from the creative music of words and phrases in the harness that is the form of the poem.

Every poem makes a statement, as all things in time and space make a statement. The artist shapes time and space and body to discover his statement. Poets seem to agree that they generally don't know what an individual poem will try to say. Some, in fact, resist knowing, as if the appearance of that knowledge too soon or at the wrong time will destroy the art-spell. Robert Frost spoke of a piece of ice melting on a stove as a figure for the poem which the poet watches until he is able to save it just at the edge of dissolution. That edge is the artist in control, but a control sufficiently tentative to permit discovery. The element of surprise, as Frost also tells us, is critical to both writer and reader. It is at the very core of the pleasure we take from a poem—but this is not surprise as trick. It is the surprise of timing, necessity, inevitability that allows one to accept the statement of the poem as emotionally valid. If the poet does not know what statement he will come to, he knows that when he has found a few compelling words he is going to find next a context. Everything is decided according to context, for it is only through context that full, clear expression is approached. Narrative is one sort of context; image and lyric are others. None exist entirely separate from the other but are matters of emphasis. At its most fundamental, poetry may be imagined as a spectrum. On one end there is the pictograph, the representational image cut into stone. On the other end is the abstract word, entirely non-visual, such as *honor* or *metempsychosis*. The poem exists most powerfully—as act and as meaning simultaneously—in the middle of the spectrum. At least the poem as ideal exists there.

Art, if it is art, makes a point. It means. The poem must mean or it is no poem. How ludicrously simple that seems. Yet there is no end of aesthetic theory to the contrary and there is a very great deal of bad poetry justified by critics who would find meaning where no meaning is. And there are those who would argue that the absence of meaning is, itself, a statement of meaning—as one poet I know who argues that a poem of hers, half a book long, is chaotic because it imitates chaos. This is solipsistic. The poem which defies referential clarity is unlikely to succeed in meaning anything to anyone, though there are examples of such poems which attain to something like a super-clarity. If a vote were taken even now, I suspect Eliot's *The Waste Land* would be regarded as massively clear by many and massively murky by an equal number. Having a point to make certainly does not make a poem but where is the true poem which makes no point? Complex and abstract expression is the human act beyond all others. A poem, like the essay, is a sort of hypothesis, a theorem of experience, but it ordinarily abandons the illusion of argument, syllogism, or proof. It exists both for and as the dramatic presentation of what it means. What would Williams' wheelbarrow poem be if it did not begin "so much depends/ upon" . . . ? It would be a non sequitur.

*   *   *

The first question of value in a poem has to do with the depth, quality, and validity of its feeling. The great poem simply tells us more, and tells it more profoundly, about what it means to be alive. This is so even when we do not accept entirely the statement of the poem. *Paradise Lost* and "Lycidas" are such poems. There are perhaps infinite numbers of ways we know the world but foremost among those ways is feeling—it is still first. We must judge a poem by the truth and size of its feeling and this feeling must be a necessary, inevitable result of the poem's resolution of its own actions. We must judge a poem by submitting it to the testing fire of individual and historical knowledge; we must find it authentic or false. Our assessment of feeling is not, however, a matter of merely agreeing with a poet's sentiment. It is a matter of emotional proportion and rightness generated by dramatic circumstance. We can be touched by melodramatic poetry but moved only by tragic poetry. I mean tragic in the literary sense, in the sense of the work which enables us to embrace great pain and great beauty and great joy because we have seen the inescapable and crushing forces of fate in combat with the largest human spirit. But the poetry is not those forces, that drama, or any resulting statement—not precisely.

The poetry is the music which evokes, creates, releases, controls, and clarifies feeling in the dramatic context.

It is, I think, impossible to separate what I would call the context of the poem and what I would call the communal function of the poem from the sound or music. The music is the poem's first order of existence. It shapes the feeling even as it rises out of the feeling, but the poetry is the music and not the feeling. Nothing is harder to speak of in the abstract than this music and it may be that nothing significant can be said of it. One reads the textbooks and the theories of sonics with a sense of hopeless irrelevance. Nothing I might say can have any specific connection to the universe of poetry any more than does, say, Paul Fussell's *Poetic Meter & Poetic Form*. Whatever Fussell or anyone may tell us of poetry's mechanics, no one can give us the next poem's blueprint. Both the reader and the writer remain the subjective unknown out of which the poem will sing or remain mute.

What is common in the sound of poetry in Neruda, Smart, Li Po, Baudelaire, and Emily Dickinson? Very little, I should guess. A comparative examination of sonic strategies employed by each might be profitable but I suspect we would miss the poetry. Much of what we are taught about how sounds operate on the individual ear seems sheer opinion and is occasionally nonsense. If the music and the meaning of a poem work as one act of the mind, these actions nevertheless impel us toward the separate directions of feeling and thinking, which are themselves never strictly divisible. The final value of a poem is to give pleasure, but in what does this pleasure consist? What in any poem pleases us, and how? If our agreement with what the poet says seems suspicious, then how much more so seems that tendency to pluck out felicitous lines or vivid images. Yet it is rare to find the poem whose statement is utterly repellent to us while its music is enchanting. The poetry is in the music, however much or little we can locate the music. But it is also true that insistent rhythmic sound, if that is the only music one speaks of, is not poetry, as Lewis Carroll proves. A friend of mine understands no German, though he has a sense of German sounds. He likes to read Rilke aloud in German—his brand of German—because the soporific rolling of syllables pleases him, just as he is pleased by Dylan Thomas. What he loves is not poetry. Clusters of sound, however sweet, constitute no poetry when there is no referential meaning.

*   *   *

All poetry asks what is valuable in life. Every aspect of a poem's organization conspires to dramatize a poet's experience of the world and reveal what is both durable and valuable. Readers are, however, too prone to think that what the poet says in a poem is precisely what *he* thinks or feels. While this may be the actual case it is also true that the poet writes through what might be called a second self, a sort of neuter, super-aware, nameless other. It is, at any rate, my experience that I am a different person at the typewriter than the person who answers the telephone or plays tennis. The first person speaker in my poems is rarely, and only then in part, the person identified with my social security number. This means that what happens to the created second self of the poem most often has not happened to me. But those events and that speaker are inventions in service of what my imagination regards as valuable, though those values arise from whatever I have been able to know of anyone's life. Poetry attempts to objectify and simultaneously dramatize with immediate force. The second self provides distance, objectivity, perspective, form, and tempering for the first self's unmediated rehearsal of experience. In words we repeat the acts of our experience and we do it because we need to know what and how we are in the world. Poetry is perhaps the most concrete and immediate way of knowing, but it must proceed through testing and resolution and speculation, for assertions of value without resistance have no force.

*   *   *

William Carlos Williams and Charles Olson claimed to create new forms of poetry in order to accommodate new thinking about human experience in general and about Paterson, New Jersey, and Gloucester, Massachusetts, in particular. Can it really be shown in specific ways how the geographical, cultural, or even sociological character of those places had a single influential moment with the formal organizations of words those poets put on the page? That is, what about Gloucester affects Olson's decisions to shape lines and stanzas as he did? It does not surprise me that the critical studies of Olson and Williams, including the several dissertations on the subject with which I have been associated, have little to say about the relationship of biography and formal choices in the area of poetic music. The tendency of such criticism is to argue for a grand form based on a socio-political argument about a reflected socio-political society. That is, to argue for a poetry composed of verbal architectures and not verbal musics, a poetics analogous in part to the Bauhaus movement. To speak of poetry in Charles Olson and poetry in, say, Anthony Hecht or Elizabeth Bishop is to confuse what is meant by the word *poetry*—or it is to make the term massively inclusive. The result is, I think, a general confusion about form wherein we are obliged to call whatever is lineated *poetry*. At what point does technical innovation collapse into mere eccentricity? At what point does poetry cease to be defined by the devices of musical organization such as lines, stanzas, or any of the pattern-making sound signallers? At what point does poetry exist as verbal architecture? At what point does it exist as feeling?

*   *   *

When we sound a poem in our heads we can experience the effect of form, of lineation, of rhythmic surge and ebb. When a poet chooses a line length, he chooses for the stop and go of a form that alters his perception and the reader's. He controls subject, poem, and reader. End-stopped lines with metrical regularity create a tight control and experience. The experience of continuity which devalues end-stopped lines and disregards the fusion of line halts and eye halts asks for a different experience. One cannot read Kinnell's "The Bear" in exactly the same way one reads a poem by Marvell or Richard Wilbur. One implication is that poetry itself is different for these poets, and not a matter of superficial options. Yet some readers and writers regard form as not merely an option but a reflection of political orientation, as if the writing of sonnets indicates a covert alignment with oppressive conservatism. Free verse, in its many varieties, is often enough described as revolutionary with the full implications of social rebellion. Where then does *form*, even each individual version, come from and what is it exactly? Does form inherently demonstrate a poet's deepest philosophical convictions? Surely rhythm lies at the heart of form—but there is no free rhythm since rhythm is possible only in systematic resistance or containment. Form, it might be said, is that set of disciplines and responsibilities to which the poet agrees with each poem and this would imply the recognition that nothing is free, that everything a poet does has its cost, its obligation, its allegiance.

*   *   *

At the center of form, whatever might be meant by that word, is that most idiosyncratic, most felt, and least describable matter: rhythm. Roethke says of it that: "We must keep in mind that rhythm is the entire movement, the flow, the recurrence of stress and unstress that is related to the rhythms of the blood, the rhythms of nature. It involves certainly stress, time, pitch, the texture of words, the total meaning of the poem." And he says also that "Rhythm gives us the very psychic energy of the speaker." We should be alert enough to recognize there are at least two, not one, kinds of rhythm in his definition. The first sort not only identifies but also creates the life in the poem, the character of the poem's speaker. It is drawn from the personality of the poem's maker, from the emotional blood-pulse of the heart. Once it is impressed in the poem, it tells the reader's heart how fast to beat, how he should pace himself through the dramatic experience. Darting us ahead, or withholding us from time, now fast and now slow, this rhythm creates immediate experience. It controls psychic pressure and emotional inevitability. This rhythm is analyzable and, as Roethke suggests, may be broken into identifiable components. It is the rhythm, for example, which may be scanned, the subject of prosodic studies.

But there is a larger idea of rhythm which Roethke implicates but does not consider. This is the rhythm of change and truth. If the rhythm above is the rhythm common to a single man, the rhythm here is that common to men. It consists of what is changeless, continuous, and may be called the truth. Each man's singular rhythm, in every poem, plays against the common rhythm and it is the resistances as well as the congruencies of the two impulses which provide tension, vision, and discovery. One might picture these rhythms in the lines on a heart-monitoring oscilloscope: the constant line there is death. Any good poem sets the local, singular rhythm against the rhythm of constants; indeed, its act of discovery is to find the constant that is not death, for that is the principle of resistance by which self-definition, self-creation, and all knowledge of self and other achieves measurable value.

This rhythm of constants lies in the imagination of the race. Constant is, perhaps, not the most accurate word for what seems to me to be far from static. Perhaps what I mean are clusters of energies verging on convictions, the images and stories which emerge in great myths as dramatized explanations of what the race considers to be continuous and true. If every poem is an attempt to create, to explore, and to expand consciousness, as I think is the case, then reason suggests every poem is an attempt to contact those constants. But every poem is also a record of the individual's encounter with resistances. The poem's greater rhythm is, then, embodiment of the human's motions in conventional time as well as his continuity out of time. Surely this is the truth of any poem: its ability to hear the heart beating in this world but also beating in synchronization with the heart of the race, or body, of all men. Flannery O'Connor says all this very plainly: "The writer operates at a peculiar crossroads where time and place and eternity somehow meet. His problem is to find that location."

In ways I am not sure I understand, the music of poetry is composed by the constant engagement and disengagement of the individual and the communal psychic energy. Where do those energies come from? To the writer, this asks: why do you write? Again Flannery O'Connor is helpful. Her answer was that she had a gift. Great poets have that gift and it cannot be taught or in any way purchased. This is, I think, why every discussion of prosody leads inevitably to vision and the location of a poem's value in what it says, and not the other way around. Poetry is poetry and not prose or drama because of its music—but is music far more than patterns of sound even when those patterns are the uncounterfeitable signatures of individual poets. Flannery O'Connor says, wonderfully, that the writer "operates" and she means he acts, participates, even cuts through the much going on around him. More than anything else he hears and he watches, giving and receiving, a rhythm within rhythms, a truth within truths.

*   *   *

Recently I read Yeats praising Rabindranath Tagore and remembered that I had bought a battered copy of Tagore's poems for a dime. I found it and read Tagore. He is what might be called a *pure* poet. Extremely lyrical and melodious, he is entirely conventional in construction and his subject is most ordinary: love experienced, love lost, love lamented. He seems more in love with the idea of love than with any person, resembling the courtly love of Provençal lyrics. His poems would gag one with their thick sighs did not a reader regard them as the practise of something like an anachronistic skill. The pure poet, insofar as such a creature actually exists, is an escapist. He seeks an ideal, a world uncorrupted, a music which has no intention of discoursing with or walking among the flesh of this world. In Tagore, a twentieth-century poet, one finds no trains, airplanes, wars, scientific discoveries, or news of the world at large. He is all expression, all veneration of a habitual and stiff decorum. He ranges from reticence before love to wallowing in rapture. There is hardly any dramatic tension or occasion; there is no presence of the tough-minded citizen. He gives himself entirely to bald statements of affection with no syntactical, rhythmic, or imagistic surprise. Let Tagore think of grazing the hem of a woman's skirt and he melts—almost literally. He is a sort of ruder Rilke. Not surprisingly, he reminds me of many younger American poets in whom the world seems too weakly embodied, too little explored, too frequently constricted to one voice and one anxiety that simply hasn't the power to sustain interest. Seeking purity, these poets refuse internal resistance.

Yet in Tagore there are the true pleasures of poetry: praise, feeling, direct expression, a cleanness of attention, a sense that the poem may be like the stilled surface of a country pond, virginal and fragrant and, well, pure. The pure poem is successful because it radiates and works exclusively. Tagore can suggest great beauty with his everpresent observation of a young girl's ankle bracelets, but one never quite feels it is a whole, mature vision. One misses entirely that girl's dirty feet, the barnyard smell, even the dailiness of village life. Because of what Tagore does not incorporate in his poem, his pure music is finally dismissable. When we read a Provençal lyric which tells us the story of a man who falls in love with a woman's image, travels years to find her and dies of love when he sees her, we nod a little. But the story adds that the woman, upon seeing this man, falls in love herself and also dies on the spot. This we cannot accept, however lovely the language. Tagore's eloquent simplicity and his transparent feeling are pure and attract us away from our existence in cynicism, knowledge, and fear—but they do not sustain us. This is also the case with some contemporary American poets. We all want the unsullied expression of quintessential beauty that would be *pure* yet to have it we must deny the poem any broad connection to this ordinary world. The purer the poem, the more it must exclude the warts and winds of our existence. The consequences of purity are limited expression, limited knowledge, limited audience, and *mere* beauty.

*   *   *

We want, all of us, the civilization of pure poetry, which is the impulse to form. Yet we want also our beasthood, which might be called pure expression. We are human more than beast because we possess consciousness. As Emily Dickinson says, we feel first, but we seek to render permanent and understandable our feeling. We do this in organizations of symbols that assert the formality of thought as preferable to brute act. We do something a white crane and a bulldozer can't do; we do something not possible for a eucalyptus or a newt. The protohuman act is to receive and respond to the world with creative thought. Not all creative thought is equal in quality. The democratic attitude which would argue against qualitative discrimination in poetry is a foolish and naive one. One mark of excellence to be sought in a contemporary poem is the balance of civilization and the beast, of disciplined form and passionate expression.

We cannot reduce what is valuable in any poem to a single aspect or idea and we cannot enlist the poem, as a measure of value, in the service of expressing what is good for the Republic. On the whole, what is valuable is the transmittable and felt human experience a poem contains. Inevitably we must test the validity of a poem against the curve of our lives. If we accept a super-natural vision, an extra-human cosmology, as did Milton and Gabriela Mistral and Mario Luzi, there is another basis for judging the poem's reality and beauty. This is also true of any poem which supports a political idea. Yet for most contemporary poets the poem has no such grounding. Our poet has himself, what he has seen and known and felt, what he has assimilated from history and culture, as touchstone and source. This tends to drive him away from grand ideas and toward the image of himself as minimal, as a voice which can be trusted with only the most local and circumscribed of truths. Yet he must find a way to make the life of his poem congruent with the lives of men. He must find a way to speak for the good of the Republic. What else is so clear in the poems and statements of the Eastern European poets such as Milosz and Herbert?

It is because we must find a way to conjoin the issues of the self with the large issues of the Republic of men that the contemporary poem must above all be emotionally accurate and tested. We should certainly, as well, suspect the poem that fails ordinary journalistic accuracy. The poem that lies must be rejected. The lie is what is wrong with poems of polemical rhetoric, however well-intended the poem's subjective attitude. Denise Levertov's anti-war poems fail as poems to the extent they become propaganda. They do not think or feel complexly enough. Among younger poets, many less skilled than Levertov, we are impelled to ask what the poet thinks and we often enough discover little evidence of thought, the kind of thought which approaches large issues. It is no answer to say, in their defense, that poetry does not think, it feels. Feeling is a way of thinking and in the poem feeling submits to formal organization for purposes of communication. Too many poets lack the necessary intensity of speculation by which poetry moves the reader from sight to knowledge. Much of our poetry is aggressively trivial, as if it feared being thought over-serious, righteous, or ambitious. The poem that is trivial asks us that we do not look too closely at ourselves, and it demeans us by that.

                                *   *   *

The polemical poem, whatever its message, ordinarily makes music subservient to program. Yet the music is the poetry. Only artful sound can lift message to art. No sentiment, however righteous or agreeable or moral, is by itself art. Sound is form, an organization of words, but when matched to an appropriate context the living and free pulse of experience may result. Context is dramatic situation, of course, but I think it is something more. It is the poem's chance for ambitious art, the opportunity for the poet to conduct experiments in ethics and morality, to demonstrate maturity and range of vision. It may be the forum for a truth, a whole truth. For the poet who wants polemic, context is a prefabricated shell meant to support an ideological statement. For others context is something freer, more alive, something which generates a statement and allows its discovery.

The contemporary poet, if we judge by the various published interviews and working papers, begins his poem with an image taken from the imagination. He does not usually know why the imagination seizes on one image rather than another. The image comes to him independent of a context and he is content, perhaps, merely to record it. But soon enough he finds himself asking why this image should matter, what it suggests, what its existence may mean for him. Put simply, he plays with the image and discovers that the imagination has been slowly locating whatever it is in a web of relationships. All things exist in a web of relationships. These may manifest themselves to the poet as compulsive sounds, vivid pictures, or the sense of a narrative; they may exist as all three, in fragments or more sustained units. The poet's process, however, is to choose or establish a context. Successive drafts frequently show the initiating image to be irrelevant and it is dropped as the poet concentrates on the forces, the possibilities invoked by the newly focused context. This is exactly what Richard Hugo describes as the triggering subject. Initially, the poet seems to have little idea of what the poem will say, what its intention is, what form it will seek as appropriate and much of his own pleasure consists in discovering these things. These discoveries, to judge from what poets commonly say, are mysterious in nature and process but are guided by unbidden sounds, words, phrases that simply arrive in the head. Once they exist they seem to generate more of their kind, until a rhythmic direction is established, until everything sonic about the poem is determined. Of course, the poet is able to enter this evolution with his own determinations but the point and force of his entry is both delicate and critical. It is what will determine art. I have, as others have, often enough made deliberate choices to impose a form on a poem and have killed the poem or temporarily hidden the true poem.

The ability to establish the triggering context and the further ability to know when to wait and when to act are perhaps the most valuable of all talents for a poet. They are, I think, the least accessible to discussion. Biographical criticism appears to assume that such contexts are drawn directly from one's lived experience but I think this is not the case. This is why invention is commonly thought to be confession. Just as mysterious to me as the establishment or discovery of context is the relationship between context and evolving music. I cannot say with certainty which precedes the other or which is the primary influence on the poem. Again, my experience is common with other poets. I respond to that overheard music, a sound pattern, and I follow it as far as I am able, always with the initial surety it will lead to the pleasure of a poem's completed act. In the end, however, I shall not be following the music but leading it, fitting it to the context which has emerged. The point at which the transfer from rapt attention to controlling agent comes is impossible to predict or to formulate. Yet I can say the poem is freely made by the music so long as I may add that the poet shapes his music in service of his meaning, a meaning that abides latent and potential in his context. The writer of the polemical poem does not expect or experience the surprise that Frost meant when he said no surprise in the writer, no surprise in the reader. The surprise is not merely how things fall out but how the sound of words leads to and rests in art.

*   *   *

The American poet wants both a private and a public language for his poem because he is saddled with a need to express the uniquely American experience and humankind's common experience. We believe there is an uninvented American wheel. We chafe at the limitations of form and the witness of history. We want a language of such purity and scope that it might say everything to everyone and all at once. This impulse toward purity is escapist. All poetry is an escape into illusion, a retreat from un-selective experience, yet it becomes art to the degree that escape meta-morphoses into penetration of that experience. Art moves from raw sensory data to and through organized meaning. The minimalist attitude toward poetry, especially toward language, is a search for pure poetry, but it fails to be more than escapist, more than locally ambitious however it may secrete self-justifying aesthetic theories. What is the appropriate lan-guage for our poetry? Is it an echo of English verse? An imitation of the Asian pictograph? A slang-flecked image composed in triadic feet? What will be the langauge that is identifiably American but not parochially po-etic? Perhaps any answer will require the single poem pointed at or un-satisfactory abstractions. Surely, at least, we want an ordinary language that is referential, connective, and visionary, words that are not *just* there but unshakably, memorably *there*.

Ordinary language is not merely the banal, the conversational, or the eccentric. Poetry is not merely ordinary language lineated. Poetry is not precisely monosyllabic or polysyllabic, concrete or abstract, personal or public. Whoever demands one or the other shills for a half-truth, a half-lie. Poetry is a dialect of the language we speak, possessed of metaphorical density, coded with resonant meaning, engaging us with narrative's plea-sures, enhancing and sustaining our pleasure with enlarged awarenesses. In comparison to ordinary uses of language, this dialect is characterized by efficient discipline: of sharper imagery, focused symbols, connotative power, deployed rhythmic suggestion. It is both affective and effective communication. We ask the reader to participate in our imaginative act but we control, by the score of the language, the limits and range of that participation. We do not attempt to hide what we mean. I can think of nothing which is more central to that actual writing of a poem than that statement: we do not attempt to hide anything. Yet every beginner and not a few experienced writers assume that is the nature of poetry. The fact is that we write as directly and forcefully and carefully as we can—at our best—because we know the complexity of emotions and the conflict of perceptions, which we are in our humanness, frustrate clarity in every word, every phrase, every implied or explicit human circumstance.

Language is a rotting corpse of what men have felt, thought, and spoken. We are nothing without the dead and what has belonged to the dead; but they constantly block our clear expression and we are obliged to shoulder them aside, however gently. We attempt to do this every instant when we speak the words that carry an accumulated freight of meaning that is the legacy of the past. We feel, all of us do, that there is nevertheless a clarity our words can reach in which we may express entirely what we feel and mean. But we despair of reaching that clarity, with reason. Some of us settle for the language the dead have left us. Some of us in frustration brutalize the language and try to explode our way beyond the dead. And some are lucky enough to attain to a clarity that is like hope itself. The poems which please us, whether we find them abandoned or finished, seem arrived at that clarity but we know the arrival is temporary. We know there is no permanently pure expression. We cannot ever get free entirely from the death-hand of language. We can only hope for a temporary accommodation and the agent of that accommodation is form, specifically a form of music.

The poem, whatever its Platonic shape in our dreams, is the way our minds ingest and use the world. It is what generates beauty. Its commands are *Look! Know! Connect!* No one of these commands is significantly valuable without the actions of the others. In that, the triad resembles the integral motions of a symphony: all the parts working for one purpose and within a unified sequence. What we hope, of course, is that these three imperatives might result in the poem by which the poet shall know himself and the world, and know what cannot be so well and fully known any other way under the sun.

We humans are enigmas, paradoxes. That is not an original thought but it is worth remembering. We live in an isolation within ourselves and with ourselves, a total and terrible isolation, because we cannot and are not, parted from the womb, truly a part of any other. We speak casually of the love that joins us each to each and we speak fervently of religious oneness. In every religious vision I know about, the ultimate rest is a condition of being where all is fused, flowing, emphatically joined. Even this belief is based on the implicit recognition that the fundamental fact of *this* exis-

tence is our division one from another, our utter isolation. We bond ourselves sometimes for life and we even speak of how in our love we become
a part of another. This is wish-ful thinking and poor metaphor. Always in
the world, we are always and essentially apart, alone. Art that is great and
true and complex affords this paradox the full dramatic reality we know.
Such art tries to help us force back the borders of the unknown. It helps
make verifiable what we can only intuit. Art's knowledge and its province
are inevitably interior. That is why the artist follows no law other than the
one he makes, though his law will be more strict, more demanding, more
impossible to keep or to understand than any exterior law. The forms he
creates act according to strictures never acknowledged until the poem is
complete. That is, I am aware, an overstatement and it obviously ignores
the influences of literary heritage as well as contemporary fashions. But I
mean not the many of us who are going into the anonymous dust of
years—I mean those poets who will alter the course of poetry, who seem
scarcely to know anything of laws until the laws have been felt, obeyed,
broken, revised, and recast.

Law is an odious word to any poet and probably has no business here. If
the poet is free of anything, he is free of external constraints. Almost, I
hear the voices of objection, citations of the terrible and all too frequent
cases of those poets bent and broken by the governments of men. I
don't forget Miguel Hernandez and Apollinaire and Mandelstam and
Akhmatova, to name only a few. Nevertheless, I believe each poet has the
freedom to choose silence or the poem's speech, whether he speaks it only
to himself or etches it in blood on his cell wall. In the poem and with the
poem, he is free; there his freedom consists in choosing how he will say a
thing as well as what he will say. Men may make their laws to govern a
publication, but no law can be imposed on the poem that the poet does
not himself accept. The poet is free even if his choice is only to die with
courage. He can choose even that in the last instant, and choice is freedom.
Because poets are the bearers of freedom and choice, governments fear
them and men love them.

*   *   *

What is a poem? What does it do? It is music and statement and feeling
and the shape of courageous thought. It says *no* to death and to pain and
to the spirit's imprisonment. It denies that it may affirm and witness and
celebrate the grace and goodness of life. To the degree that it sacrifices full
and complex witness to experience, that it begins to moralize, it is rotten
and useless. Art, poetry, does not promulgate a social design nor does it
yield up constitutions. It shows us a man in the motions of his life. The

poet believes he must seek for life in art but he must first seek for the possibilities of art in life. Art may and usually does improve the quality of life. It may even affect human behavior for the better—but we had better not hold our breath.

Baudelaire says poetry exists only to be poetry. That is like the great wheeling hawks I have loved since my boyhood. The hawks exists as itself above all sophistry or explanation. Its nature is to rise and fall, to be silent and to sing. The hawk belongs to the high air where he circles and everything seems part of a force whose only intention is to keep the hawk what he is and where he is, mysterious, serene, and compulsive. Almost I want to say the poem is that hawk's voice riding out like a final sound of defiance in a final place. Yet a poem is not a hawk nor a place. It is an organization of formed words made by a man or a woman, an undeniable, strongly sounded music of human crying-out, sometimes in joy and often in sorrow, which comes to rest and to live in an apparently natural but always artificial form. In a poem a man may rise and fall with the beauty of a hawk, but he is not a hawk. A man must do and he must be in the world but he cannot, if he would fulfill his destiny as a man, refuse the attempt to know the meaning of himself and the attempt to render it permanent in the memory of his kind. Melville spoke with admiration of the "whole corps of thought-divers that have been diving and coming up since the world began." The hawk, as much as I love him, is a pitiful and limited creature in comparison to the thought-divers, the poets, whose pursuit of clarity and form is nothing less than the will to live for beauty and to make it the meaning, the noble energy by which we shall be enabled to live and to know the fullness of that living.

(Woman) Writer

JOYCE CAROL OATES

I

What is the ontological status of the writer *who is also a woman*?

She experiences herself, from within, as a writer primarily: she does not inevitably view herself as an object, a category, an essence—in short, as "representative." In the practice of her craft she may very well become bodiless and invisible, defined to herself fundamentally as what she thinks, dreams, plots, constructs: in contrast, that is, to what other persons see her as *doing*. Life consists, to adroitly paraphrase Emerson, of what a person is thinking day by day.

Perhaps it follows, then, that when the writer is alone, when she is alone with language, with the challenging discipline of creating an art *by way of language alone,* she is not defined to herself as "she"—? Does the writer require the specification of gender? Is memory itself gender-bound? Are impressions filtered through the prism of gender? Is there a distinctly female voice?—or even a feminine voice? Or is "gender" in this sense an ontological category imposed upon us from without, for the convenience of others?—a category which dissolves the uniquely individual in the Abstract, in what Melville called, in quite another context, "hideous, intolerable Allegory."

All artists are idealists and romantics; even cynicism, as you may frequently have noticed, is artful. It has been said that the artist requires a special and even secret world to which he alone has the key; and it is also true that an incalculable faith, innocent and unwilled as the color of our hair or eyes, and prior, certainly, to both reason and experience, underlies all motives for sustained creativity. "Faith" is notorious for attaching itself to virtually any object, visionary or hallucinatory or "real": but the possi-

---

Keynote address, Twentieth-Century Women Writers Conference, Hofstra University, 1983.

bility of being deluded—one might almost say, the *hope* of being de-luded—is one we must accept, if we are going to continue to write. If the ideal reader experiences the classic "enlargement of sympathies" by way of serious fiction, it is to be assumed, perhaps to be taken on faith, that the writer, immersed in these sympathies, experiences a similar enlargement of vision.

Here is a genderless meditation upon the secret motive for art, by a twentieth-century writer, in English, who was absolutely obsessed—which is to say, fascinated, intoxicated, redeemed—by language in its infinite variations, coaxed and threaded into the most formidable of struc-tures: coldly mandarin and nearly unreadable to some, cherished as one of the literary geniuses of our time by others:

> Whenever I start thinking of my love for a person, I am in the habit of immedi-ately drawing radii from my love—from my heart, from the tender nucleus of a personal matter—to monstrously remote points of the universe. Something impels me to measure the consciousness of my love against such unimaginable and incalculable things as the behavior of nebulae (whose very remoteness seems a form of insanity), the dreadful pitfalls of eternity, the unknowledgeable be-yond the unknown, the helplessness, the cold, the sickening involutions and interpenetrations of space and time. . . . When that slow-motion silent explosion of love takes place in me, unfolding its melting fringes and overwhelming me with the sense of something much vaster . . . then my mind cannot help but pinch itself to see if it is really awake. I have to make a rapid inventory of the universe, just as a man in a dream tries to condone the absurdity of his position by making sure he is dreaming. I have to have all space and all time participate in my emotion, in my mortal love, so that the edge of its mortality is taken off, thus helping me to fight the fact of having developed an infinity of sensation and thought within a finite existence.[1]

This eloquent statement attests not only to the little-understood connec-tion between private emotion and the impulse for art, the mysterious mo-tive for fiction and metaphor, but speaks frankly of the "edge of mortality" that underlies it: our sense, which increases with the passage of years, that the present moment, undeniably and perhaps wonderfully real as it feels, is not, in its swift retreat into the past, so "real" as we might wish: and arguably less real than the experience would be, for instance, of slipping quietly away, and opening a novel written many decades ago, in a "pres-ent" now otherwise lost. Time is in love with the productions of Eternity: or with those creations one hopes will at least seem eternal, within the span of our culture's life. Writing is not antithetical to "experience," and it is certainly not an escape from such: it *is* experience: but one which looks, however hazily, into the future. The effort that is *now* will endure *then*.

So the days pass and I ask myself sometimes whether one is not hypnotised, as a child by a silver globe, by life; and whether this is living. It's very quick, bright, exciting. But superficial perhaps. I should like to take the globe in my hands and feel it quietly, round, smooth, heavy, and so hold it, day after day.[2]

This insatiable desire to write something before I die, this ravaging sense of the shortness and feverishness of life, make me cling, like a man on a rock, to my one anchor.[3]

*   *   *

There are writers, born women, who do not think of themselves—at least by their testimony—as women, when they write; and there are other writers, born women, who believe their writing to be conditioned at all times by their gender. Much is made of the elusive Female Voice without regard for the fact that Voice always means voices, if we are being at all attentive to subtleties of pitch and nuance. As for content—hasn't it been a heady consequence of Modernist aesthetics, that one is free to write about anything?—that even the most ignoble and despicable of subjects is soluble in art?

What is the ontological status of "Virginia Woolf," who died more than forty years ago? The woman does not exist; the woman-writer does not exist; we have only a number of books—novels, essays, sketches, letters, a diary. The "Virginia Woolf" of the public writings is a fastidious craftsman, even when it is her intention to simulate the spontaneity of life (so "fluent and fluid," one observer worried her by saying, "it runs through the mind like water"); the "Virginia Woolf" of the diaries and letters impresses us as being less postured, less willed, less *self*-conscious. But how can we judge? Where does personality reside—in a resolutely artful (and artificial) utterance, or in a presumably unpremeditated speech? Diaries and letters are after all art-forms, their energy in the present tense, but their gravitational centers in the future. And there are biographies. An immense sea of biographies. There are anecdotes, thumbnail portraits, curious allusions that would altogether astonish those to whom they allude. (As in the title of Edward Albee's "Who's Afraid of Virginia Woolf?") Thus, not one "Virginia Woolf" exists, now that the woman herself is dead, but a vertiginous multitude. They are all assemblages of words; a considerable number are works of supreme art; but where can personality reside in such a phenomenon as—words! Yet more crucially, where can gender reside? If not even handwriting communicates sexual characteristics, can the printed word?—can typeface?

One can become deluded into thinking that one "knows" Virginia Woolf in some fundamental way, but in fact one knows only diverse texts by diverse hands. The writer "Virginia Woolf" exists, now, not only primarily but exclusively as an assemblage of words; and it might be argued that the language of Virgina Woolf, however capably translated into another language, is not hers: cannot be *her*. (How curious they are, these books of ours, translated into foreign languages!—we may sense an oblique kinship but know, perhaps with a sense of poignancy and loss, that the language is not our own: the book is therefore by another author.)

Our immediate response to a book, to what must be called an artful assemblage of words, is therefore wholly a response to language, not unlike a response to music heard for the first time: are we fascinated by it?—at least interested in it?—disturbed by it?—provoked?—amused?—irritated?—confused?—bored?—angry?—indifferent? Along a similar spectrum the student of any art-form finds himself vis-à-vis a certain work of art at various stages in his life. A genuine response is incalculable—unpredictable—unwilled. Should we be predisposed to "like" a work of art because its creator (distant, legendary, perhaps long dead) was identified, during his or her lifetime, as *male* or *female*? And what, considering the evidence of moldering bones in remote graves, does *male* or *female* now mean?

Most artists, and certainly the writer, aspire to invisibility by way of art, however blatantly, and often vulgarly, they exhibit their visibility in a consumer-oriented culture. Most novelists—though not of course all—really do attempt to refine themselves out of existence by way of an immersion, a systematic and disciplined immersion, in language. (If this were not the case, the writer would be something else: a politician, a preacher, a dancer, an actor: one, that is, who performs in public, in person, in the personalized flesh. But to be a writer is to abrogate that public identity or persona for the time one is in fact writing. The craft is often said to be a lonely one, and we should be astonished if it were not.) My faith in the craft of writing, in the writer's role, most succinctly put, is that it is—as others have noted—a form of sympathy. And, being mimetic, being bodiless, consisting solely of words, it necessitates no displacement or intrusion in the world; it exults in its own being.

II

Luxury of Being Despised*

> *In revenge and in love, women*
> *are more barbaric than men.*
> —Nietzsche

The sneering shout in the street, the anatomical female
stretched wide across the billboard: St. Paul's contempt.

Montaigne instructs us that poetry belongs to women—
a wanton and subtle art, ornate and verbose,
all pleasure
and all show: like themselves.
And Freud, that women have little sense of justice.
And De Kooning, in these angry swaths of paint:
how crude, how magnificent, such monster women!

The fiery sightless eye which is your own.
The booming breasts, the maniac wink.
All is heat, fecundity, secret seeping blood.
Flesh is here: nor are we out of it.

   What bliss, to be so despised:
the closed thighs all muscle,
the Church Fathers' contempt,
the Protestant chill, what freedom
since we have no souls!—
what delight.

The angry swaths of flesh which are your own.
The blank stare,
the cartoon heart.
Virginity a mallet.
Mad grin worn like a bonnet.

   Though it is true that the writer is bodiless, and transformed by craft
into invisibility, what of the (woman) writer? Does she occupy a significantly different space? What is the *objective*, as opposed to the *subjective*,
state of her ontological existence?
   A woman who writes is a writer by her own definition; but she is a
woman writer by others' definitions. The books she writes are indeed artful assemblages of words—she does have immense, and at times naive,

---

* "Luxury of Being Despised" originally appeared, in a slightly different version, in *The Bennington Review*, June 1982. Copyright © 1982 by Joyce Carol Oates.

faith in their worth—but her sexual identity is not thereby dissolved or transcended. Books are neuter objects, *its:* writers are *he* or *she:* for this is the ontological fact of flesh, nor are we out of it. Of course one can speak casually of "Virginia Woolf" when, strictly speaking, one means a book ("I have been reading Virginia Woolf"): one can make elaborate critical judgments, or reduce all complexity to a blunt statement (by saying, for instance, "Are we not somewhat over-saturated with Virginia Woolf?"): and here there is some confusion of *it* and *her,* but none that violates a convention of usage. As one moves farther and farther away from the actual, existential, minute-by-minute immersion in specific passages in specific works by Virginia Woolf, one may readily confuse her prose with that of prose written about her, by biographers, memorists, critics, reviewers. Our sensibilities become blurred; dulled; lazy. Soon everything that pertains to "Virginia Woolf" is saturated with the biographical fact (perhaps significant, perhaps not) of her femaleness.

Since I am a woman who writes, I see that, in the eyes of most observers, I must be a "woman writer," though there are, so far as I can determine, no "men writers." Sometimes the extraordinary praise is thrown at me, like a bouquet of roses that lands in one's face instead of in one's arms, that *I write like a man.* (One wants to inquire—which man?) It was once a central issue in a fairly vicious negative review of a novel by a contemporary writer that he was a "male Joyce Carol Oates"—an insult of the most sombre dimensions, quite apart from the fact that, in some quarters, it is seen to be a despicable thing to be a female Joyce Carol Oates.

As a (woman) writer, consequently, I find myself (which is to say, *I am found:* I do not will, or wish, or invent myself) in an impersonal category that is my birthright for better or worse. Not all women are despised by all men, at least not all of the time, but it is a fairly commonplace dilemma—whether it is consciously articulated or not—that a man's quarrel with the feminine in his own nature will be a quarrel with women: the impulse may be abstract and psychological, but its fruition is always concrete. One need not consider the misogyny of the ages—for one thing, it is too familiar, and too depressing—since there are examples close at hand, in even the most well-intentioned of literary forums: too many, indeed, to contemplate. (For instance, in the *Harvard Guide to Contemporary American Writing* of 1979, clearly a standard reference text, one finds chapters titled "Intellectual Background," "Literary Criticism," "Experimental Fiction," "Drama," etc., and "Women's Literature"—a potpourri of virtually everyone whose name might come to mind under this rubric, with an inevitable emphasis, the heart sinks to see, upon those books by those writers who write about "female subjects." Being thus ghettoized feels like an insult

until one stops to realize—the (woman) writer stops to realize—that a
ghetto, after all, is a place to exist: dissolve it, and one may find oneself
with no place in which to live at all.

In the general adulation of John Berryman there seems rarely to have
been space for an examination of the tacit prejudices of (male) poets regarding their respected peers:

> Them lady poets must not marry, pal.
> Miss Dickinson—fancy in Amherst bedding her.
> Fancy a lark with Sappho,
> a tumble in the bushes with Miss Moore,
> a spoon with Emily, while Charlotte glare.
> Miss Bishop's too noble-O.
>
> That was the lot. And two of them are here
> as yet, and—and: Sylvia Plath is not.
> She—she her credentials
> has handed in, leaving alone two tots
> and widower to what he makes of it—
> surviving guy. . . .[4]

That was the lot, Berryman casually informs us: the grotesquerie of the
situation being the ease with which, in a drunk's babyish prattle, centuries
of women poets are dismissed; and those who are deemed worthy of attention are nonetheless "lady poets"—a despicable or quaint category, de-
pending upon the degree of one's charity.

And there is Robert Graves's famous declaration: "A woman is a Muse
or she is nothing."

And—I open a book at random, this very instant, to feel my eye at once
snagged by the remarkable observation, "What is mere confession in a
female writer [Doris Lessing] amounts to intuitive genius in Knut
Hamsun."[5]

Clearly, the (woman) writer who imagines herself "assimilated" into the
mainstream of literature, the literature of men, is mistaken, or deluded, or
simply hopeful: or is her faith based upon a stubborn resistance to what *is,*
set beside what *may one day be?* To pretend that one is not what one is, in
the flesh, in the historical flesh, is naive; to brush lightly aside the evidence
of being despised is symptomatic of that interesting variation of hysteria
called denial. Yet—must one insist upon it?—must one focus upon injustice, and loss, and insult, and pain? The luxury of being despised is an
embittered and satirical one, yet it allows for a certain energizing of forces,
away from the self, perhaps, and into the work: away from the distractions
and the immediate gratifications of visibility, and toward the semi-
permanence of art.

So it is, the (woman) writer has faith in the nobility of the craft to which she has dedicated herself; but she is, we might say, no fool, in gauging her relative position in it. One moves between the poles of idealism and pessimism, well within the limits of euphoria and despair, steering a middle course, as the handy cliché would have it, and trying to maintain a sense of humor. A writer may be beleaguered by any number of chimeras, but only the (woman) writer is beleaguered by her own essential identity. *How can the paradox be accommodated,* one asks, and an answer might be, *With difficulty.*

NOTES

1. Vladimir Nabokov, *Speak, Memory: An Autobiography Revisited* (New York: Pyramid Books, 1968), p. 219.

2. Virginia Woolf, in *A Writer's Diary,* edited by Leonard Woolf (New York: Harcourt Brace Jovanovich, 1954), p. 135.

3. *Ibid.,* p. 117. (An amusing counterpoint to Modernist preoccupations with the redeeming nature of the "permanent" word can be found in a novella by an early contemporary of Woolf's, H. G. Wells. This is that sobering parable *The Time Machine,* in which, in the year Eight Hundred and Two Thousand Seven Hundred and One A.D., the Time Traveller happens upon a library in the vicinity of what had once been London. He discovers brown and charred "rags" that appear to be the decaying vestiges of books. "They had long since dropped to pieces, and every semblance of print had left them. But here and there were warped boards and cracked metallic clasps that told the tale well enough. Had I been a literary man I might, perhaps, have moralised upon the futility of all ambition. But as it was, the thing that struck me with keenest force was the enormous waste of labor to which this sombre wilderness of rotting paper testified.")

4. John Berryman, *The Dream Songs* (New York: Farrar, Straus & Giroux, 1969), p. 206.

5. From John Updike's *Picked-Up Pieces* (New York: Knopf, 1975), p. 151.

An Interview with
Theodore Weiss

The following interview took place on Sunday, March 27, 1977, at Theodore Weiss's house in Princeton, New Jersey. Colette Inez is the interviewer.

INTERVIEWER: Do you see the poems you'll be writing in the next decade as going in any special direction? Do you see a pattern?

WEISS: If I did I probably wouldn't want to tell you. I have many directions I want to pursue: the dramatic, the convergence or collision of the dramatic and meditative, and the lyric dramatic. Of course, the problem of pattern is something for the critic and reader, not for the poet. The silkworm does not measure the silk, he's too busy spinning it. The critic, hungering for patterns, may find them where they don't exist.

INTERVIEWER: Do you have thematic obsessions?

WEISS: I do, but I distrust them. They're often limitations, not violent illuminations.

INTERVIEWER: If you were asked to select one poem that you did not write but wished you had, which poem would you choose and why? It can be a poem from any period.

WEISS: Terribly important to me is Wordsworth's "Tintern Abbey." It's a kind of touchstone, one of the happiest melanges of the lyrical, the meditative, and the dramatic, because of the way Wordsworth's mind moves at its own pace, then is accelerated by the world around it, by the stimuli of its own thinking and the past. This kind of contemplative intricacy has always engrossed me.

INTERVIEWER: Why do you prefer the dramatic to the lyric?

WEISS: I've always been impatient with the single, simple lyric, despite its purity of voice, because it's a little too one-dimensional. It has to put everything in one emphasis and hope that that will blow the walls down and let in the world. Whereas a poem as subtly complicated as "Tintern Abbey" wonderfully employs not only the furniture of the poet's mind, but the different rooms the mind lives in. Although Wordsworth's chief dialogue is with himself—"I am myself, the soul and I"—and he restages that old debate of body and soul, the vigorous old battered world invades his mind. I resent the confinement of a single voice. We live limited enough and sleepy lives. I'm eager to reach out beyond myself, living inside another's life enlarges mine. As even Stevens said, "We might have invented sight, but who could have invented the things we see?" Much as I'm enamored of sight, it's the things we see, and the processes that entails, which finally are more impressive than what my own processes might come to.

INTERVIEWER: If you were to give one piece of advice to a young poet, what would it be? Would you recommend poetry as a profession?

WEISS: Be in touch with excellence. Don't get lost in your own moods, they wear out too easily. It's a rough profession, not easy at all. Most of us are drawn into it because of the surface glamour that we see.

INTERVIEWER: When did you write your first poem?

WEISS: Oh Lord, that's hard to say. I suppose I began to fumble toward it in my high-school days. I remember a dear friend of mine, rather more advanced than I in reading and writing, had published a little essay on Robert Frost in *Scholastic*. I was awed by him. While I had known some Frost poems, I was startled by the idea of a live poet, a man of my own time, writing poems. In those days poets were all dead. We were walking downtown between the library and the main book store, the only literary spot in Allentown, when he stopped, stared at me, and said, "You know, Ted, you really ought to write poetry." I was flabbergasted. It had never occurred to me before. I began to write purple prose, influenced by Walter Pater. Then in college Muhlenberg was small and congenial enough so that I could substitute poems for assigned essays. I worked into a kind of primitive poetry. It wasn't until I went to graduate school that I fell into an absolute stupor of writing, living in a tense, hallucinatory cloud. After going to a few classes at Columbia, I found them so desolate that I soon abandoned all of them, except for Mark Van Doren's and Meyer Schapiro's that I sneaked off to regularly, despite the English Department's warnings against any wandering. They were lifesavers. I would sit in my room and write most of the day. A lot of gas and hot air, I'm sure, before I hit oil, I covered huge notebooks full of things I've never dared to look at. There were no workshops to encourage the young apprentice then.

INTERVIEWER: In those days poets weren't generally found in universities teaching literature.

WEISS: They were *persona non grata* in most schools. I remember one important moment at Muhlenberg. Chapel was required and I hated to go. Somehow, through their own administrative ignorance, the school brought Middleton Murry, an unfrocked minister, and he gave a talk on *Antony and Cleopatra*. I was listening to incense, as they say in the East. It was pure rapture. Now all the heavyweight poets are teaching and students, wooed and cosseted, come flocking on all sides. And it is troubling because they know considerably more than we did. They know us! Worse than that, they learn it easily. Many think they're instant poets. And since so much of what's being published, even by people whose names are rather respectable in the world, is poor, why shouldn't they?

INTERVIEWER: Would you advise the young poet, then, not to choose literature as a career but to work, say, as a lawyer or architect?

WEISS: Well, it's interesting, isn't it, that Williams and Stevens, two magnificent poets, were both happy griping endlessly about having to work. In fact, Stevens maintained that his insurance kept him on a steady keel. Williams' practice was palpably important . . . his energies, experience, and understanding came from his medicine. The university's a place for the artist to hang out in without paying the dues that bohemianism levies. Still, teaching has nourished me. It's a wonderful place for a ready-made, often eager, exuberant audience, one through which to discover and explore essential realizations. I don't know how much my students have learned in my classes, but I do know how much I have!

INTERVIEWER: Painting motifs run through your poems, which leads me to suspect that you're a painter as well as a poet. Do you find any relationship between those disparate loves? Does one enterprise influence the other?

WEISS: Alas, I'm not a painter, though I keep edging toward it now and then. Just last year Renee brought me a sketchbook which I have on my desk in all its virginity. When I was young I drew a great deal. In fact, for a long time, I thought it would be my profession. I'm not sure how and when words overtook drawing, but they did. The notion of taking something as simple and primitive as colors, putting them together, and making a world . . . the immediate visual world of painting astonishes me, in particular the compositional quality. You know this problem of how many modern poets struggle against time in order to turn time almost into a space; they do resent the runningness away of a poem. Just think of Whitman's catalogues. It's clear he expects you somehow, as he describes each person in a different profession, to secure them all at once. If he could have employed a great sheet three hundred feet wide, then you could step back and see all those people going on. That's why they're not differentiated as individuals. Whereas the compositional play of a painting lets you take in everything at once. . . . Of course my poems draw heavily on the visual so that it threatens to beggar the other senses. It's a great American spectator tradition. Emerson called himself a transparent eyeball.

INTERVIEWER: In a recent *New York Times* review of *Fireweeds,* William Stafford mentioned the surreal effect of some of your poems and the holding off, as he put it, of the ordinary world. Do you agree with this assessment? If not, would you say why?

WEISS: Well, Stafford addressed himself almost exclusively to one long poem, "The Store Room," that grows out of Homer's *Odyssey.* I wanted to convey my deepest sense of that superb poem by being true to Penelope's nature and Odysseus'. After all, the *Odyssey* is a poem of fits and starts, and Penelope is located in the middle of the world of the poem, holding off the suitors, holding off her own aging, keeping a world going so that her wayward, many detoured husband will somehow find his way back to her. But it's not a holding off of the ordinary world. After all, both Odysseus and Penelope, especially Odysseus, are creatures of appetite; they love the world, they don't want to use it up too soon; they have a certain amount of aesthetical quality that Homer gave them, and part of that is the admiration we put into the thing before we devour it. So "The Store Room" is a multiple way of studying that world before finally acknowledging it. . . . As for surrealism, I generally have little sympathy with it. I'd say only that at moments of high intensity in any poem, where suddenly many things converge and you have a kind of incandescence that almost blinds you to the things there, a kind of surreal effect does occur.

And that occasion I like. If that's what Stafford meant by surreal, I'll accept it.

INTERVIEWER: The term "surreal" has come to cover so much. . . .

WEISS: Yes, exactly. It's too often a mechanistic approach to poetry, which I abominate. But I do believe in this: when the mind begins to go, when it begins to ignite, everything becomes the right fuel; it doesn't matter whether it's an ash or an oak or a junk pile, it seems to be what you need. Now whether it is some magnetic attraction, or it is that the mind has reached such a high pitch of accomplishment that it can make everything seem right, I don't know. There's also luck in this business. Teaching Pound recently, I ran across an introduction by Yeats to the *Noh* plays, where he says the following: "All imaginative art keeps at a distance, and this distance when chosen must be firmly held against a pushing world." Now that's pretty much what I've been getting at. Especially in a time like ours, the poet must not compete with the clamor of the age. One yearns to surround words, even opulent ones, with silence so that they have a space for their resonance, a space to breathe in and to exert the full amplitude of their powers. But then there's the other side, mainly that I want in poetry as mixed and abundant a mash as I can find. It's sometimes a matter of delaying a poem until it can collect its own crescendoes and then suddenly break out, as at the end of "The Store Room" there is the great bow which has been bent; it's been bent for however many pages and years before Odysseus shoots it.

INTERVIEWER: What would you say to poets and critics who accuse you of being bookish, of not writing about common subjects, such as going out for a walk, taking your shirts to the laundry?

WEISS: Let me be autobiographical. For a long time I shared this democratic fix, the notion that you must not attempt anything other than your own immediate world; I resisted the literary as strongly as I could. And then one day I began to admit to myself that I was being hypocritical. I felt it a fraud to pretend, as Hemingway had to do apparently, that he had never read a book when he was one of the better-read men of his time. I had to confess to myself that in *The Tempest* and *The Odyssey* I was in a world more real to me than most people I know. Since these works affected my imagination as much as they did, it would be foolish and spendthrift not to use them. After all, it's the absorption that counts. My poems about Caliban and Penelope are of no consequence if all they do is remember abjectly and studiously the originals, but I feel I'm writing modernly, not just my diction but my accent, stress, and focus. The Caliban poem, for example, is really under it all a comment on the excess of power that Prospero exercised. Caliban finds Prospero's book and is reading it and he begins to do the magic and it works, but he isn't in total charge of it. A bit of the island is blown off in a big storm and he thinks he did it. Well, I was thinking of nuclear energies. We are monkeying around with powers that are unlimited, scary, and may be final.

INTERVIEWER: Would you explain what you mean by the word "democratic?"

WEISS: I still think our country is a fairly noble enterprise (I will use the old word); its ideals remind us that we have nobler impulses than our ordinary ones. I love poetry's giving itself impossible assignments. Writing a democratic poem is an almost impossible assignment because by its very nature poetry is elitist; it means using words in a special way to talk specially about something. That is elitist, no matter what you say. Yet I love the idea of poetry's obliging itself to open up to include more than was there before. If it does, then it's magnificently democratic.

INTERVIEWER: I see in poetry today a kind of tyranny of plain folks, people who aren't plain and whose minds are complex assuming they're "just folks." Would you comment on that?

WEISS: If, as Williams sometimes suggested, the ordinary is the fundamentally important element in us, not just the casual, not just the accidental, not just the weak, I'll accept it. Otherwise, I see no reason to write poetry, and I know why many poets are collapsing into prose poems. They are gradually giving up altogether; they've given up rhyming—okay; they've given up meter—okay; there are those who are giving up metaphor—okay. Now, it's the verse line. They're writing lots of things which are often neither fish nor fowl, neither prose nor poetry, and offering them—a sort of final collapse into what they can do. I have no great sympathy for such writing.

INTERVIEWER: You mentioned Williams and Stevens. In an earlier interview you once said that they were perhaps the two American poets who most mattered to you. They seem to have shadowboxed each other a lot. I can see much more of Stevens than of Williams in your rich abundance of language and in your meditative impulses. How did they influence you?

WEISS: Williams was an eye-opener, as he was for a lot of my generation, because he said, "Look, America's possible. It's a poetic world if you can use it." I admired him because he wasn't imposing earlier views on it. I loved, as I've written of him in a poem, his vulnerability, his availability. He probably came closer to being at the mercy of his time and place than any other American poet. Now one has to accept the difference of temperament. He was, as I knew him, a nervous, almost shrill, yet open man thoroughly captivated by his practice of medicine. Obviously Stevens was a man dealing with the most abstract of all things, actuarial tables. Imagine inviting your muse after spending a day with life and death. And yet it worked.

INTERVIEWER: Maybe he wrote a policy for immortality.

WEISS: He did. The make of my temperament is closer to Stevens than to Williams, yet what Stevens called "the anti-poetic" in Williams, much to Williams' chagrin, appeals to me. I love the idea of defying easy poetizing. I want the hard things in life that will challenge us and say, "ah-hah! Can you make a poem of this?" I share the age's appetite for the thing-in-itself. Stevens cared for it, too, despite his often-noted detachment. Maybe he was more interested in the thirteen ways of looking at a blackbird because there's no blackbird there. The poem is a mosaic of looking made up of his own eye, and like a fly's eye, he's caught different glances and assembled them. I adore the facticity of Williams, his ability to become a sycamore tree. There it is. If a tree can be translated or transcribed, he's done it. On the other hand, I wouldn't want to relinquish Stevens' playfulness, zaniness, and colorful abstractions, that mind enamored of its own powers and able to do virtuoso things. Like Stevens, I'm a sedentary man; I'm not engaged in life and death practices. My hands aren't, as Williams' were, every day in the muck of existence. He was pulling out babies and pushing in corpses; that makes a difference. Certainly Stevens was a lonely, isolated, private man in a way that I don't think I am. There was a kind of Emily Dickinson spirit in that big, burly body. As you can see, I'm caught somewhere between the two men.

INTERVIEWER: In his review Stafford says that you offer every relief from heightened language. James Dickey, in his review of *Outlanders*, says quite the opposite: "Weiss arrives at a clear, intense verbal life through the most analytical processes, and it is apparent he could not have achieved the intensity of these poems by any other means." How do you respond to the contradiction?

WEISS: I think they're both right *(Laughs.)* If I can't write unheightened language, why should I write heightened language? In some poems I want low-keyed words, to lead the reader in casually and then unexpectedly present him, perhaps, even without his knowing it, with much more than he ever thought. I knock on a dull-seeming, anonymous door; it opens and, my God! it's not a door to a little house at all. There are many paces and spaces possible. I don't like modern poetry's crazy notion that a poet must find his voice and be stuck with it. I want many voices, not just one lumpy little dull voice! Look at Creeley. He has to write the same poem over and over. He's got a prison uniform he'll never get out of unless he realizes his predicament. But I don't care to live all my life in a cell. I want a many-vistaed house if I can manage it; I may not have the salary for it, but I'll try anyway. It's fascinating. For years I was attacked for being too rich, too dense, and now I'm being told I'm too simple and discursive: in Stafford's term, "He's slow." Slow? People have usually complained that I move too fast, they can't make my connections. If this age likes a plain style, a slow style, even—I hate to say it—a drab style, I'll prove I can work in those surfaces, too. But the poems won't, if I can help it, end up being plain, slow, and dull.

INTERVIEWER: Your syntax intrigues me because it reflects your way of talking. It's mobile and digressive. You use the colon, as if to say: "I have an allegiance to process. Don't try to pigeonhole me." Your syntax intimidates some people. Would you talk about it?

WEISS: Years ago I read a lively interview with Pound in *Paris Review* that shook up my head. Out of nowhere, in his inimitably knowing style, Pound said, "Well, the true characteristic of American poetry and American writing is the parenthesis. And it's in Henry James." That delighted me no end because mine is a kind of parenthetical, portmanteau mind. I hate to give things up and I hate to be one-dimensional, so I keep the poem open as long as I can to contain everything.

INTERVIEWER: Long vestibules of your own.

WEISS: That's right. And Joycean multi-compartmented valises! Or a gallery with many pictures on the walls. It's a hard medium to manage and it's often a precarious medium for readers to manage. It can break easily. Especially break the lyrical rhythm or flow. It's an all-inclusive ambition not to cut things off—or to cut down—and in that I think I'm rather democratic. Even though it sounds aristocratic in James, the idea of a parenthesis, a covered wagon going over the vastness of the Plains but keeping everything as it goes along, beguiles me. I've written simpler poems, again to prove that I can, and recently I did a series of poems I've called "Minims"—I can write short if I have to; I'm long enough to do that—poems which I first titled "Haikus, Lowkus, and Cuckoos." But I decided I couldn't since there wasn't a haiku among them, only cuckoos. Another thing, syntax is a conserving impulse. If you give up metric, at least conventional metric, and to a large degree I have, syntax then becomes especially crucial. It's trying all the time to accommodate itself to the true nature—either of the words or the image or even the larger pattern—of the thing said. For me syntax is the lifeline of a sentence or a poem. Syntax and its play of syllables—the skimming skein of sounds, rippled at times to the surface, at others caught deep down in the undertow, yet swaying insinuatingly as in a dance—helps to ensure the shape and unity of a poem. Syntax satisfies both sides of me, the voluptuary and the puritan.

INTERVIEWER: Your poems are markedly sensuous, "The Fire at Alexandria" springs to mind, yet never frankly sexual or confessional. Do you have any comment?

WEISS: All my poems are confessional, but I try to confess salient things, not the gossip of my life. I am a voyeur, as far as my poems are concerned, of vision. I want to catch the larger and more difficult things in their moments of cohabitation, rather than the casual, logistical fact of a man and a woman going to bed together. The confessional poets cash in on the accidental, for like many people today they believe that the world is little more than a series of accidents. Anything that happens along may have a certain amount of sensationalism and outrage to it, and that's what they'll write about. Frankly, it's the triumph of journalism. But for me, details, while wonderful in themselves, are also keyholes, if I may continue the voyeur image, and leisurely entries to a vast something else, celebrations of consciousness and the world out there.

INTERVIEWER: I'd like to ask you about revisions.

WEISS: First it's vision, then it's endless revision. I discovered some time ago something which really startled me. My longest poem, *Gunsight*, was originally a twenty-line poem—imagine, a twenty-line poem! Obviously as I looked at these lines, I saw they made up a scenario, each line a scene. I worked intermittently on it for almost twenty years. Since I write so easily, to begin with, I have forced myself to write with terrible anguish thereafter. Maybe it's the puritan: first syn, then tax. Not only did I have to fill every rift with ore, I had to fill the aura with riffs. . . . It's remarkable how as you trim your little garden plot you recognize possible avenues to explore, great parks and mazes hiding under every bush.

INTERVIEWER: Marvin Bell called Robert Bly a Norwegian-American commentator on Oriental poetry. How do you respond to the new, if it is new, internationalism on the poetry scene?

WEISS: It isn't new. Who was more international than Pound and Eliot? They were the source of my internationalism, and the fact that Americans don't really live anywhere. When I was a child, we moved at least every year around Allentown. Where has my home been? Where my job has taken me. We lived in Bard, in the Hudson River Valley, for twenty years, a lovely spot which gradually became visible in my poems. The negative develops slowly, slowly. But it seems foolhardy of me to affect being a deeply-rooted man. I live in all kinds of literature: English, French, Russian, Greek; they're homes, too. I don't know why modern man, particularly in the arts, is so frightened of admitting that the mind is a place he lives in and that works are also places he lodges in. How poets who write poems can hate poetry as much as they do astounds me! But this is only self-protection. First of all, they haven't read; second, they're too lazy to read or can't read; third, they claim to be original. And that's the last thing they are because we aren't original alone. Everything about us, our world, our words, is inherited. And, if we're good, we learn to make the most of what we inherit.

INTERVIEWER: Your books don't contain many translations the way a lot of contemporary poets' books do. Why?

WEISS: I haven't time for them. I'm busy writing my own poems. They're translations enough. I'm translating all the time: translating me, translating the world, finding the words for it that might almost fit it. I teach, which keeps me busy. And I edit. As you know, that's rather exhausting. To go back to the subject of internationalism: you know the opposite trend is at least as strident in the country. Poets are settling for and investigating local regions: Snyder in California, Hugo in Montana, Berry in Kentucky. There are poets digging in, burying themselves in their own shtetls. I'm uneasy about it because it seems to me that unless you've been in this place more than in your one own life, your roots are likely to be shallow. I can sympathize with their hunger for a land of their own. But given our world and its problems, I'm for internationalism altogether.

INTERVIEWER: A number of your poems refer to Christian dogma and tradition, with polite nods to Jacob and Moses, Eden and Jerusalem. I suspect you'd be more comfortable in Athens than in Tel Aviv. Why haven't you tackled Jewish themes more vigorously in your poems?

WEISS: I would feel uncomfortable perhaps because I'd be too much at home in Tel Aviv. A modern man like me is probably at home only where he's not at home. I speak more Yiddish than ever before here in Princeton. Maybe it's in self-defense. Many of my multi-lingual colleagues talk in languages that I don't understand, so I retaliate with Yiddish! And that really puts them on their backsides.

INTERVIEWER: Was Yiddish spoken in your family?

WEISS: My grandmother spoke it. I lived with her for a year, and Yiddish was the only language she had, so I learned it. I had to come to Princeton to find *Yiddishkeit*. I went to England to find out I was an American, so I come here to find out I'm a Jew. That makes sense, doesn't it? Also, there's another side to it. I'm not a joiner, and that also makes me a modern man. I'm very eager to visit Israel and to see Jerusalem. My parents seldom went to synagogue; I wasn't even Bar Mitzvahed. I did fall in love quickly with Greek, the language as well as the literature. And Homer is the poet who most matters to me, because, notwithstanding Shakespeare, he says the world most accurately. I love the Hebrew prophets because they take language farther than it's ever gone before, and they surprise it with unprecedented antics and unequalled splendors. On balance, though, I'm more Hellenist than Hebraist. After all, the Jews were anti-image; the aesthetic grace of Hellenism bewitches me. Also, I prefer multiple gods. I find one god boring . . . even if, aside from his heavy-handed moralism, he's as good as they claim he is. I like the graciousness and indignity of the Greek gods. However, the Hebraic and the Hellenic happily dovetail for me in the following way: this world exists finally for goods and use, and the great old Jews loved the world not just because God had made it, but because he had made it good.

INTERVIEWER: What do you think of the current fragmentation of poetry in America, the splitting of poets into discrete groups: Women, Third

World, Black, Deep Image, Zen, Surreal, Academic, Raw, and Cooked? Do you think there are any major poets calling the shots?

WEISS: A lot of poets are potshotting each other to death. If all these categories you mention suggest a richness, a reaching out to more and more of the world, I'm all for them; the more kinds, the better. The only thing I object to is that any one group should think it's supreme. I'm grateful to have people sacrificing themselves, experimenting with styles, testing resources. Perhaps they'll enrich the compost. As for major poets, "major's" a tricky word to use. This time is terribly rich, almost frighteningly so, in capable poets.

INTERVIEWER: How do you feel about what's called the raw school of poetry?

WEISS: I don't like raw poetry because it gets very close to being the tyranny of the sensational; the idea is boring that unless you bring up images dripping with either sweat, blood, or shit, you haven't got a real image. Obviously overcooked poems are boring, too. As I like to say sometimes when I read, I think of myself as medium rare.

INTERVIEWER: You say in your article, "Towards a Classical Modernity and Modern Classicism," that you regretted poetry's surrender of immense sectors of the world to prose, most of all to the novel. Have you tried your hand at novel writing? Or does the lyrical and narrative drive in your poetry satisfy the latent novelist in you?

WEISS: The novel overwhelms me. Trying to keep that much going is more than I can understand, let alone even at times read. Bill Humphrey, my old friend, said, "You don't know how to read a novel. You try to read it as a poem. That's a mistake." And he's probably right. Just as I try to read it as a poem, I try to write it as a poem.

INTERVIEWER: Yet narrative is very important to your poems.

WEISS: Yes. Narrative is a difficult matter in our age. The novel has almost abandoned it. Somehow, I'm sorry to say, we have lost either the appetite or the talent for story.

INTERVIEWER: Why?

WEISS: We're distracted. Then too stories are based on cause-and-effect relationships, and we're suspicious of most logical procedures. Anybody who tries to tell a straight story in a poem is regarded as a throwback, Stephen Vincent Benet *redivivus*. But the impulse is strong in me, which may explain why the long poem allures me, its management and development. One solution I've tried is the suite of seemingly disparate poems, which are always looking toward a common center, even though it's not visible at once. It's a floating metaphor beyond the larger one which attempts to accommodate all the others. Sustaining a long poem without conventional narrative or meter taxes one's stamina and imagination. I'll have to satisfy my narrative hungers in monologues.

INTERVIEWER: Nineteen seventy-seven marks the thirtieth year that you and Renee have been putting out the *Quarterly Review of Literature,* surely one of the most distinguished literary journals in our history. Would you comment on the ways the *Quarterly* may have influenced poetic taste?

WEISS: It's impossible to say with any accuracy what impact a little mag, appearing sporadically over thirty years, may have had. Certainly it's not up to its editors to say. But one virtue we have striven for and, we believe, sometimes attained: providing space for poems remarkable for one quality above all others: quality. Whatever our personal prepossessions, we have shied away from schools, have distrusted theoreticians and polemicists who flaunt poems as illustrations. We appreciate partisans (it is probably necessary for an artist to think that what he is doing is the only thing to do), especially when the passion of their partisanship inspires vital poems, uniquely authoritative in themselves. We rarely care what prompts the poem; it's the poem that matters, that must make its own way, be a pleasure in its own right. As a consequence, poems of all variety swarmed into *QRL;* and it became, we think, a center of good writing. It hasn't advertised or pushed anything beyond the delight of honest, accurate composition; at the same time it has, by what it has published, militated against the merely propagandistic, the sensational, the chaotic, the destructive. In short, we've done what we could to keep the mansions in poetry's realm open. Encouraging innovation, we have sought no less to keep alive hard-won past accomplishments, always in danger of being lost. Possibly also we have made some exchange likely—if just by juxtaposition in our pages—among otherwise rival camps and thereby exhibited to oncoming poets new possibilities of coupling, even fertile miscegenation. In conjunction with this, we have strongly stressed translations of works worlds and times away, for themselves and to enrich the local brew. Poetry, we feel, is one of the few true homelands for all nationals. *QRL*'s business and chief *raison d'être*, therefore, has been to found one instance of such a paper state.

INTERVIEWER: Given so much exposure to other poets, how have you kept your own voice?

WEISS: Such exposure may afford a kind of protection, the privacy, the little clearing even, of a headlong crowd. Also, one measures and defines himself through the assertive presence of others. Reading countless poets has probably quickened finding my own voice, the need to identify myself, to speak up and emphatically. In choosing among myriad poems I have clarified not only my own notions of poetry, what it is or might be, but what I want my writing to be. Furthermore, editing underwrites the excitement of "replying." New work is not, some recent critics notwithstanding, merely a product of earlier literature; but a real part of it is response, the endless dialogue between past and present (my personal interest and my teaching immersed me also in past great literature), and present and present. Even the most outlandish poets, these perhaps most of all, are reacting to—and so part of—"tradition." Poems arriving hot off the typewriter—good ones, discovering new parts of our world or redeeming the banal; great ones, insisting on as they demonstrated our abundance, depth, extraordinariness—surely have filliped me to regions of myself I might otherwise not have attempted. Writing by its nature, particularly in a country huge as ours, is a solitary occupation. Willy nilly we in *QRL* developed a superior company and so ensured crackling postcards from poetry's volcanic core. We indeed established a "school" but of all grades, classes, distinctions. This school, challenging, summoned me forth.

Recitations

MAXINE KUMIN

In the spring of 1910, my mother, wearing her handmade best blue silk skirt, recited a poem called "The Curfew Bell" from the stage of the town hall in Radford, Virginia.

"England's sun was slowly setting o'er the hill-tops far away," she declaimed with appropriate gestures, "Filling all the land with beauty at the close of one sad day." On through all sixty lines of Rose Hartwick Thorpe's now-forgotten tale of a young heroine who saves her lover from execution by shinnying up the rope and stifling the clapper of the curfew bell that is to toll the hour of his death. "Not one moment paused the maiden, but, with cheek and brow aglow, / Staggered up the gloomy tower, where the bell swung to and fro. . . . / See! The ponderous tongue is swinging; 'tis the hour of curfew now, / And the sight has chilled her bosom, stopped her breath, and paled her brow."

Luckily, the old sexton who rings the bell each evening is too deaf to note the absence of its sound on this occasion. Cromwell rides into the story toward the end. Touched by Bessie's heroic deed, he pardons the young prisoner, whose name is Basil, and whose crime is never specified. Ah, Basil and Bessie! "In his brave, strong arms he clasped her, kissed the face upturned and white, / Whispered, 'Darling, you have saved me; curfew will not ring tonight.'"

My mother's skirt, which she had sewn herself, was made from material sent forty miles to Roanoke to be pleated. This detail was never left out of her retellings. Body English played a large part in the recitations of her day and the skirt, falling in knife pleats to the ankle, belled out satisfactorily around her as she writhed, imitating brave Bessie's climb up the belfry, up the slimy ladder. Then, as Bessie springs onto the rope itself and swaying through the air hangs onto the bell's great tongue, the skirt alternately flares and clings seductively to the prize-winning elocutionist who acts out the part.

This, at least, is how I recreate the scene. I can see my mother's demure on-stage curtsey and hear the applause of her parents and eleven siblings, although, to my sorrow, I never found out what the prize was.

At the time that she confided these scraps of her personal history I was approximately the age she had been that day in the town hall. I listened grudgingly. What I wanted most in the world was to be totally unlike her. I had broken out in the itchy, surly eczema of adolescence. Immersed in Dostoievski and Saint Teresa of Ávila, I discounted my mother's verbal skills. Privately, I thought her a butterfly and a social climber, and perhaps she was. But she was adept at nonsense rhyming and could frequently coax me out of a dark mood with her impromptu couplets.

My mother lived into her eighty-fifth year, long enough for us to become friends, long enough for me to praise her ability to have poems by heart. I am grateful to her for the memory-genes she passed on to me. I'm grateful, too, for the adept and ridiculous rhymes, and for the nonsense language she often tickled me with, a gibberish that imitated the inflections of speech but conveyed nothing, except tonally; all useful idiosyncrasies for the poet.

I also was lucky in adolescence to have two pedagogues of the Old School as different from my stylish, modish mother as Rose Hartwick Thorpe's poems are from, say, Louise Bogan's. Juanita Mae Downes, my Latin teacher, battle-scarred by the Depression, alternating her wardrobe between the all-purpose black dress and a similar model in purple crepe, wore her hair in one of those visible-invisible hair nets originally designed for the kitchen staff. She was a large, square, ungainly woman in her thirtieth year of teaching *hic, haec, hoc* in the same public school system. She espoused not only the reasonable and orderly processes of conjugation and declension, but etymologized ardently and wittily along the way.

Tidal waves of this efficiently designed language and its root meanings washed into my life. Surely not the worst way to endure the seething introversions of adolescence, translating Ovid and Virgil, memorizing whole chunks of the *Aeneid,* the *Metamorphoses* and *Tristia,* locating the caesura in each line and breaking the lines into their appropriate measures by scansion.

> Arma vi/rumque ca/nō // Trō/iae qui/ prīmus ab/ ōrīs
> Ītali/am fā/tō profu/gus // Lā/viniaque/ vēnit
> lītora,/ multum il/le et ter/ris // iac/ tātus et/ altō
> vi supe/rum // sae/vae memo/rem Iū/nōnis ob/ īram;

I muttered, marking the hexameter lines into their dactyls and double-lining the caesuras. Long afternoons I stayed late to unravel the mysteries of the elegiac stanza with its alternating hexameters and pentameters, its diaereses followed by pauses:

cum subit/ illi/us // tris/tissima/ noctis i/mago
qua mihi/ supre/mum—// tempus in/ urbe fu/it. . . .

It was better than crossword puzzles. Sometimes the subject matter grew racy: Dido and Aeneas in the cave, for instance. Miss Downes guided my endeavor, censoring nothing, for if it was written in Latin, how could it be unsuitable for a high school senior? Ovid—*Metamorphoses* in particular—got me through a terrible year in which cheerleaders and football players and planners of the senior prom (I didn't go) mocked me in my dreams.

In English class, Dorothy Lambert, as soft and powdery as Miss Downes was regal and rigorously corseted, shepherded me through parts of speech, the parsing of the sentence, and gloriously(!) the undiluted rules of prosody. Lambert's own Poetry Yardstick graced every student's copybook. Its measure was applied from metonymy to terza rima, from sonnet to synecdoche. Under her watchful eye I read Donne, Marvell, Shakespeare, Arnold, all with the same enthusiasm. Every week we wrote out another fifty lines we had committed to memory. A minimal amount of groaning accompanied this process; accreting poems was then considered a respectable pursuit and it began in grammar school. I remember in "Evangeline" my confusion over the "Druids of eld," which I took to be a distant place. And how these trees could stand "like harpers hoar" was an unsolved puzzle. For a long time I concluded that these were a species of animal, "with beards that rest on their bosoms," something like the walrus's mustache. In public assembly the sixth grade did the "Deacon's Wonderful One-Hoss Shay," or else Poe's "The Bells."

But in high school, pink, powdery, motherly Mrs. Lambert who was divorced and had secret sorrows, let loose on us masses of British poetry. She was mild and she was funny; even the restless, would-be dropouts at the back of the room sat still for her. "Would Sleepy Hollow please to come to order?" she'd say, and magically it came to pass. We wrote out sonnets by Shakespeare, Milton, Keats. Mrs. Lambert was much taken with the poets of World War I and put us onto Wilfred Owen and Siegfried Sassoon. In fever, I found Housman's *A Shropshire Lad* in my mother's bookcase and, without ever intending to, memorized most of it. After that, I fell upon Hopkins as upon a box of chocolates.

At Radcliffe, in Theodore Spencer's class, we again wrote out a poem a week from memory. On the side, I began to take in poems that especially pleased or devilled me—Yeats, Auden, Eliot, MacNeice—antidotes to the early large doses of Longfellow and Poe and James Whitcomb Riley. Sunny afternoons in the spring, on the roof of Cabot Hall, some of us combined sunbathing with reading poetry aloud, a dual sensuality I am no longer up to, wanting even the least sweaty poems in a cool, dry place.

There were no women role models at Radcliffe in the forties, no spinsters or matrons exhorting us to go forward. By 1943, thanks to wartime austerities, classes were no longer taught twice, once in Harvard Yard, once in the Radcliffe Quadrangle. Not that we were no longer deemed so distracting that we should be isolated, but that the male-professor-power could not be spared. My favorite professors were of course all male—there were no others, except for Maud Cam.

The three I liked best were all foreign, either from birth or at one remove: shy Michael Karpovich, who had served in the short-lived Kerensky government; Elliot Perkins, who exactly satisfied my image of an Oxford don; and most wonderful of all, Albert Guerard. In my freshman year, Guerard, then a young instructor lecturing in the survey-of-English-literature course, struck me as eloquent, witty, and urbane. He chain-smoked, which was then a delicious habit, he had read everything from *Piers Plowman* to T. S. Eliot, and he did not condescend to his students. Five years later, I was privileged to be a member of his graduate seminar in Conrad and Gide.

"There was a man so poor / he fell in love with jail," a line I cannot attribute. Something quoted by Camus? Still, it says precisely how we adapted to this curious world of letters. Women poets were for the most part three-name ladies who wrote Victorian verselets about God and butterflies. Knowing no other world outside these confines, we accepted as givens the awful sexist compliments of that era. *You write like a man. You drive like a man.* Sylvia Plath typed Ted Hughes's poems for submission along with her own; obviously, men don't type. I can even blushingly remember a lover who used to say to me, only half-teasingly, "You're okay, for a girl," though I didn't type for him.

In the late fifties, when I began to publish poems in the littlest of the little magazines, then gradually in literary quarterlies of larger circulation, and finally in the prestigious pages of *Harper's, The Atlantic, Saturday Review, The New Yorker,* I had an editor (male) say to me more than once, "I really liked this poem, I wish I could have taken it, but I printed a woman just last month." As if we were some rare species of flightless bird to be sighted on special occasions. How dangerous we must have seemed, then! Undependable, hysterical; in short, female. And how tacky and sad this story feels to me now, looking back on it.

I remember my second daughter, age three, covering a picture of a merry-go-round horse lost from the carrousel, saying, "Don't read that page. It's too poor." An emotion I share. In the early sixties, the published women poets could still be counted on the fingers of two hands.

Sometimes on college campuses or at academic or arts symposia I meet poised, cheerful professional women who assure me that the women's movement is irrelevant now. They're terribly wrong, of course, but in a sneaky way I cherish the smug rectitude of their position. I admire their style, their briefcases, their credentials, the insouciance with which they cross a room, take up an embattled position in an argument, order wine in a restaurant, and make sure that the company's secretaries are not only referred to as staff people but are given equal opportunity to rise from the ranks along with the senior executive's nephew.

My daughters, both of whom attended Harvard during an era of co-ed dormitories, unisex bathrooms, absent parietals, and the bombing of Cambodia, have chosen more worldly careers than their mother. Perhaps growing up in a house full of intemperate poems and crumpled rejection slips, uncollated manuscripts and round-robin workshops had something to do with their choices. "Company?" they'd ask, seeing the glasses set out on the sideboard, the whiskey bottles and coffeepot brought to the table. "Company? Who's coming?" And, on being told, a chorus of groans: "The poets! Oh God! Now we'll never get any sleep."

But watching their yeasty comings of age, the long pull they endured to get their law and jurisprudence degrees, the noblesse oblige they exhibit in their public positions, I realize that they have, paradoxically, been models for me in my middle years. Who is mothering whom?

A jocular professor in an outstanding graduate program asked a woman Ph.D. candidate, "Are you ready for your oral exam? Good. First, take off all your clothes," only to be coolly advised: "Not only is that completely unfunny, Dr. X, but it's certifiable as moral turpitude."

Thirty years ago, could I have said that?

And yet, I confess it, each of these daughters has taken me aside to say that the women's movement is too narrow, does not address the global issues. Hunger. Survival. The absence of hope in refugee camps everywhere.

Zero population!

Nuclear freeze!

Humane resettlement policies, immediate distribution of surplus foods; put that in your poetry, they are saying. Get with it, Ma. Write about the Love Canal, the challenge to safe abortion, food stamp cutbacks. Clitoridectomies. Poseidon submarines.

"'The great Overdog,'" says one, "'that heavenly beast / with a star in one eye, / gives a leap in the east.' Remember that one, Ma? Remember when you used to write out poems on the breakfast-room wall for us to memorize? How we couldn't have dessert unless we knew the poem?"

Now *that* is a canard. The poems were chalked on the wall, all right, and changed fortnightly. They were to be absorbed osmotically, without any discussion. The Freudians have a term for this misremembered anecdote.

"'Loveliest of trees, the cherry now,'" says the other, dreamily, before I can defend myself, "'is hung with bloom along the bough.' That was the one I liked best," then looks at her watch. She's late for a meeting, she's off in her running shoes, carrying her corporate high heels in a chic little box.

It's a comfort that they have poems in them, too. Poems, even imperfectly recalled, keep me company. My head is stuffed full of bits of poems from many periods and persuasions, and I am glad of it. In an age when creative non-violence must stare down the nuclear first-strike fanatics, many of us may well go to jail for our convictions. Whatever the setting, poems are furniture in the mind. One I mean to take along with me is Marianne Moore's "In Distrust of Merits," for, as she put it:

> The world's an orphans' home. Shall
>   we never have peace without sorrow?
> without pleas of the dying for
>   help that won't come? O
> quiet form upon the dust, I cannot
> look and yet I must. . . .

The Tradition of Total Experience

WILLIAM STAFFORD

Becoming a Writer Back Then:
Some Memories of the Iowa Workshop

It must have been the fall of 1950 when my wife Dorothy and I, and our two tiny boys, rolled into Iowa City in our old green Chevy, pulling the Stafford estate in a two-wheeled trailer. Dorothy had a teaching job in the city schools, and I had a grad assistantship paying $700 a year and remission of fees. Our affluence enabled us to move into Quonset Park.

Those days, as I remember, the poetry workshop met Monday afternoons for a couple of hours. Between fifteen and twenty poets would sit around the main room in the barracks building beside the Student Union, and Paul Engle would begin a tantalizing minuet of remarks, and jugglings of multigraphed copies of student poems, and establishings of occasional insights that kept me excited and hopeful. I had to learn backgrounds that structured the Engle remarks, which often alluded to publications or rivalries that were out of my ken. I soon caught some of the sly remarks. And from the first I liked the Workshop, and throughout my two years I served easy time.

Fiction workshop had about the same format, but it was larger, and I found it less exciting: in poetry we were always within a syllable or two of something overwhelming; but in fiction there were discouraging numbers of pages elaborating a structure that—maybe, later—might come to something.

John Crowe Ransom was to visit Workshop one week, and a ludicrous thing happened. Our poems were submitted and then multigraphed in the office, and my poems for that week (Engle must have suffered from how many poems I poured into the sessions) got shaken down to two, and these for reasons of economy were pushed close together on one page. Mr.

Ransom kindly fished my page out and began an analysis with so much finesse and care that I began to realize that I was the only one present who knew that the page was supposed to be *two* poems. That afternoon the new criticism welded my poems brilliantly together, and I was too gratified, and too timid, to pull them apart.

Dee Snodgrass and his wife Lila and their little girl lived in a quonset just beyond the garbage house from ours, and I profited from Dee's guidance; from the first, he seemed to be around Kenny's or The Airliner, or wherever the main gossip was, more than I; and he enjoyed the high regard of a number of our noted visitors—I remember Whittemore, and Penn Warren, and Jarrell. Jarrell in particular I remember for one of Dee's remarks—"It's fun to have a gee whizz critic now and then, after these austere visitors." (But I remember that Jarrell said, gee whizz, my poem was a nineteenth-century poem.)

It was along about this time that Dee began a pattern that was to make a great difference in his life: he stayed up later and later, making it necessary to sleep later and later; by the time the year was over he was living at night and Lila was keeping their child quiet through the day so that Dee could sleep.

Partly through Dee, and partly just through the closeness and informality of those Workshop days, I became pretty well acquainted with insiders, people who then or later enjoyed high places in the pecking order—and there always was a pecking order. Bill Belvin was an insider, and Donald Justice (whose insights I early learned to respect) was, and James B. Hall, and Don Petersen, and Leonard Woolf. And there was a girl whose talent gained Workshop respect—she confided to me during one time when The Romantics were getting their usual demolition, "But I *like* Shelley." No one else heard her, and she throve. Later, when Penn Warren visited she was so excited that she spent her grad ass't pay for a dress to wear to class. Warren made his greatest impression on me when he glanced magisterially through several pages of poetry manuscripts and said, "I do not understand these poems." I had been studying Brooks and Warren in order to be able to understand *any* poems.

Shapiro came, and the poets had a party at the Engle place in Stone City. For Dorothy and me it was a wondrous time—those rolling hills looking just like the pictures, and the big stone barn, and the rooms full of writers. I even had a chance to ask Shapiro something that had been troubling me. He was editing *Poetry* at that time, and I was afraid that my habit of sending stacks of poems to editors might lead them to rate me by the poems they liked the least. Shapiro said, "Don't worry—we get bad poems from everyone."

Now I remember an influence that was always present at Iowa during those years, not heavily present, but continuous, and so remote now that it might be missed and thus left out of assessments that could be puzzling for the omission: many students then were veterans. They were back from a Just War. And I was a pacifist. At the gatherings, some of the zing of sociability came from that shared past, for the others. They told me my stand was all right, and Dorothy and I caught up social momentum by attending Friends Meeting, held often in the Student Union on First Day.

The student with social concerns most like mine was George Bluestone. He was very successful while at Iowa; I believe lately he has gone astray into Film. I remember that one time he sold a story to *The Atlantic,* and was holding a party to celebrate his check. When he telephoned Norm Springer to invite him, Springer said, "Oh, George, don't you know that news of your success is ruining my enjoyment of dinner?" This feeling of rivalry was all around us, partly a joke, but felt. I remember going over to the library to look at James B. Hall's thesis, a collection of short stories—I intended to try for my degree with a book. I felt frightened when I read the stories—they were so good. And other writers were in the library studying like mad; for a PhD we could use our writing for a thesis, but we had to match those fanatics in the regular English Department, on the tests. The attrition rate was high. Many writers settled for various adjustments, and no doubt for most the big inducement was thought of a strike in publishing.

During my second year my way eased by the friendship and guidance of a lucky sequence of teachers. Engle forgave me the spate of poems. Ray West was reassuringly there. And Walter Clark came in to teach and to share his great sociability. He was to read his story "The Wind and Snow of Winter" at the first meeting of the fiction workshop. When he finished, he was asked about his revisions in the story, the craft that went into it. He held still and considered and then said something like—"It's just a tale. I might have changed a few words."

Herb Wilner came over to our quonset and said Clark had consented to come over for dinner, and they didn't know whether they could adequately entertain him. Clark came, and late, late—far into the morning hours—he was telling his wonderful tales, relaxed, at home.

By the end of that second year, our family had become Iowans. We loved the place. We had packed the two-wheel trailer and tied the boys' little car on top of the load. I hurried for my orals, crossed the river, passed where Dee used to live, past the garbage house—and there was Dorothy coming to meet me, pulling the boys in their wagon: Paff, on the orals committee, an ogre, they said, who tripped up writers on their Old English, had telephoned to let Dorothy know I had made it.

With The Degree, and all that knowledge, and a box of manuscripts, we rolled west.

Having Become a Writer: Some Reflections

Why did it take so long for the world to tell me the crucial thing about writing?

Back in the graduate school, around the quonset at the University of Iowa when I was learning to write, I would hear the kids uttering all kinds of wild, imaginative wordings. Our boys were talkative, at the stage when they would try to say anything, but without really knowing how grown-ups were saying it. The language got a continuous going over.

I would come home from graduate sessions, maybe a lesson on T. S. Eliot's "Tradition and the Individual Talent," and there would be the boys, flourishing in their ignorance. Without being conscious of it at the time, I was being diverted from the normal graduate school commitment to tradition.

At supper the boys would mimic what they had heard, but put some English on it: "Have you studied your Steakspeare?" "Let's go to the University." One of them carried on an elaborate folk-legend analysis of the creation—God made the world, but "ants made His hands, and the hands made everything else. . . ."

One of them came out from his nap, stretched, and remarked: "I dreamed God is dead."

Further, some of our neighbors who were the most interesting talkers had never read T. S. Eliot or the people he quoted or the people his quotes relied on. A grad student in dentistry was one of the best talkers. With his teeth, he made a wonderful sound. Down our row lived a talented writer, but his wife was more inventive with language. The world was conspiring to teach me the lesson that is upon us now in the current literary scene: a new poem or story or novel or play can be traced back through earlier poems etc., and endless games can be played with analyses of influences from literature; but the plain truth of the matter is that any literary work must rely for its effect on bonuses and reverberations that derive from the original resonance between human beings and their total experience, not from that little special tangent that comes from the Literary Succession.

The tradition from which the individual talent diverges and from which the individual talent derives strength is much greater and more immediate than literary tradition alone. And even the literary tradition has no power because of its being literary, but only because of its being linked to wide, daily-language meanings and overtones.

At that time—and earlier, I realize now—I was being prepared to jib at the assumption artists around me had. Years later, in a quick interchange about "what writer most influenced your work?" I was compelled into a response that surprised both my questioner and myself: "My mother." And with that answer I began to accept a stance that I now fully accept.

Not the voices at the center of your cultural monuments, not the lessons learned under conditions set for you by teachers distanced from your own talk, not the whole weight of the library—but the talk around you by those near your own ways, the early conversations in your home, the relaxed interchanges with your friends—these language encounters are the most helpful, the most sustaining, the most harmonious and crucial for anyone.

We may regret our circumstances—and no doubt many of us should. We may wish our associates were more vivid and informed (and certainly my mother had limitations and odd, feisty quirks in her character). We may hold before us an ideal of a world where everyone has maximum encounters with some kind of established standard of excellence. But the way toward a fuller life in the arts must come by way of each person's daily experience. To deny that experience—even to veer from it in a minor way—is a false step.

When our family left graduate school, it was in a cocoon of our own feelings, with college life behind us and the boys excitedly talking about what was "behead of us," and our car avoiding no parking signs but aiming for "yes parking." One of the boys asked, referring to a playmate left behind in Quonset Park: "Is our sky fastened onto Donna's sky?" And I realize now that our sky was not only fastened onto Donna's sky, but onto everyone's sky.

Through the following years, writing day after day, going wherever the lines led, I have found that lesson of nearness to be lasting. You write from where you are. When Stephen Mooney of *The Tennessee Poetry Journal* asked for a statement on being regional or local, I found it easy to take a stand, in Tennessee, or Oregon, or Iowa, or wherever:

> All events and experiences are local, somewhere. And all human enhancements of events and experiences—all the arts—are regional in the sense that they derive from immediate relation to felt life.
>
> It is this immediacy that distinguishes art. And paradoxically the more local the feeling in art, the more all people can share it; for that vivid encounter with the stuff of the world is our common ground.
>
> Artists, knowing this mutual enrichment that extends everywhere, can act, and praise, and criticize, as insiders—the means of art is the life of all people. And that life grows and improves by being shared. Hence, it is good to welcome any region you live in or come to or think of, for that is where life happens to be, right where you are.

The Pursuit of Suffering

DANIEL HALPERN

Why is it that the love literature we love best is that which evokes the greatest sorrow? The whole tradition of romantic love in literature is based on this seeming paradox. From the troubadours of the eleventh century to the poets and fiction writers of the 1980's, the path of love in literature has never been smooth. It is difficult, beset by obstacles, fraught with painful emotions as well as pleasurable ones. And this literary tradition is not a mere intellectual, scholarly notion about how romantic love must be treated in poetry and fiction; rather, the tradition derives from a set of emotional priorities that exist in the human condition. Paul Valéry saw this condition clearly when he wrote:

> Passion of love secretes a fatal poison that is, at first, only faintly active, easily eliminated, and passes unnoticed. But a few trifles can quicken it so that, suddenly, it can overwhelm all our powers of reason, and our fear of men and gods. By this I mean that in becoming strongly enamored of someone, we unconsciously invest the object of our love with a power to make us suffer which far surpasses the power we grant him or her (and look for) to make us rapturously happy. And if the need to possess some one person takes such complete hold of us as to form the condition of life itself (which is the way absolute love works), this now-vital affection, once it is torn by despair, sets little store by life. It familiarly entertains the idea of murder. This soon mingles with the idea of suicide; which is absurd, thus natural.

C. S. Lewis says that "French poets in the eleventh century discovered or invented or were the first to express that romantic species of passion which English poets were still writing about in the nineteenth." Of this passage Maurice Valency, in his book *In Praise of Love,* writes, "Formulations of this sort are perhaps unduly stimulating. What is meant is simply that the system of love poetry developed by the troubadours of the eleventh century differs in certain important aspects from those amatory patterns which we find reflected in the literature of antiquity. Unquestionably this is true." Whether love as a poetic mode was "discovered" in the eleventh century by the troubadours, or by classical poets such as Ovid, Sappho, Catullus, and Horace, who certainly understood the vicissitudes of romantic love, is a question for scholars interested in defining tradition and style. Most of us will agree that love does exist, in one form or another, from time to time in our lives, and this has always been true regardless of literary styles or fashions.

Perhaps it is not surprising that during this period of unsurpassed woman-worship in the poetry of medieval poets, a paradoxical countermovement of misogyny flourished. Petrarch, who swore by the every movement of his Laura, was a self-professed woman-hater. It seems to me that our current literature is troubled by the same ambivalence toward women as was present in the attitudes of the troubadours. There continues a basic, and deeply rooted, confusion of attitude, a legacy of ambivalence, toward love that finds its way into the vocabulary of romantic love in our fiction and poetry—a rhetorical vocabulary that could theoretically form a literature that addresses itself not to adoration and frustration regarding the love object, but, given a different emphasis, could easily become a celebration of respect and understanding.

The mandate for poets is always to find a new idiom—to articulate what is most private and specific, and to communicate it without making the poetry exclusive or tedious with a reliance on the literal. Part of this new idiom ought to be able to address itself to the connection between love and respect. It is noble to believe that the characters of fiction and poetry respect those they believe they love, but this is not necessarily the case. Montherlant addresses himself to this:

> The need to respect the object of desire . . . is doubtless one of man's most noble needs. It is not a natural phenomenon. There is no natural connection between, on the one hand, desiring and possessing, and on the other bestowing, not love in the modern sense of romantic passion, but that fundamental approval, based on respect, which is worthy of the name of friendship.

From the point of view of traditional romantic love, the tension between men and women, which has always existed, is not altogether negative; in fact, it is often assumed that this conflict is necessary to maintain the passion in our romantic literature. We might begin now to understand and agree with de Rougemont's passion-therefore-suffering theory. He points out in *Love in the Western World* that "we have no history of happy love, and romance can thrive only in a situation where love is fatal, illicit, and doomed by life itself." He contends that "what stirs lyrical poets to their finest flights is neither the delight of the senses nor the fruitful contentment of the settled couple; not the satisfaction of love, but its passion. And passion means suffering." In developing his thesis he comes to understand that when we find ourselves in a difficult love relationship, we are not aware of the suffering that passion puts forth, but only that the relationship is thrilling. He goes on to say that passionate love, given its reliance on the illicit, is a misfortune—adultery, or the Tristan and Iseult myth, being the prototype.

Dante, according to Eliot, believed that poetry not only must be found through suffering but can find its material only in suffering. In the same essay, Eliot writes that Shelley believed that our sweetest songs are those composed of the very saddest thought.

However, in this state of suffering and passion a heightened consciousness or awareness of the external world is often achieved. At the end of Alberto Moravia's novel *The Empty Canvas* the central character, after attempting to kill himself because he cannot possess the young girl he has fallen in love with, suddenly sees, suddenly *senses*, the tree outside his window—and therefore the physical world—for the first time. The irony is that what normally comes to life in the external world is everything but the realistic perception of the lover. It is a heightened awareness of the world that is addressed, and the paradoxical emergence of the real in the midst of fantasy.

The obvious question raised here is of the veracity and depth of emotion in a relationship described as passionate, especially since we associate passion with the fleeting, the transitory, and much in romantic relationships appears to be in the service of the imagination. We can ask, Do the lovers respect each other, can they allow themselves to know each other? In romantic love each loves the other from his or her own standpoint. Therefore, if it is to last, they need to invent a *love,* a *text,* something objective and neutral. Only what preserves the illusion of the Other can be entertained by the lovers; they will never heed Ovid's warning: "As for the act of love—keep passion away altogether." This is not to suggest that all relationships established in the literature of romantic love are slight and without depth; simply, they are often romanticized, and therefore inevitably falsified, versions of the way things are.

Narcissism plays a part in romantic literature. As a way of discussing it, let us imagine a poem in which a man sees his loved one as a body of water he can look into. We can see how she becomes a handy vehicle for the transportation and screening, in the cinematic sense, of the self. She is a necessary agent, a mirror who presents him with himself—she in effect takes what is seductive about him—and to him—and gives it back. What is given back is the self.

Established here is a kind of sexual or romantic narcissism. It is the projected self the self falls for, the projected image passion attaches itself to—and in so doing, sets up for itself the possibilities of suffering.

Here the self of the *lover,* as distinguished from the *loved one,* becomes the obstacle that passion requires to survive. Not only is it necessary that the self be identified and recognized in the loved one, but it allows the lover to redefine and in many ways overlook the loved one, because the former is effectively standing in front of the latter.

In regard to language it has been pointed out by numerous love-philosophers that there is a considerable discrepancy between the language we use when in love and the language we use when we're not. Roland Barthes suggests this might be because in love we use a language addressed to ourselves and to the person we imagine and usually believe we love. What results is a language of solitude. This too the writer inherits.

In the poem of sexual narcissism, the loved one, or Other, is negated, cannot be *present,* and the self of the lover seduces itself. The woman is the man's reflection in the above hypothetical poem, the water that is looked into. In the literature of self-regard, the self is the only obstacle. Jung has an interesting discussion of narcissism and sentimentality in art in his essay "On the Relation of Analytical Psychology to Poetry." He writes: "The psychologist would call "sentimental" art *introverted.* The introverted attitude is characterized by the subject's assertion of his conscious intentions and aims against the demands of the object." Such sexual narcissism, in some ways, represents the romantic fringe, an extension of romantic love—or, from another perspective, romantic love at its very purest, and most obvious.

The aim of romantic love is to preserve and heighten passion and intensity of feeling, and this is accomplished at the expense of reality, the "real" identity of the other. The object of passion is the emblem of emotion, but the lover as symbol surrenders his or her independent human integrity.

Objectivity and perspective are not things people in the throes of passion are eager to experience; in fact, the very idea of perspective would, by definition, minimize the intensity of the passionate experience, if you subscribe to the theory that passion means suffering, something undergone, the mastery of fate over a free and responsible person.

It is certain that poems of unhappy love are by far the majority. I've picked

poems of this kind, within the tradition of romantic love poetry, capable
of transforming the personal love situation, using the emotional event of
the poem to elicit a parallel (even if imaginary) pathetic event in the
reader. Good love poems manipulate memory, they place us back in time,
they make us recall and reestablish momentarily such feelings of love that
were operative in that privileged moment outside of time, with all the
attendant dangers, agonies, narrow escapes, and joys. The following is a
poem by Cummings in which the narrator appears willing to place himself
in the position of giving his love and total happiness over to another, in
effect turning the other cheek so that he suddenly finds himself far away in
the land of disenchantment.

> it may not always be so; and i say
> that if your lips, which i have loved, should touch
> another's, and your dear strong fingers clutch
> his heart, as mine in time not far away;
> if on another's face your sweet hair lay
> in such a silence as i know, or such
> great writhing words as, uttering overmuch,
> stand helplessly before the spirit at bay;
>
> if this should be, i say if this should be—
> you of my heart, send me a little word;
> that i may go unto him, and take his hands,
> saying, Accept all happiness from me.
> Then shall i turn my face, and hear one bird
> sing terribly afar in the lost lands.

In this poem bitterness is transformed into a Christian unwillingness to
become embittered—the loved one is imagined to have found another,
and the suffering narrator wants to congratulate him, to present him with
"his happiness," before he turns to hear the terrible song of the distant
bird, when he faces his loss alone. But it is very likely that he can allow
himself this generous act only because it is an imagined event—she has,
after all, not yet found someone else. One might question the validity of
the narrator's perception of, and his need for, his loved one—the complex
configuration behind his acceptance, on one level, of the possibility of her
falling in love with another. How easily he congratulates that Other, how
easily she is given over. So much for passionate love.

I would suggest that however moving and lovely the Cummings poem
is, it participates in the sentimental, sentimentality being symptomatic of
romantic love, as well as one of the most overworked words in the vocabulary of literary criticism. There are various ways of thinking about senti-

mentality. J. D. Salinger says it's "giving to a thing more tenderness than God gives to it." That's catchy but it doesn't help us much in thinking about sentimentality. The clearest statement I know is in I. A. Richards' essay called "Sentimentality and Inhibition": "A person may be said to be sentimental when his emotions are too easily stirred. A response is senti-mental if it is too great for the occasion, [or] if it is inappropriate to the situation that calls it forth." The emotion and suffering in the Cummings poem finally have nothing to do with the loved one; they are in excess of the imagined scene. In this sense the poem can be considered sentimental. The narrator is concerned with the fascination and subsequent seduction of—and finally betrayal by—the self. Betrayal because the demands of the self lead the narrator to suffer what hasn't occurred. This partakes of ro-mantic narcissism, the notion of the self as loved object married to a dis-torted idea of the loved one. Of course, it could be said that what we call sentimental in art is sometimes called neurotic in life.

Cummings' poem is about potential unhappy love, the loss of love. If it is moving, is this because we as sympathetic readers are ready, even eager, to be moved by the possibility of loss and ourselves participate in the sentimental? Aren't we very often ready to react emotionally to a "pathetic situation," a situation not personalized and therefore abstract? "These re-actions," writes Richards, "are certainly sentimental on the part of the reader." Perhaps it is loss, or misalliance, that we secretly desire, and re-main, as Cummings demonstrates here, ever ready to invent. We must remember (for Tristan) that to possess her is to lose her—to lose every-thing. "When love no longer fights, then it has ceased," writes Kier-kegaard.

In this next poem, "A Letter," by Anthony Hecht, the narrator has in fact lost her.

> I have been wondering
> What you are thinking about, and by now suppose
> It is certainly not me.
> But the crocus is up, and the lark, and the blundering
> Blood knows what it knows.
> It talks to itself all night, like a sliding moonlit sea.
>
> Of course, it is talking of you.
> At dawn, where the ocean has netted its catch of lights,
> The sun plants one lithe foot
> On that spill of mirrors, but the blood goes worming through
> Its warm Arabian nights,
> Naming your pounding name again in the dark heart-root.
>
> Who shall, of course, be nameless.

Anyway, I should want you to know I have done my best,
    As I'm sure you have, too.
Others are bound to us, the gentle and blameless
    Whose names are not confessed
In the ceaseless palaver. My dearest, the clear unquarried blue

    Of those depths is all but blinding.
You may remember that once you brought my boys
    Two little woolly birds.
Yesterday the older one asked for you upon finding
    Your thrush among his toys.
And the tides welled about me, and I could find no words.

    There is not much else to tell.
One tries one's best to continue as before,
    Doing some little good.
But I would have you know that all is not well
    With a man dead set to ignore
The endless repetitions of his own murmurous blood.

This is a poem in which the sadness is fully realized and articulated—the woman is gone but the poet treats her with great delicacy and reverence, which is immediately evident from the phrasing, the resignation in the voice, in the opening: "I have been wondering / What you are thinking about, and by now suppose / It is certainly not me." He is even protective of her: "Naming your pounding name again in the dark heart-root. / Who shall, of course, be nameless."

It is a poem with as much sentiment as the Cummings poem, but it is not constrained by an imagined event. The loss seems actually to have occurred; he addresses himself directly to the pain he is experiencing. In both poems the last lines make clear the emotion of loss. The Cummings poem ends: "Then shall i turn my face, and hear one bird / sing terribly afar in the lost lands." Consider how much more convincing the Hecht poem is for all its directness and lack of artifice: "But I would have you know that all is not well / With a man dead set to ignore / The endless repetitions of his own murmurous blood." In tone, construction, and phrasing, the Hecht lines seem to me exemplary. They imply a sort of internal betrayal, a murder perpetrated by his own blood and pulse.

Another poem of loss is "From a Survivor" by Adrienne Rich:

    The pact that we made was the ordinary pact
    of men & women in those days

    I don't know who we thought we were
    that our personalities
    could resist the failures of the race

Lucky or unlucky, we didn't know
the race had failures of that order
and that we were going to share them

Like everybody else, we thought of ourselves as special

Your body is as vivid to me
as it ever was: even more

since my feeling for it is clearer:
I know what it could and could not do

it is no longer
the body of a god
or anything with power over my life

Next year it would have been 20 years
and you are wastefully dead
who might have made the leap
we talked, too late, of making

which I live now
not as a leap
but a succession of brief, amazing movements

each one making possible the next

The poet is, in the very act of the poem, reconstructing herself, making it, through her strength and control, slowly back into life—a blossoming of movements, first one, then the next. Rich's poem is, compared to the Hecht and Cummings poems, harder, more insightful, and ultimately the most instructive. While Cummings out of happiness projects the end, and Hecht agonizes for both of them over their loss, Rich operates outside of sentimentality, places the man of *that ordinary pact* in time and continues to live—if not in the leap, in the succession of amazing movements forward. I have ordered these three poems so that the creation of obstacles by the self happens to a progressively lesser degree, so that the self, in the Rich poem, finally gives way to the realistic exterior world.

We can like, and be moved by, all three of these poems. A question that I've already raised is, why do we get such pleasure, as in the Hecht and Cummings poems, from so much sadness? Why do sad situations carry so much more weight and meaning than states of contentment and happiness and so define things more poignantly? Graham Greene writes: "The sense of unhappiness is much easier to convey than that of happiness. In misery we seem aware of our own existence, even though it may be in the form of a monstrous egotism. But happiness annihilates us; we love our identity." We empathize with difficult love and in so doing unburden our psyches. There is something appealing about sharing the poet's loss, especially since it is vicarious and carries the pale odor of nostalgia; that is, it recalls a time when we felt emotionally engaged—a moment when loss was clearly registered. In the Cummings poem it is the imagined threat of losing the loved one. In Hecht's poem it is the loved one's actual departure, and in Rich's poem it is the refusal to mourn and the subsequent transcendence over loss, the ultimate obstruction that finally dooms all love. In the first two poems, romantic love is clearly in evidence; the third poem, though a poem of loss, rejects the narcissistic principle I've been discussing. Rich takes what might be called a practical (or a pragmatically enlightened) stance; and, as the title informs us, it is from a survivor in the active sense of that word. She is not interested in maintaining or extending or luxuriating in the memory of the loved one who might have participated in Rich's more gradual progression into understanding. He is remembered, almost coldly, in the bitter objectivity of those stark lines that open the poem—there is no romanticism here. This is not meant judgmentally. These opening lines, because they are unwilling to surrender *the other* as he was, are powerful in their refusal of pathos, and in this refusal create a sense of sadness, of real mourning.

Perhaps writing happy love poems is more problematic. The vocabulary of sadness seems richer than that of happiness. Even poems that advertise an extreme of happiness, that exist without a realized misery, are very often tinged with the idea that to love, passionately so, is to suffer, passionately—thus the bittersweet poem of love that is about to suffer. As love poems get happier, the verse often gets lighter. Of course we do have numerous happy love poems in the language, not to mention songs of love, if lyrics count, such as these by Howard and Windsor that Mabel Mercer sings: "Though you're not my first love, baby, / you will be the first to last." And then there is Elizabeth Barrett Browning's memorable "How do I love thee? Let me count the ways." Perhaps the true narcissist would reply, "One, myself, two, myself," and so on. Once you begin the ebullient, numerous lines spring to mind. Irwin Shaw wrote, "Every time I make love with you I forget one more bad thing that happened in my life." Durrell in *Justine* writes, "A city becomes a world when one loves one of its inhabitants." And Kierkegaard, in a classic of romantic love, *Diary of a Seducer*, says, "Outside the door stands a little carriage which to me is large enough for the whole world, since it is large enough for two."

One could argue that the poems of happy love have had less impact than the tradition of sad poems, poems that prevent the celebration of contentment and continuity. This is not to say that there are no memorable happy love poems—certainly Shakespeare's comedies and Elizabethan love lyrics are sacred. But we want Orpheus and Eurydice, Tristan and Iseult, Romeo and Juliet, Abelard and Heloise, Daphnis and Chloe. Frustrated love must be more interesting. Tolstoy opens *Anna Karenina* with: "All happy families are like one another; each unhappy family is unhappy in its own way." *The Good Soldier* begins with the sentence: "This is the saddest story I have ever heard." We are apprised right off—and as readers, are we not a little excited by the prospects of misery?

We more readily share the lot of the betrayed, of Rich and Hecht and even Cummings in his fantasy. We are most tempted by those love relationsips in literature that opt for unhappiness because that is an easier emotion to evoke—one need only create an obstacle. To dramatize a state of contentment within the context of happy love is a baffling task. The plot of happiness certainly engages us less, and certainly does not evoke a state of happiness in the way that unhappiness evokes a sympathetic feeling. If we share the elation of the happy lover, we take little away with us.

If we hear a happy love poem, we don't participate much in the happy event the poet experiences; on the contrary, we are reminded, through personal experience, of how transitory and vulnerable states of happiness are. It's worth remembering Marvell's "The Definition of Love," which plays on the Platonic definition of love as a longing that is unfulfilled. It starts out:

> My love is of a birth as rare
> As 'tis, for object, strange and high;
> It was begotten by Despair
> Upon Impossibility.

Happiness can seem to have a smugness about it, an exclusiveness and independence that undermines our ability to identify, while misery, on the other hand, loves company. Misery creates tension, and tension can be quickly established. In *Leisure, The Basis of Culture,* Josef Pieper writes, "A state of extreme tension is more easily induced than a state of relaxation and ease although the latter is effortless." This speaks to contented love and difficult love—the relaxed and the tense.

In Louise Bogan's "Song for the Last Act," the loved one is absent and only his *presence,* which has been memorized, survives. This seems the logical place for love to move and re-pitch its tent—now that the person is gone, the memory of him can be memorialized and thrive in the imagination forever. The poem allows the images to accrue into a celebratory and elegiac tone.

Now that I have your face by heart, I look
Less at its features than its darkening frame
Where quince and melon, yellow as young flame,
Lie with quilled dahlias and the shepherd's crook.
Beyond, a garden. There, in insolent ease
The lead and marble figures watch the show
Of yet another summer loath to go
Although the scythes hang in the apple trees.

Now that I have your face by heart, I look

Now that I have your voice by heart, I read
In the black chords upon a dulling page
Music that is not meant for music's cage,
Whose emblems mix with words that shake and bleed.
The staves are shuttled over with a stark
Unprinted silence. In a double dream
I must spell out the storm, the running stream.
The beat's too swift. The notes shift in the dark.

Now that I have your voice by heart, I read.

Now that I have your heart by heart, I see
The wharves with their great ships and architraves;
The rigging and the cargo and the slaves
On a strange beach under a broken sky.
O not departure, but a voyage done!
The bales stand on the stone; the anchor weeps
Its red rust downward, and the long vine creeps
Beside the salt herb, in the lengthening sun.

Now that I have your heart by heart, I see.

In Bogan's poem the narrator has the Other by heart; that this memory might have little to do with the person as he was, which is now at least once removed by the passage of time, is irrelevant. How different this is from Rich's memory. For Bogan death functions as a final *romantic* obstacle. It brings us back to the idea of the negation of the loved one in order to maintain the romantic stance. In this poem the memory is frozen, fixed, and offers little chance of alteration.

This is something we've come to expect in most of our romantic literature; it is in the interest of the various characters in fiction as well as in poems to refuse knowledge of each other in order to maintain their romantic relationship as well as keep the obstacles operative. In D. H. Lawrence's *The First Lady Chatterley,* Constance half-heartedly attempts to understand Parkin, the gamekeeper, for who he is. In this passage she is addressing him: "I can't live with you. And I couldn't live with him if he had thoughts about you . . ." Parkin's prospects at this point in the novel

are not looking up. He is damned to the illicit and secretive. The passage
continues in the great tradition of approach-avoidance: "He was silent for
what seemed a long time. 'Yer wouldn't fret, like, if yer went away somewhere an' niver seed me again?' he asked. She glanced up at him and saw
the pondering eyes. 'I should mind,' she said, 'but what else could I do?'"
There is only one answer.

In Elizabeth Bowen's *The House in Paris* Karen has little sense of Max.
In fact, when he commits suicide after their assignations, she is as sur-
prised as we are—we having seen Max through her eyes. In the passage
I've chosen, Karen is speaking:

> We have been people darting across the sea to each other; there has been no
> time yet to be anything else. There has been no time to feel anything but com-
> pulsion. If I had known you loved me I would not have dared come. That
> goodbye in the train only happened because those people jammed us face to
> face. When you touched my hand, I knew one kind of meeting was possible, but
> I still thought you loved Naomi. When you were asleep last night, I thought
> you should be beside her. I didn't ask what I felt; I wanted *not* to know.

In this conversation the obstacle, a fiancé, is addressed, acknowledged,
suffered for, then ignored. After this little speech by Karen, Max asks,
"Would you marry me?" And Karen answers, true to form: "You said that
was not possible: after that I never let myself think." Which means of
course that it is not too late for her to reconsider, now that she has almost
been asked—almost because Max said *would*, not *will*.

The narrator in Benjamin Constant's novel *Adolphe* writes: "I was distressed when she seemed to question the love which was so necessary to
her; I was no less distressed when she seemed to believe in it. It is a fearful
misfortune not to be loved when you love; but it is a much greater misfortune to be loved passionately when you love no longer." It would seem
that nothing is going to satisfy this character. Imbalance must at all costs
be maintained.

I said earlier that the mandate for poets is always to find a new idiom, to
articulate what is private and communicate it without making an exclusive
poetry. Most of the above discussion deals with relationships established
and held in a frenzy where very little mutual knowledge between people is
involved—both in our literature and, because art imitates life, in the relationships we make before the fact of literature.

"False lovers deserve false love," wrote Montanhagol in the thirteenth
century. And Andreas Capellanus said:

> Oh, what a wonderful thing is love, which makes a man shine with so many

virtues and which teaches everyone, no matter who he is, so many good traits of character! There is another thing about love which we should not praise in a few words: it adorns a man, so to speak, with the virtue of chastity, because he who shines with the light of one love can hardly think of embracing another woman, even a beautiful one. For when he thinks deeply of his beloved, the sight of any other woman seems to him rude and rough.

Perhaps true and contented love is possible, perhaps unlike beauty in the mind it need not be momentary.

But the momentary appears to be what we want, at least for the moment—the "perpetual moment," the "suspended moment." There's even a tense for it in the English language: the imperfect. The happy ending is a wonderful device in our literature, but no matter how far into the sunset the lovers ride, the sun eventually goes down.

Politics and the Mode of Fiction: A Conversation with E. L. Doctorow

The following interview took place in Philadelphia and New Rochelle in the autumn of 1981. The interviewer is Richard Trenner.

INTERVIEWER: I'd like to talk with you about your political beliefs and activities, both because they interest me and because I think they deeply inform your writing. I see in your work an explicit political rhetoric and an insistent concern with how political and social forces help shape the lives of your characters.

A timely way into this subject might be your recent testimony before a subcommittee of the House Appropriations Committee. As I understand it, P.E.N. asked you to testify against the cuts the Reagan Administration planned for the budget of the National Endowment for the Arts. Your testimony—and the testimony of other advocates of federal funding for the arts—very likely kept the cuts from being as drastic as the President would have liked. And your remarks received a lot of publicity. You spoke memorably and forcefully *for* public support for individual artists and *against* the vast increases in military spending Reagan successfully sought. I think of the almost passionate language and the self-acknowledged sense of futility of your going to Washington to testify. Let me quote just the final two paragraphs. They are fine and strong, and they lead to my first question, which concerns the forms a writer's engagement in the work of political and social change can or should take.

. . . I cannot avoid the feeling that it is senseless for me to testify here today. People everywhere have been put in the position of fighting piecemeal for this or that program while the assault against all of them proceeds across a broad front. The truth is, if you're going to take away the lunches of schoolchildren, the pensions of miners who've contracted black lung, the storefront legal services of the poor who are otherwise stunned into insensibility by the magnitude of their troubles, you might as well get rid of poets, artists, and musicians. If you're planning to scrap medical care for the indigent, scholarships for students, day-care centers for the children of working mothers, transportation for the elderly and handicapped—if you're going to eliminate people's public service training jobs and then reduce their unemployment benefits after you've put them on the unemployment rolls, taking away their food stamps in the bargain, then I say the loss of a few poems or arias cannot matter. If you're going to close down the mental therapy centers for the veterans of Vietnam, what does it matter if our theaters go dark or our libraries close their doors?

And so in my testimony for this small social program I am aware of the larger picture and, really, it stuns me. What I see in this picture is a kind of sovietizing of American life, guns before butter, the plating of this nation with armaments, the sacrifice of everything in our search for ultimate security. We shall become an immense armory. But inside this armory there will be nothing, not a people but an emptiness; we shall be an armory around nothingness, and our true strength and security and the envy of the world—the passion and independent striving of a busy working and dreaming population committed to fair play and the struggle for some sort of real justice and community—will be no more. If this happens, maybe in the vast repository of bombs, deep in the subterranean chambers of our missile fields, someone in that cavernous silence will remember a poem and recite it. Maybe some young soldier will hum a tune, maybe another will be able to speak the language well enough to tell a story, maybe two people will get up and dance to the rhythm of the doomsday clock ticking us all to extinction.

My first question is: What *should* a writer do who wants to be politically effective in these days of growing militarism and social divisiveness throughout the United States and other parts of the world?

DOCTOROW: That is a question that you struggle with every day. It's an infernal question—the degree of engagement. We're all pretty well educated in the dangers to one's writing of ideological piety, of a fixed political position. Every writer knows how dangerous it can be in terms of doing something good. But I'm rethinking the whole thing. In view of the emergency—I think that it *is* an emergency—is some kind of new aesthetic possible that does not undermine aesthetic rigor? A poetics of engagement.

INTERVIEWER: I'm not sure why you can't have a very powerful political work that is also aesthetically excellent.

DOCTOROW: You can. But it would usually end up acknowledging, by its very nature, the ambiguities of what it's talking about. The works that have been destroyed by ideological commitment are, by and large, obscure today, like a lot of the novels of the thirties. Political sentimentality is as bad as any other kind.

The failure arises from diction. What very often happens is that the novelist or the poet assumes the diction of politics, which, by its very nature, tends to be incapable of illumination. If you use political diction, you're not reformulating anything. You're telling people what they already know. Your rationale is your own language, and the danger of explicit politics in a book is in giving that up.

INTERVIEWER: Yes, but I see *The Book of Daniel,* for instance, as more than a political book. It's a deeper book, not only in its subject matter but in the sense of the characters' dire spiritual and psychological predicaments. The rhetoric of the novel is political, and yet it's certainly not the sort of sterile and deceptive language that you see in straight political writing. So maybe you have already managed to combine something that is aesthetically good with a strong political statement.

DOCTOROW: Maybe so. But one has to invent each time a way to do that. For instance, when I was in Peru recently, someone asked me an extraordinary question at a lecture I gave. All the questions had been very literary—informed, thoughtful. There were writers there, and academics. It was a civilized audience with elegant manners. And this guy piped up and said, "When are you going to write about the neutron bomb?" Everyone was embarrassed. But it was a good question. "I've been writing about the neutron bomb all my life," I told him. And in one way I have. But what he was talking about was, What are you going to do *now*? How can you feel (and I don't, of course) that anyone's written anything since it's still there? It's your bomb! When are you going to write about it?
  I've been thinking about the question ever since it was asked. It's the only one of the evening I remember.

INTERVIEWER: Isn't the novel insufficiently active and direct for the kind of threat that the neutron bomb represents? Maybe what's called for is a lot more direct political action, or at least more direct rhetoric.

DOCTOROW: I don't know what's called for. I think it was Robert Jay Lifton who discovered that anyone who talks about nuclear bombs has twenty minutes. You can talk about these things for twenty minutes before people numb out. I don't know if it's even *that* long.

INTERVIEWER: On the other hand, what is the alternative to writing about the neutron bomb—about the ever more dominant militarism of our time? What more important subject is there right now?

DOCTOROW: Let me talk about this from the inside of the novelist's mind. In here it's not a subject at all, not to be formulated in moral or ethical terms. In here, as I think about it, the bomb loses its political character entirely. The unsettling experience in writing fiction now may be in finding that the story of any given individual, and I don't care who it is, may not be able to sustain an implication for the collective fate. There's a loss of consequence, that's what I mean. The assumption that makes fiction possible, even Modernist fiction—the moral immensity of the single soul—is under question because of the bomb. To write fiction now as it has been written may be to misperceive or avoid the overriding condition of things, which is that we're in the countdown stages of a post-humanist society. On the other hand, if that's true, I wouldn't mean to imply that the problems of writers of fiction aren't the least of our problems.

INTERVIEWER: Have you been politically active outside of your writing? Or have you used your writing as the main way in which you respond to hard political and social facts?

DOCTOROW: I have generally stayed away from any kind of consistent political activity. I have given benefit readings. I have given my name to various groups and ad hoc committees and causes of one kind or another—peace, trade unionism, civil liberties, getting foreign writers out of prison, and so on. They are all quite specific. And I don't go out and look for them. They are available to me all the time. I'm actually quite selfish. I do relatively little. Going down to Washington to testify on behalf of the National Endowment is, I suppose, an example of direct political action. Or testifying for P.E.N. on the issue of conglomeration in the book industry—the heavy commerce that is coming into the book industry, the effect of that in First Amendment terms. But I'm not a well-organized person and I don't write efficiently. I need a great deal of time in order to get my day's work done—which is a very small number of words—probably between five and six hundred words a day. I have to give myself six or seven hours. It might all happen in fifteen minutes, but not until the end of the sixth hour. You never know. So I'm always very conflicted about doing public things. Sometimes this shows up as bad spirit, a reluctance to be interviewed. Or I will feel I have made a mistake and that in this particular situation I'm being exploited. Or I will think that what I am doing is quixotic and of no real value or consequence at all. I was very much for that writers' congress held recently in New York and lent my name from the beginning to promote and publicize it, but I participated rather marginally on one panel, and then with great reluctance. I'm personally disposed to privacy and a low profile and constantly have to deal with issues of publicity as if I've never dealt with them before. I always feel ill-equipped when someone calls up and says, "Will you do this? Will you speak? Will you give an interview?" I don't learn. It's as if I've never had an experience of this sort before. I can never really adjust to it or think of myself as a forum for any social ideas that I have.

INTERVIEWER: I must say, your interview with Paul Levine [in *E. L. Doctorow: Essays & Conversations,* ed. Richard Trenner] has a clear and useful political content. You talk at length about your political views and your sense of history. So sometimes giving an interview works. It's just very hard to predict when one will.

DOCTOROW: I always have the feeling that my mind has no distinction, except possibly in the book I'm writing. In other words, whatever I have to offer only emerges or is realized through the act of writing. My political opinions are quite ordinary. Fiction is really a different mode, an illuminated way of thinking. And every time I give an interview or write or deliver a speech or do anything like that outside of my work, I think I'm hurting myself. I'm not being in myself, I'm being out of myself. And this shows up in the conflicted feelings I have. It's so easy to become an expert in this country. There's such a sucking thirst for expertise and authority. So if you sit down and think for a couple of days and write something about the National Endowment, then you get dozens of requests because you're an expert, you're a voice of authority on money to artists. But whatever you knew, you've said. And you've only been able to say it because you could sit quietly in your room and work it out.

INTERVIEWER: I appreciate that your truest work, politically, is as a writer. I believe that. I've seen it in your books.

DOCTOROW: And yet, if you asked me, "What *are* your politics?"—I'd have a tough time.

INTERVIEWER: Well, let's start with the obvious. You're on the left.

DOCTOROW: I would say I'm a leftist. But of the pragmatic, social-democratic left—the humanist left that's wary of ideological fervor. It's a very exhausting place to be. I think the clear, definitive ideologies have all discredited themselves by their adherents.

INTERVIEWER: What is the genealogy of your politics? Are your political values largely the result of personal experience, or what you've seen in the streets, or of your reading over the years? A combination of all three?

DOCTOROW: Victor Navasky wrote about me that I have a kind of primitive politics, almost a primitive sense of what's fair and what's not fair, what justice is and what injustice is. There's something true about that. So to go on to answer your question, in one sense I don't think of my ideas as political because they're so basic, the perceptions so fundamental and indisputable—like the most glaring sort of prophecy. It's at the level of, "Don't do this. This is wrong. God is going to punish you." It's that simple-minded. All the analysis is built on it: Stealing is wrong. Therefore tax laws which favor the wealthy are wrong. Murder and torture are wrong. Therefore the foreign policy which funds and supplies murderous torturing dictators is insupportable. I've been called an idealist and naive and a pseudo-Marxist. But in this country the reference has to be the Constitution; and the political analysis, Marxist or otherwise, will have to develop from just such elemental biblical perception, from what we are in our mythic being, not from what Europe is.

INTERVIEWER: As a preface to my next question, let me tell you something about myself. I grew up in a prosperous Republican family in a prosperous Republican town, but my politics, which are not very articulate, are strongly different from the politics of most of the members of my family and the people of my hometown. Why? Difficult to say, but I like to think they are different because I've had glimpses into the lives of both the rich and the poor, and I've had a couple of years during which I was supporting myself and making a bad job of it. And I think I began to connect with what it means not to be protected and supported by money, class, and school affiliations. I wonder, what are the personal antecedents of your political philosophy, however unevolved, in a beautiful theoretical sense, that philosophy may be?

DOCTOROW: I immediately think of my grandfather and my father. Mine was not an experience like yours. I grew up in a lower-middle-class environment of generally enlightened, socialist sensibility. My grandfather was a printer, an intellectual, a chess player, an atheist, and a socialist. His was a kind of socialism that represented progress, the coming into the light from centuries of darkness. He had emigrated from Russia as a very young man. He learned the English language and read Ingersoll and Spencer and Jack London. It was a very Jewish thing, somehow. Humanist, radical, Jewish. The sense of possibility. All the solutions were to be found right here on earth, and the supernatural was not taken seriously. I remember my grandfather giving me Tom Paine's critique of fundamentalism, *The Age of Reason,* when I was ten or eleven. And this continued with my father. My father was a romantic, a dreamer. He was born in New York and lived there all his life, but loved best the real downtown, the docks, the import-export firms, the ship chandlers. He liked to bring home exotic foods. He never traveled but I think he must have dreamed about the sea. He was a midshipman in training in World War I. Toward the end of his life, he routinely read every newspaper, magazine, and journal from every corner of the left.

INTERVIEWER: Did your grandfather and father work in politics?

DOCTOROW: No. My grandfather was a printer and, by the time I played chess with him, he was retired and quite elderly. My father owned a record and radio and musical instrument store in the 1930's and lost the store later in the Depression. He then became a salesman for a jobber in the same industry—home appliances and, later on, TV sets and stereo equipment. His politics were expressed through the papers he read at the kitchen table, the lectures he attended, and the sentiments he expressed when the news was read over the radio. I think he belonged to some sort of fraternal Jewish socialist organization that had a very good insurance program, burial benefit.

INTERVIEWER: Is there something deeply Jewish about your political convictions?

DOCTOROW: I suppose so, though I don't think my kind of vision is *only* Jewish. Historically, there's been a kind of tradition among Jews—often very embarrassing to mainline, establishment Jewish thinking. Emma Goldman is a perfect example of that tradition. Her father was a rabbi. Somehow what she did—when she got over her bomber phase, at a relatively early age—had a Jewish-prophet character to it. Think of the terribly unpopular and personally dangerous positions she got into all her life. The connection between one's precarious position in society and the desire for some analysis that would change society is not exclusively Jewish, but it runs all through modern Jewish history. Yet there's more to it than that. In *Prophets Without Honor,* his book about the renaissance of German-speaking Jews in the thirty or forty years before Hitler, Frederic Grunfeld shows this tradition at work. It's in Freud. It's in Kafka, Schoenberg, in some of the poets killed by Hitler, in the critic Walter Benjamin. Whether they were that radical or not, there was some sort of system to thought—a humanist critique, a social or political skepticism, whatever you want to call it—that had to come from their inability to be complacent or self-congratulatory.

INTERVIEWER: Aside from whatever anti-Semitic impulses at work in some people on the far right, there may be the fearful recognition that radical Jewish humanism is very dangerous to their position.

DOCTOROW: The Nazis used that. The Jews they went after—the Jews who most enraged them—were the assimilated Jews, the families who had lived in Germany or Austria for hundreds of years. Einstein, for instance, infuriated the Nazis. Einstein was coming up with a universe in which nothing stayed the same very long. Things kept transforming and there was no space without time, and energy became mass and mass became energy. They saw all this relativism as a great threat to their psychic security and a typically Jewish maneuver to undercut and destroy the Aryan race. It was not the pious, practicing Jews who kept to themselves who so much enraged the Nazis at the beginning. It was the Jewish professors and composers (like Mahler) and scientists, all of whom had assimilated to one degree or another. The number of poets, novelists, critics, painters, and musicians whom they destroyed. Migod. That's the other connection you make between art and social criticism.

To get back to the idea of a radical Jewish humanist tradition, if I was not in that tradition, I would certainly want to apply for membership. Years ago in New Rochelle, I gave a talk at a Conservative synagogue. This was at a breakfast meeting of a men's club or something like that. The title of my talk was "Other Jews." And it was just this I was talking about: the expression of Jewish rectitude in humanist political terms. I mentioned Emma Goldman. And I mentioned Allen Ginsberg, this Buddhist, homosexual, Beat poet. Ginsberg is right smack in the middle of that tradition. I thought a suburban synagogue was a good place to talk about it.

INTERVIEWER: To move away from the especially Jewish quality of your vision, how would you summarize abstractly your social ideals?

DOCTOROW: There is a presumption of universality to the ideal of justice—social justice, economic justice. It cannot exist for a part or class of society; it must exist for all. And it's a Platonic ideal, too—that everyone be able to live as he or she is endowed to live; that if a person is in his genes a poet, he be able to practice his poetry. Plato defined justice as the fulfillment of a person's truest self. That's good for starters.

INTERVIEWER: To bring that about would, of course, require a tremendous reorganization of the social and economic structure of our society. Would you say that we'd have to have a socialist reorganization to make possible the kind of justice you describe?

DOCTOROW: Probably, yes. But it would come up out of us, our best illusions about ourselves. It would be pragmatic and honest and plainspoken. We would build on what we already have, we would go out in the barn (which is the Constitution) and tinker. And it's the failure to recognize *that* which has always brought programmatic radicals up short in this country. You want to achieve some degree of genuine enlightened social control of production and services—but without creating a bureaucracy that turns oppressive, and without relinquishing any of the political freedoms that exist now.

INTERVIEWER: Do you think the shift in the opposite direction that Reagan represents is a temporary aberration? Or is it (coming from some deep impulse in the American political character) likely to endure?

DOCTOROW: The great political contests in this country since Franklin Roosevelt have been between the center and the right. So in that sense Reagan is not an aberration. On the other hand, there is something new about him: the abandonment of the liberal rhetoric by which we've always disguised our grubby actions from ourselves. This president is saying the conflict between our democratic ideals and our realpolitical self-interest is over; that the conflict between our constitutional obligations and the expediencies of economic capital reality is over; the crackling contradiction between our national ideals and our repeated historical abuse of those ideals is over. It turns out after all we were not supposed to be just a nation, but a confederacy of stupid murderous gluttons. So there's a terrible loss of the energy you get from self-contradiction, from the battle with yourself. If there was a way of taking a national EEG, you'd find that the brain waves have gone flat. That's new. The religious fundamentalists and the political right have made explosive contact, and in the light of their conjunction it says Armageddon.

I Write for Revenge Against Reality

FRANCINE DU PLESSIX GRAY

A nightmare recurs since childhood:

Facing a friend, I struggle for words and emit no sound. I have an urgent message to share but am struck dumb, my jaw is clamped shut as in a metal vise, I gasp for breath and can not set my tongue free. At the dream's end my friend has fled and I am locked into the solitide of silence.

The severe stutter I had as a child, my father's impatience and swiftness of tongue, his constant interruption of me when I tried to speak?

Or perhaps another incident which also has to do with the threat of the Father and the general quirkiness of my French education: One day when I was nine I was assigned my first free composition. From infancy I had been tutored at home in Paris by a tyrannical governess, the two of us traveling once a week to a correspondence school whose Gallically rigid assignments (memorization of Asian capitals and Latin verbs, codifying of sentence parts) were hardly conducive to a fertile imagination. "Write a Story About Anything You Wish," Central Bureau suddenly ordered. Filled with excitement and terror by this freedom, I began as a severe minimalist:

"The little girl was forbidden by her parents to walk alone to the lake at the other end of the long lawn. But she wished to visit a luminous green-eyed frog who would offer her the key to freedom. One day she disobeyed her parents and walked to the lake and immediately drowned." (The End)

"Pathetic dribble!" the Father stormed on his daily visit to my study room. "You dare call that a story! What will become of you if you can't ever finish anything!"

It was a warm May evening of 1939, the year before he died in the Resistance. The love of my life (my father was himself an occasional scribbler) was warning me that I should never write again. I still remember the hours I spent honing those meager sentences, the square white china inkwell into which I squeezed the rubber filler of a Waterman pen, the awkwardness of ink-stained fingers as I struggled to shape my letters (I was born left-handed and had been forced to use my right), the tears, the sense that my writing was doomed to be sloppy, abortive, good for naught.

So it may have begun, the central torment of my life, my simultaneous need to commit fantasies to paper and the terror that accompanies that need, the leaden slowness of the words' arrival, my struggle with the clamped metal jaws of mouth and mind. An affliction deepened by that infatuation with the written word that possesses most solitary children. For books had been the only companions of my childhood prison, particularly such stirring tales of naval adventure as *Captains Courageous* or *Two Years Before the Mast,* which fueled dreams of running away to sea and never being seen again.

Then came the war, the flight to America, the need to learn a new language. English was learned as a means of survival and became a lover to be seduced and conquered as swiftly as possible, to be caressed and rolled on the tongue in a continuous ecstasy of union. English words, from the time I was eleven on, were my medium of joy and liberation. I fondled them by memorizing twenty lines of Blake when ten had been assigned; I wooed them so assiduously that I won the Lower School Spelling Bee within ten months of having come to the United States. (I was the only foreign scholarship student at the Spence School; shortly after the contest a delegation of Spence parents descended on my mother, who was supporting us by designing hats at Henri Bendel's, to verify that we were true emigrés and not usurpers from Brooklyn).

I continued to court my new tongue by struggling for A's in English, by being elected editor of the school paper, which a predecessor had artfully named *Il Spenceroso*. Omens of a "literary gift" continued to accrete—a prize in Bryn Mawr's Freshman Essay Contest, the Creative Writing Award at Barnard for three stories of a strictly autobiographical nature. Such portents brought no security. I fled from myself by being a compulsive talker, a bureaucrat, polemicist, hack journalist. I had taken no more than two courses in literature beyond Freshman English, thinking I was smartass enough to learn it for myself. One of the other courses had been a creative writing class that earned me a C- for first-person fictions about situations I knew nothing about—I seemed always to be a middle-aged alcoholic actor seeking salvation in a Bowery church. After that fiasco I had sought refuge in rigor and formalism—physics, philosophy, medieval history. There was a curious furtiveness about the way I continued to carry on my love affair with literature. I copied entire paragraphs from Henry James or T. S. Eliot into private notebooks out of sheer delectation in the texture of their prose. In a stretch of a few solitary vacation weeks I would memorize two hundred lines of Marvell for the pleasure of speaking them to myself during nights of insomnia. Why all this reluctance and covertness?

"You're writing pure junk," Charles Olson had stormed at me during a summer workshop at Black Mountain when I'd handed him my prize-winning college stories. "If you want to be a writer keep it to a journal." The giant walrus rising from his chair, 6 feet 7 inches of him towering. ". . . AND ABOVE ALL DON'T TRY TO PUBLISH ANYTHING FOR TEN YEARS!" Another paternal figure had censored me into silence, perhaps this time for the best.

I followed Big Charles's advice. I kept my journal in New Orleans where I dallied as if I had ten lives to squander, drinking half a bottle of gin a night as I followed a jazz clarinetist on the rounds of Bourbon Street. I remained faithful to my secret vice in the dawns of New York when I worked the night shift at United Press, writing World in Briefs about Elks' Meetings and watermelon-eating contests in Alabama. I remained loyal to my journal through a myriad of failed aspirations while flirting with the thought of entering Harvard's Department of Architecture, of going to Union Theological Seminary for a degree in divinity. I persevered with it when I moved to Paris to earn my living as a fashion reporter, dallying with a succession of consummate narcissists to whom I eventually gave their literary due. I continued to write it when I fulfilled one of my life's earliest dreams and spent five years as a painter of meticulously naturalistic landscapes and still lifes.

By then I was married and had two children. And since I lived in deep country and in relative solitude, encompassed by domestic duties, the journal became increasingly voluminous, angry, introspective. The nomad, denied flight and forced to turn inward, was beginning to explode. One day when I was thirty-three, after I'd cooked and smiled for a bevy of weekend guests whom I never wished to see again, I felt an immense void, great powerlessness, the deepest loneliness I'd ever known. I wept for some hours, took out a notebook, started rewriting one of the three stories that had won me my Barnard prize. It was the one about my governess. It was published a short time later in *The New Yorker,* one year past the deadline Charles Olson had set me. It was to become, twelve years and two books of nonfiction later, the first chapter of *Lovers and Tyrants.* The process of finishing that book was as complex and lengthy as it was painful. It entailed a solid and delicate psychoanalysis which forced me to accept my father's death. Epiphany achieved, I was able to write the novel's three last chapters—my first genuine attempt at fiction—in a mere six months. I may have had to bury my father to set my tongue free.

*   *   *

And yet what kind of writer have I become, six years and two novels later? Few scribblers I know have struggled so hard for so little. I am too many things I do not wish to be—a Jane of all trades shuttling back and forth between scant fiction, voluminous reporting, innumerable and unmemorable literary essays. I feel honored by yet undeserving of the appellation "novelist." I am merely a craftsperson, a cabinetmaker of texts and occasionally, I hope, a witness to our times. My terror of fictional invention has denied me that activity which from childhood on has been the most furtively longed for, which has proved to be (when I finally began to tackle it) the most deeply satisfying.

Might I remain brainwashed, along with many of my generation, by the notion that fiction is the noblest, the most "creative" of all genres of prose? No avocation has better clarified that issue or my identity as a writer than the business of teaching. I stress to young colleagues that some of the greatest masterpieces of our time have been works of nonfiction or hybrid forms which defy classification—James Agee's *Let Us Now Praise Famous Men*, Edmund Wilson's criticism, Peter Handke's *A Sorrow Beyond Dreams*, all of Roland Barthes' work. I urge them to shake loose from the peculiarly American fixation on novel-writing. I tell them that the obsession to write The Great American Novel might have done more harm to generations of Americans than all the marijuana in Mexico. The syllabus for the course I taught at Yale last fall sums it all up:

THE WRITING OF THE TEXT: This is a seminar in the reading and writing of literature which I hope can remain untainted by the word "creative." It is dedicated to the premise that a distinction between "fiction" and "nonfiction" is potentially harmful to many aspiring writers who will progress more fruitfully if they are encouraged to think of their writing as pure "text" without worrying about what "form" or "genre" it will fall into.

Reading Assignments: F. Scott Fitzgerald's *Crack-Up*, Max Frisch's *Sketchbooks*, Flaubert's *Dictionary of Accepted Ideas*, Elizabeth Hardwick's *Sleepless Nights*, Boris Pasternak's *Safe Conduct*, William Gass's *On Being Blue*, Maureen Howard's *Facts of Life*.

The first thing we must do when we set out to write, I also tell my classes, is to shed all narcissism. My own decades of fear came from my anxiety that my early drafts were ugly, sloppy, not promising enough. We must persevere and scrawl atrocities, persevere dreadful draft after dreadful draft in an unhindered stream of consciousness, persevere, if need be, in

Breton's technique of automatic writing, of mindless trance. And within that morass of words there may be an ironic turn of phrase, a dislocation that gives us a key to the voice, the tone, the structure we're struggling to find. I am a witness to the lateness of my own vocation, the hesitation and terrors that still haunt all my beginnings, the painful slowness with which I proceed through a minimum of four drafts in both fiction and nonfiction.

Question:

Why do I go on writing, seeing the continuing anguish of the act, the dissatisfaction I feel toward most results?

Flannery O'Connor said it best: "I write because I don't know what I think until I read what I say."

I write out of a desire for revenge against reality, to destroy forever the stuttering powerless child I once was, to gain the love and attention that silenced child never had, to allay the dissatisfaction I still have with myself, to be something other than what I am. I write out of hate, out of a desire for revenge against all the men who have oppressed and humiliated me.

I also write out of love and gratitude for a mother and stepfather who made me feel worthy by hoarding every scrap of correspondence I ever sent them; love and gratitude for a husband of exquisite severity who still edits every final draft that leaves my typewriter. I write out of an infantile dread of ever disappointing them again.

I write because in the act of creation there comes that mysterious, abundant sense of being both parent and child; I am giving birth to an Other and simultaneously being reborn as child in the playground of creation.

I write on while continuing to despair that I can't ever achieve the inventiveness, irreverence, complexity of my favorite contemporary authors—Milan Kundera, Italo Calvino, Günter Grass, Salman Rushdie, to name only the foreign ones. They are certain enough of their readers' love (or indifferent enough to it, since the great Indifferents are the great Seducers) to indulge in that shrewd teasing and misguiding of the reader, that ironic obliqueness which is the marrow of the best modernist work. It is not only my lesser gift that is at fault. Behind my impulsive cataloguing, my Slavic unleashing of emotion, my Quaker earnestness to inform my readers guilelessly of all I know, there still lurks the lonely, stuttering child too terrified of losing the reader's love to take the necessary risks.

Yet I remain sustained by a definition of faith once offered me by Ivan Illich: "Faith is a readiness for the Surprise." I write because I have faith in the possibility that I can eventually surprise myself. I am still occasionally plagued by that recurring nightmare of my jaw being clamped shut, my mouth frozen in silence. But I wake up from it with less dread, with the hope that some day my tongue will loosen and emit a surprising new sound which even I, at first, shall not be able to understand.

The Question of Poetic Form

HAYDEN CARRUTH

. . . 151. Sometimes when manufacturers go into business for the first time they give their products high model numbers, as if to suggest that they are old companies with long experience in similar antecedent productions. Well, in somewhat the same spirit, though I hope for reasons less specious, I begin here with paragraph no. 151. God knows I'm an old company, and perhaps only he knows the number of my antecedent productions. But, more specifically, what I want to suggest by my high model number is the time that has gone into the preparation of this particular product; my years of random "scholarship," my amassed notes, fragments, citations, experimental pages, scattered bibliographies, and so on, with which I sit surrounded now—more than enough, I assure you, to fill up 150 introductory paragraphs. Then rejoice with me, for they are all jettisoned. No footnotes, no quotations, and as few proper names as I can get by with: that is how I have decided to proceed. Let the thing be abstract, subjective, principled. Academic critics and philosophers have their reasons, I know, but their reasons are not mine; nor are they the reader's, at least not if my readers are the people I hope to address, my fellow poets and lovers of poetry.

152. Yet aside from the fact that I would find it personally too disheartening not even to mention my labors, a further point arises from these missing 150 paragraphs. For a long time I shuffled my papers, sorted them, fumbled them, trying to make my notes fall into some pattern that would be useful to me, until at last I saw the truth: there is no pattern. And the reason is clear; I knew it all along, but was intimidated from applying it by the manners of the very scholars whose works I was reading. Virtually every important theory of poetry has been invented by a poet. That is the nub of it. And each theory has sprung from the poet's own emotional and esthetic needs in his particular time and place—or hers, for many important statements have come, especially recently, from women, though I must submit to grammar by masculinizing the métier hereafter—

and moreover each theory has been derived from what the poet has observed of his own psychology and method in his own workshop. In short, the theories are subjective. Each theorist begins by returning, not to "first principles," since in art they do not exist, but to experience. The scholarship is irrelevant. And no wonder the theories are inconsistent and often in conflict; no wonder there is no pattern and the categories break down, so that the scholars end, as one of them has, by calling Pope a neoclassical romanticist or by using every term in their catalogues, ineffectually, for Ezra Pound. Yet the statements of Pope and Pound and other poets remain crucial, the indispensable documents of our poetic understanding. In them I find both urgency of feeling and the irrefragability of knowledge, the real knowledge of what happens when a poem is written. Both qualities are what keep art and the artist alive.

153. There is no pattern then; quite the contrary. And consequently what I am doing here above all is asking for . . . but I don't know what to call it. It is neither reconciliation nor toleration. Among genuinely conflicting views reconciliation is impossible, while toleration implies indifference or a kind of petrified Quakerish absolutism of restraint. These are not what I mean at all. Yet it is true that I abhor sectarianism in the arts, or dogmatism of any kind. What I am asking for, I think, is the state of mind that can see and accept and believe ideas in conflict, without ambivalence or a sense of self-divisiveness. Call it eclecticism if you will. I have been accused ot it often enough, the word flung out like a curse. But just as I, a radical, distrust other radicals who are not in part conservatives—i.e., who are ideologues—so I distrust poets who cannot perceive the multiplexity of their art, perceive it and relish it. Poetry is where you find it. I am convinced of this: convinced as a matter of temperament, as a matter of thirty years' intensive critical reading, and as a matter of my perception of human reality—the equivalence of lives and hence of values. So if you find poetry in Blake but not in Pope, or the other way around, that's OK, you are better off than people who find it in neither. But if you find it in both, then you are my kind of reader, my kind of human being.

154. Moreover poetry is a mystery. I don't mean the poem on the page, though that is difficult enough. I mean what went before: poetry as process, poetry as a function of what we call, lumping many things together, the imagination. Think how long science has worked, thus far in vain, to explain the origin of life, which appears to be a simple problem, comparatively speaking, involving few and simple factors. Then think of trying to explain the imagination: the factors are incalculable. I believe it will never be done. Hence what anyone says about poetry, provided it be grounded in knowledge, is as true as what anyone else may say, though the

two sayings utterly conflict. Yet they can be held in the mind together, they can be believed together. And still the element of mystery will remain.

155. What about Aristotle? He was no poet; far from it. It shows unquestionably in his theory of poetry. He wrote about art from the point of view not of the artist but of the spectator, the playgoer. He described the psychology of esthetic experience; pity and woe, the notion of catharsis. This is interesting and useful, and from it certain ideas may be extrapolated about the work itself, the play. But about playwriting, about art as process? No. And Aristotle's attempt to do it—the feeble theory of imitation—as well as the attempts of a great many others after him, have produced confusion and irrelevance for nearly twenty-five hundred years. To my mind this is the giveaway. A real theory of art begins with process and accepts the inevitability of mystery; it rests content with its own incompleteness. A spurious theory of art begins somewhere else and tries to explain everything.

156. The word that seems to incorporate most fully the essential idea of imaginative process is the word *form*. But at once the element of mystery makes itself known, for the word has been used in so many different ways, with so much looseness and imprecision, that clearly people do not know what it really means; or perhaps the word itself really means more, implicitly or innately, than the people mean, or can mean, when they use it. Hence the imprecision can never be eliminated; the craftiest philosopher will never produce anything but a partial definition. Yet this is no reason for not trying. A few years ago I was attacked by an eminent poet, publicly and bitterly, because in a short piece on another topic I had said that the staggered tercets used by Williams in his later poems are a "form." Granted, I was using the word imprecisely, which is what one must do with these large, complex, mysterious terms, especially in short pieces, if one is to avoid a breakdown of communication. I am sure my readers knew what I meant. But the eminence was not satisfied; apparently he was infuriated. No, he said, the staggered tercets are merely a style; the form is something deeper, the whole incalculable ensemble of feelings, tones, connotations, images, and so on that bodies forth the poem; and I purposely, if somewhat quaintly, say "bodies forth" rather than "embodies" because I think this exactly conveys my attacker's meaning, and the distinction is worth attending to. Of course he was right. I agree with him; I agreed with him then and before then. But at the same time he was only partly right, and he was being dogmatic in just the sense I have referred to, that is, by insisting arbitrarily that part of the truth is the whole of the truth, and by pinning everything upon an understanding of terms. This is what dogma is. Yet often enough in the past the meanings of our terms have

been exactly reversed. *Form* has meant the poem's outer, observable, imitable, and more or less static materiality; *style* has meant its inner quality, essentially hidden and unanalyzable, the properties that bind and move and individuate. Indeed this was the common usage of the two words in literary theory from Lessing and Goethe to T. S. Eliot. And all that is proven by this is that poets are always talking about the same things, but with different names, different tones, different emphases, and different perceptual orientations. How could they otherwise, when each returns to his own experience for the knowledge from which he writes?

157. The danger is, as we have seen, that experience which leads to knowledge will lead further to dogmatism. It happens all the time, by no means more frequently among poets than among others. Yet it isn't necessary. Neither in human nor in categorical terms is this progression inevitable, and it can be interrupted anywhere by reasonableness and humility. What do we mean by the word *form* in ordinary speech? What is the form of an apple? Certainly it is not only the external appearance, its roundness, redness, firmness, and so on. Nor is it only the inner atomic structure. Nor is it the mysterious genetic force that creates appleness in the apple. It is all these things and more, the whole apple. The form *is* the apple. We cannot separate them. In philosophical terms it is the entire essence of the apple plus its existence, the fact of its being. I think that when we use the word *form* in reference to a poem we should use it in just this way. It means the whole poem, nothing less. We may speak of outer and inner form, and in fact I think we must, provided we remember that these are relative terms, relative to each other and to the objectives of any particular inquiry. An image, for example, may be an element of outer form at one time or of inner form at another: it depends on how you look at it. But the form *is* the poem.

158. As for style, to my mind it is not something different from form but something contained within form, a component of form. True, it is unlike other components. But they themselves are more or less unlike one another, so why should this cause difficulty? The best definition I can make is this: style is the property of a poem that expresses the poet's personality, either his real personality or his invented personality, or, most likely, a combination of the two. It is manifested in the concrete elements of form: syntax, diction, rhythm, characteristic patterns of sound or imagery, and so on; and if one has sufficient patience these elements can be identified, classified, tabulated, they can be put through the whole sequence of analytic techniques; yet style will remain in the end, like the personality behind it (though not on the same scale), practically indemonstrable. Style consists of factors so minutely constituted and so obscurely combined that

they simply are not separable and not measurable, except in the grossest ways. Yet we know a style when we see it, we recognize it and are attracted or repelled by it. One reason for this is the fact that style is a continuing element in a poet's work, it remains consistently itself from one poem to another, even though the poems in other respects are notably dissimilar. We speak of the "growth" and "maturity" of a poet's style in the same way that we speak of the growth and maturity of a person. This is an interesting fact; it may even sometimes be a crucial fact, as when we are attempting to explain the incidence of poetic genius. But it can also be a dangerous fact, for it leads to the state of mind in which style seems to be abstract from the poem, abstract from form itself. This is a delusion, I think, and moreover a delusion that brings us near the heart of the question of poetic form.

159. Some people will say that my assertion regarding outer and inner form is sloppy. I don't see why. I am comfortable in my radical relativism, and am frankly unable to explain why other people shouldn't be comfortable in it too. Yet I know what they have in mind. Some kinds of outer form, they will say, are repeatable. Sonnets, villanelles, that sort of thing; and of course it is quite true that the structures of meter and rhyme in some such poems may be indicated roughly but schematically by stress marks and letterings, and then may be imitated in new substances of words, images, feelings, experiences, and so on. My critics will say that this repeatability of certain elements of form makes them absolutely distinct from other elements that cannot be repeated. Again I don't see why. To me the poem in its wholeness is what is important, and I do not care for classification. Besides, absolute classifications are a myth. Simply because we can state that two poems written a hundred years apart are both Petrarchan sonnets, does that make them the same? Obviously not. Moreover the statement itself seems to me to have only the most superficial classificative meaning; it is virtually useless. Oh, I know what immense complexes of cultural value may adhere to the Petrarchan sonnet or to other conventional classes of poetic structure, and how in certain contexts, outside the discussion of form, these values may be most decidedly *not* useless. OK. But here I *am* discussing form, and the point I want to make is that in reality no element of form is perfectly repeatable and no element is perfectly unique. Outer and inner form may approach these absolutes at either end, but they cannot reach them. They cannot reach them because the absolutes lie outside the poem. A rhyme scheme is not a poem; it is a complete abstraction, which has only the absoluteness—if that is the right term—of a Euclidean triangle existing nowhere in nature. Similarly the combination of vital energies and individual referents at the heart of a

poem, its inner form, may be almost unique, almost unanalyzable or indis-
cerptible, but it cannot be absolutely so, for then the poem would cease to
be a product of human invention and would assume a status equivalent to
that of the creaturely inventor himself, a part of *natura naturata;* and that,
I believe—I fervently hope—is impossible. (Though I know many poets
who claim just this for their own inventions and their own inventive
powers.) In short, it is not a question of repeatability but of imitation.
And it is not a question of facsimile but of approximation. All we can say
about the abstractability of form, including style, is that some elements of
form, chiefly the outer, are more or less amenable to imitation, and that
other elements, chiefly the inner, are more or less resistant to it. Yet this is
saying a good deal. The form *is* the poem, and all its elements lie *within* the
poem. Repeatability is a delusion. Finally, even style, though I have noted
its continuance from poem to poem, does not continue by means of repeti-
tion but by means of self-imitation, that is to say, imperfectly, hence
changeably and developmentally; an unchanging style would be a dead
style, or no style at all, and certainly not a part of poetry.

160. I don't know if what I have written in this last paragraph is clear.
Let me reduce it to an analogy. By examining a number of apples one can
draw up a generalized schematic definition of an apple, and by using modern methods of investigation one can make this definition account not
only for the apple's external appearance but for its invisible internal structure and its animate energy, the forces that determine both its specificity
and its individuality. Conceivably this definition might be useful, since by
referring to it one could recognize another apple when one saw it. Beyond
that, if one were inclined to make classifications the definition would help
in distinguishing the apple from other classes of fruit. But no one, not
even the most ardent lovers of definitions, would say that the definition *is*
the apple. Obviously the definition is only a definition. And yet some people say that the definition is the *form* of the apple. Can this be? I don't see
how. Can a form exist apart from the thing it forms, or rather apart from
the thing that makes it a form, that informs it? Can we have such a thing as
an unformed form? No, a definition is only a definition, a generalization,
an abstraction; and a form, by virtue of being a form, is concrete. No part
of the apple's form can exist outside the apple.

161. When I put the matter in these terms the source of difficulty becomes clear right away, and of course it is the Platonic ideal. Well, it seems
to me that Plato made a very shrewd observation of human psychology
when he conceived his ideals—if he was the one who actually conceived
them (I am ignorant of pre-Socratic philosophy). Unquestionably our
imaginations do contain an abstracting faculty, with which we derive and

separate ideas from things, and often these ideas become ideals in both the Platonic and modern senses. They are universals, though that is not saying as much as people often mean when they use this word. They are what enable us to be perfectionists, knowing the ideal is unattainable yet striving always toward it; which is what accounts for human excellence, in poetry and in everything else. Every poet has in his head the "idea" of the perfect poem, though it has never been written and never will be. But to infer from this useful but passive quality that ideals—definitions, "forms"—are active or instrumental in the realm of practice, in poetry or in nature, seems to me mere fancy.

162. I should think poets ought to see this more easily than most people. A form is an effect, not a cause. Of course I don't say that in a chain of cultural actions and reactions a form, or rather the abstract definition of a form, may not play a causal role; without doubt it may, and obviously the element of convention in literature is large and important. But considered in conceptual purity, a form is not a cause. Do we work from the form toward the poem? That is the mode of the set piece, the classroom exercise—and we know what kind of "poems" come from that. No, we work from the thing always, from the perception or experience of the thing, and we move thence into feelings and ideas and other cultural associations, and finally into language, where by trial and error we seek what will be expressive of the thing. If we are lucky we find it, and then only then do we arrive, almost by accident or as an afterthought, at form. In one sense form is a by-product of poetry, though this is not to deny its essentiality. Naturally I do not mean either that the actual complicated processes of poetic imagination can be reduced to any such simple progression as the one I have indicated. The whole transaction may occur in a flash, literally simultaneously. Formal intuitions may appear at the very beginning. I am convinced that no method of analysis will ever be contrived which is refined enough to isolate all the energies and materials combined in the poetic act. Yet at the same time I do suggest that form in itself is never the cause, and certainly never the instrument (the efficient cause), of real poetry, and I believe this is something all real poets can verify from their own experience.

163. Until now my strategy has been to avoid using the two words that in fact have been the crucial terms in all my speculations about poetic form for several years, the words *organic* and *fixed*. Yet they are my reason for these paragraphs, as well as my incitement. The notions I have set down here must have been set down thousands of times before, I'm sure, frequently by writers more skillful and gifted than I. Hence what impels me is my awareness that each age attacks the perennial topics from the stand-

point of its particular need, with its peculiar angle of vision and edge of feeling. And our age, speaking in terms of poetry, seems to revolve predominantly around these two terms. Organic form v. fixed form: that indicates how we look at the question of poetic form, and it pretty well suggests the quality of our feeling about it. Certainly we are earnest and combative, we are very acutely caught up. Have poets in earlier times worried themselves quite as much as we do about form in poetry? Even the word itself—*form*—has about it now a flavor of ultimacy, almost a numen, that I don't think it possessed in ages past. Of course there are good reasons for this, at least in terms of literary evolution. Anyone who has lived through the past thirty or forty years of poetry in America knows exactly how the conflict between fixed form and organic form came about, and why. But I am not interested here in the history or sociology of poetry; I am interested in the thing itself, and I hope what I have written so far indicates that I think both terms, *organic* and *fixed*, as they appear in common usage among poets today, are misapplied. Clearly this is the case with fixed form. If form cannot be abstracted it cannot be fixed; at best it can only be turned into a definition, a scheme. The case with organic form seems less clear, because in some sense the concept of organic form is close to what I have been saying about form as the effect or outcome of poetry. But frequently the advocates of organic form go further; they say that the forms of their poems are taken, if not from the ideal forms of Plato's heaven, then from forms in nature, in experience, in the phenomenal world. But forms in the phenomenal world are no more abstractions than any other forms, and transference is impossible. At best poetic form is an analogy to nonesthetic form, but a very, very remote analogy; so remote indeed that I think it serves no purpose, and the citing of it only beclouds the issue. If what I have argued here is true, that is, that form is the poem, then form is autonomous—it can be nothing else; which is only what poets have said in other ways for centuries. (Though this does not mean, I would insist, that the poem in its totality of feeling, meaning, and value is separable from morality or ordinary human relevance.) Well, if form is autonomous then let us treat it as such.

164. But if form is autonomous it is also indigenous. A particular poetic form is solely *in* a particular poem; it *is* the poem. Hence it inheres solely in the materials of that poem (which by extension or implication may include the poem's origins). From this I conceive that if an analogy exists between a poetic form and a form in nature, this analogy is solely and necessarily a coincidence; and it is meaningless. After all, what true or functional analogy can exist between the forms of generally differing mate-

rials? To say that a poetic form is analogous to a form in nature is the same as saying that a horse is like a pool table, or a dragonfly like a seraph.

165. Going back to *outer* and *inner*, these are the terms I prefer, applied with strict relativism. I think they are more exact than *fixed* and *organic*. Moreover I like them better because they imply no conflict, no war, but rather a consonance. To my mind warring poets, because they are dealing with the very substance of truth, that is, our vision of reality, are almost as dangerous and a good deal sillier than warring generals.

166. Of course I do not mean to deny what is as plain as the nose on anyone's face: for example, that Alexander Pope wrote virtually all his poetry in closed pentameter couplets. But I would say three things. First, the misnamed "heroic couplet," which seems to us the height of artifice, was just the opposite in the minds of those who used it. Dryden chose the couplet because he thought it the plainest mode available, the verse "nearest prose," and he chose it in conscious reaction against the artificial stanzaic modes that had dominated English poetry during most of the sixteenth and seventeenth centuries. In short, he and his followers thought they were liberating poetry, just as Coleridge and Wordsworth liberated it a hundred years later, or Pound and Williams a hundred years after that. The history of poetry is a continual fixing and freeing of conventions. It follows that these poets, Dryden and Pope, really were engaged in a liberation; and it follows too that we ought always to pay at least some attention to history and fashion, the worldly determinants, in our consideration of any poetry. Secondly, I do not think the couplet was a fixed form. I do not think it for the same reason that I do not think any form can be fixed. Granted, it was a pattern that was imitated by many versewriters. But among the best poets it was a form like any other poetic form: the natural, spontaneous (which does not mean instantaneous) effect of the causal topics, feelings, and attitudes from which their poems derived. It is evident in the best of Pope. He himself said: "I have followed . . . the significance of the numbers, and the adapting them to the sense, much more even than Dryden, and much oftener than anyone minds it. . . . The great rule of verse is to be musical." Today we do not like "numbers" and "rules"; but I get from this the distinct feeling that when Pope spoke of "adapting," he was thinking about poetic form in a way close to my own. And I know for certain that what he meant by "musical" had little to do with rhyming and everything to do with the total harmony of language and substance. Think of the material of Pope's poems. Could it have engendered any other poetic form? I believe the closed pentameter couplet was natural to Pope, "organic" if you like, and if his poems are not as well unified *poetically* as

any others of a similar kind and scope, if the best of them are not *poems* in exactly the same sense we mean today, then I don't know how to read poetry. (But I do.) Thirdly, in another sense of the word, different from the sense I have been using, every poetic form is fixed. It cannot be otherwise. Unless a poem is destroyed as soon as it is written, its form exists as a thing in the world, to be observed by anyone who wishes to observe it, particularly by the poet who created it. Thus every poetic form exists in its permanent concreteness—relatively speaking, of course—and thus it gives rise to influence. It produces a convention, and this convention may reenter the poet's sensibility and become part of the apparatus of imagination. It happens with all poets. After all Whitman continued to follow the conventions of his poems quite as narrowly as Pope followed the conventions of his; and in this sense the "organic" poets of today are writing in forms as fixed as any, as fixed, say, as the heroic couplet. I grant it would be difficult in practice to discriminate between what I am here calling a convention and what I earlier called a style; yet in theory it must be possible, because a style is what is expressive of a poet's personality, whereas a convention is a generalized "feeling" about language and structure, often with broadly cultural associations, which can enter anyone's sensibility, not just its creator's. It would be silly to deny a connection among James Wright, Galway Kinnell, and W. S. Merwin, for instance, or among Denise Levertov, Robert Creeley, and Robert Duncan. And I suspect that in part these connections consist of the poets' common and mostly unconscious awareness of conventions that have arisen from the multiplicity and multiplexity of their own created, "fixed" poetic forms.

167. Poetry is where you find it. Its form is always its own. The elements of outer form, such as language, tone, or texture, may move sometimes from and sometimes toward the elements of inner form, such as structures of imagery and feeling, symbols, or scarcely revealed nodes of imaginative energy. But if the poem is a real poem its whole form will be integrated. No element of outer form, considered apart from the rest, can signify whether or not a poem, an old poem or a new poem, is real; nor can any element of inner form, so considered. Hence the classification of poems, old or new, is a hurtful, false endeavor. Let the warring cease.

A Conversation with Mark Strand

The following interview took place in 1977. David Brooks is the interviewer.

INTERVIEWER: I'd like to ask first about your translations—like a number of your contemporaries, you've done a great many of them. Do you think the experience of translating is a valuable one to the modern poet?

STRAND: Yes. It gives him a chance to read poems in other languages rather carefully, and means that he casts his net further out. So much more is available to you if you can read more than one language—Spanish poetry, for example, has been terribly rich in this century. When you begin translating from another language you begin to read in an entirely different way.

INTERVIEWER: Has any of the poetry you've translated significantly influenced your own? Were you conscious of something changing after a certain amount of work, say, on Alberti, or Drummond?

STRAND: Not on Alberti. First of all, the translations of Alberti really span my whole career as a poet. I've worked on them when my own writing hasn't been going well, and it's given me something to do. I don't feel particularly close to Alberti, but Drummond is a poet I feel an enormous kinship with. Alberti's a kind of wizard or magician whose poems are interesting in a formal way, but Drummond is so charming and tells such terrific stories, and writes more often than Alberti the kind of poems I would like to write.

INTERVIEWER: Do you find that you can turn to other poets as touchstones, to somehow get you started again when your own poetry isn't going well?

STRAND: Yes. I do it both in translation and when I read poets in English. The reading of other poets always serves as grist for my own mill.

INTERVIEWER: Are there any poets in particular that have worked for you in this way?

STRAND: It changes at different times. I know, for example, that I read Lorca's "Lament for Ignacio Sanchez Mejias" when I wrote "Elegy for My Father." Right now I'm rereading Yeats. I wrote a poem for my daughter, and I know that many of those who read it are going to think of Yeats: it's clear that there are certain echoes—not only of his "Prayer for My Daughter," but from "Nineteen Hundred and Nineteen," which I think is the better poem.

INTERVIEWER: A last question on translation: your *18 Poems from the Quechua* is a curious volume—can you tell me something of how that came about?

STRAND: I did those from a Spanish translation of the original. They're very slight, and very folkloric, and quite unrelated to anything else that I've done, but not unrelated to something that was going on in American poetry at the time, and that was the search for pre-literary America. There were a lot of translations of Indian poetry being done—religious chants, ritualistic prayers, things like that—and the poems from the Quechua were my way of being influenced by what was going on in the late sixties and early seventies.

INTERVIEWER: If we can move on to your own poetry: do you believe, as do many close contemporaries, that the age demands a particular kind of nakedness in the forms of its poems?

STRAND: I think the proponents of "nakedness" are kidding themselves.

INTERVIEWER: You don't see yourself as seeking an appropriate form for the age in your own work?

STRAND: No—because for one thing I don't consider my poetry "of the age." I'm a product of my times, and I'm writing in a time, but the clues I get to help me in my own verse are from poems of the past, and not especially from my contemporaries. I feel much closer to certain people who have lived in the past than I do to many of my contemporaries.

INTERVIEWER: And one of those poets of the past is Kit Smart? What was it that first attracted you to his poetry?

STRAND: The *Jubilate*. It was one of the ways in which I broke the tyranny of writing those little pseudo-narratives that I was writing in *Reasons for Moving*. I wanted some kind of rhetorical, accretive effect in my poetry, rather than the kind of plain, narrative, reductive, pinched thing I had been doing. I began writing lists, using them to introduce images that were discrete, yet connected. It was a way for me to open up, expand. I used the *Jubilate* as a rhetorical model, though I think Whitman also influenced me in the change . . . and a few rather more obscure people—a Greek poet named Gatsos among them.

INTERVIEWER: You can see Smart's influence in the litanies of *Darker*. That's a more strident, emphatic book than *Reasons for Moving*, and the use of such a public form as the litany seems to betoken a more confident and representative voice—was that your aim?

STRAND: It was an attempt to be more direct than *Reasons for Moving*; to confront issues head on instead of writing the little parables I had been writing in the earlier volume. The public nature of the poems in *Darker*, when they are public, has to do with the times in which I wrote them. The last poem in that book, "The Way It Is," is an attempt to write a very public, apocalyptic poem.

INTERVIEWER: How closely related were those public concerns to the more personal ones of that and the earlier volumes? Sometimes certain of the public declarations seem to emanate from things which have appeared in the private poems, and seem very contiguous to them.

STRAND: That might be a sign of the degree to which I felt public issues in my personal life. I think a lot of us felt very involved with what was going on then. It stopped, we all got tired, saw that it wasn't doing much good. I began to mistrust some of the things that I wrote long before I might have, and there were a lot of public and anti-war poems that I chose not to put into *Darker*, not because I didn't believe in their stance, but because I no longer believed they worked as poems.

INTERVIEWER: Was there some crystallizing of ideas, something which, by *Darker*, had increased and broadened what Richard Howard calls your sense of "jeopardy"?

STRAND: Yes. That sense was in my first book, *Sleeping With One Eye Open,* and was there again in *Reasons for Moving.* It was a strange, pervasive anxiety, yet the source of the fright or anxiety didn't have a name. In *Darker* it did—it had a public and a private name. The public name was Lyndon Johnson, or the government of the United States, and the private name was the failing marriage.

INTERVIEWER: I suppose "Violent Storm" is one of those "little parables" you were just talking about. Though it probably pre-dates this "naming" of your anxieties, it raises an interesting question, for there you imply that there once was a time when we could sun ourselves "in a world of familiar views," when we *could* take ourselves and what belongs to us for granted. Are you referring there to some period of innocence in the life of every man, or to something which you feel has happened to society at large?

STRAND: Both. That poem is a good example of what we've just talked about. In it I also talk about the safety of the dream world—its speaker is one of those who can't sleep because he's tortured by what's going on outside and is not allowed the luxury and safety of the dream, the world of innocence, whether it be childhood or Arcady.

INTERVIEWER: *Darker* was a more public volume than you'd yet produced, yet in the next, *The Story of Our Lives,* you seemed to retreat once again into the private world. It's a closed volume, an inward spiral, and if one were to be harsh, it might be described as displaying a kind of intellectual agoraphobia. Your poems since then show a markedly different trend. Does this new direction imply some dissatisfaction with that volume?

STRAND: I'm not sure just how much I have changed; if people look back on my work in fifty years' time, they'll say Strand changed remarkably little. But it's true that I've never been satisfied with that book, largely because of what you describe. It's too inward, very much an inward spiral, or, as I used to think, one moment blown way out of proportion. I wrote those poems in a rather sad period of my own life, and it was really an attempt to figure out what went wrong, what was happening. Of course, as I say in a few of the poems, the more I tried to find out what was wrong, the less I did find. Part of the problem of inwardness is that the more inward you become, the less there is. You can't draw only on what's inside, you have to look around you, focus on external objects, so that you can draw yourself out.

INTERVIEWER: Were there any poets that you turned to for some kind of framework for those poems?

STRAND: No, and that's the good thing about the book. It is kind of an original book. I don't think it works, but I don't think there are many poems quite like those poems. They are in a way related to the *fictions* of Borges, I think, but I don't know of any other *poems* to which they are closely related. I mean, there is no other poem quite like "The Untelling," in which the man is writing the same poem four different ways.

INTERVIEWER: You are very concerned with ravelling an experience in that poem, examining it almost to the point of refashioning.

STRAND: Well, it's a fact that that image of the people on the shore is my first memory. The source of that poem is really a rereading of "The Prelude," yet here again the idea of influence is a difficult one. I don't know to what extent Wordsworth influenced my poem, but I do know that as I read "The Prelude" it occurred to me that I wanted to write a poem in blank verse, and the poems that the man in "The Untelling" writes are all in blank verse—he's chosen that as the means back, the way back. For him it's the second time around, he's revisiting that childhood situation, and in effect that's what Wordsworth does in "The Prelude."

INTERVIEWER: *The Story of Our Lives* was a necessary thing to do, something that you had to go through?

STRAND: Yes, absolutely . . . and I wanted to write longish poems, made myself write them. I threw away short pieces that I'd written in that period, just wouldn't have anything to do with them. I *willed* that book, and that's another reason I don't like it any more.

INTERVIEWER: Is there any classification of your work that you find yourself able to accept? Some have placed it as part of a new American surrealism; how do you react to such a label?

STRAND: I don't believe that much of what is considered surrealism is surrealism. Surrealism was a very definite movement in Europe some fifty years ago. There may be surrealist-like poetry being written now, but I don't consider myself such a poet. I don't think it's an appropriate term when applied to American poets. To a certain extent we all depend on free association, and we all use the suggestions that come from our subconscious.

INTERVIEWER: Still, I can see how a reader encountering an isolated poem of yours might be tempted to see in it something of the irreality of Borges.

STRAND: The *ir*reality of Borges? I'm not really prepared to talk about that. I loved reading Borges, and he was undoubtedly an influence on me—his prose, not his poetry—but just what I got from him I don't know. There were other writers I read at the same time—Kafka, Landolfi, Calvino—and all of them deal in that twilight zone of experience. There are American painters, too, who deal in that twilight zone, and who aren't surrealists. Edward Hopper is one of them; a great, great painter. How it was that I brought my talents to bear in that area I don't know, I guess it's always fascinated me.

INTERVIEWER: When one is able to read the full volumes of your poetry, imagery which seems rather eccentric in the individual poem appears to become a language through which you are making more readily accessible statements. Are your poems consciously interrelated in this manner?

STRAND: They're not consciously interrelated, no. I consciously put a book together—that is, I will sometimes leave out poems if they don't fit—but I write each poem individually, and I'm not aware of overlapping them or hooking them into each other. When I finish a book I realize that I've been preoccupied with one or two themes, and that's when it's time to quit them.

INTERVIEWER: You don't feel that your imagery is systematic?

STRAND: I think it's probably unconsciously so. I think that what poetry is for me happens to be closely tied with the words I use. Alas, unless there are certain words or a certain atmosphere in my poems, they aren't quite poems for me, and that's a severe limitation. If it's true that you need the words *moon, dark,* and *mirror* in a poem, then all your poems are going to sound fairly similar, and it becomes tiresome. It's a limitation I'm just now trying to break.

INTERVIEWER: I've a question about words. In *Reasons for Moving* you write of words that cloud the "bland, / innocent surface" of a mirror, in

Darker you tell us that "breath is a mirror clouded by words," and early in *The Story of Our Lives* you suggest that, at its best, speech can *be* that mirror. Are you trying to tell us something you feel about the nature of words, the nature of language?

STRAND: Those phrases you quote are, of course, my own, and I suppose I'm responsible for them, but as far as a systematic or developed idea of what language means to me is concerned, I really couldn't say. I do think this: that very often poetry strives for experience that is pre-verbal, or beyond words. There are certain things that we feel that can't be articulated.

INTERVIEWER: And the attempt to articulate them is somehow damaging?

STRAND: I think it's a necessary part of the poem. It helps to create the sense that there's something beyond the poem. Then, on the other hand, it's something that can damage a poem unless the poem is otherwise self-sufficient; it can make the poem seem rough or ragtag in some way. I don't know what the answer is. I often feel that words get in my way, but then I have nothing but words. The unsayable must remain unsayable, and the unsayable certainly isn't a part of poetry.

INTERVIEWER: Yet isn't much of *The Story of Our Lives* a pursuit of un-sayables?

STRAND: Yes. Here again, no matter how deeply one investigates his own life, as I do in "The Untelling," its ultimate meanings are elusive. The moment you arrive, you see another place to get to, and when you get there there's another place to get to. There's always something you've overlooked, always something you haven't understood, always a mystery in the center of the known, something you hadn't reckoned on, and I think that if the poem can exist with these spaces of ignorance in it, though not so apparent that they ruin the poem, it's marvellous. Poetry, to a certain extent, is a dance around a void, a debate with nothingness. In the sense that there was nothing before it, all writing is writing against the void. Before that particular poem there was nothing, a blank sheet of paper.

INTERVIEWER: I think it is Richard Howard who suggests that the in-creasing simplicity and directness in your style after *Reasons for Moving* represents a conscious attempt to get away from the duplicities of lan-guage. Was this so?

STRAND: You can reduce them and manipulate them, but I don't think you can ever eradicate the duplicities of language. For me, unless I speak in a very simple, pared-down way, I don't believe in the voice that I hear, which of course is my own voice. I certainly don't use the resources of language as Richard Howard does, but on the other hand I think there's something to say for the resources of the simple.

INTERVIEWER: What do you feel your poetry offers to the reader?

STRAND: That's a good question. I'm not very clear what my poems offer the reader. I rarely think of that. I really think of getting them out of myself.

INTERVIEWER: They function as a kind of personal therapy?

STRAND: No, not as a therapy or a personal release. After all, I make my poems with a great deal of care. I suppose they're meant to move the reader, put him in touch with certain areas of his experience which may seem cloudy to him, and which may through reading my poems become clarified. I hope that that might be the case with a sympathetic reader. Sometimes they're meant to delight, sometimes they're deliberately funny, though they may not seem so. They exist as moments of perceptual and emotional clarity.

INTERVIEWER: Do you intend them to be in any way prescriptive? Is there a sense in which they might be seen as recipes for a certain kind of individual psychological survival?

STRAND: Yes, I do think my poems have to do with survival, but I would hope that they speak not only for my own experience, that they speak for that of enough people that the survival isn't an idiosyncratic one. My poems are not at all didactic. I've written a few homiletic poems, but they were intentionally comic. I have no grand sense of my mission as a poet, as a carrier of the torch.

INTERVIEWER: How do you feel now about the pessimism of many of your earlier poems?

STRAND: I don't regret my pessimism at all. There's nothing to regret. I regret having written some of my poems, but it's not a regret that eats me up or lasts a long time. I think that I have been pessimistic, and I have moments of pessimism now, but I think that I'm much more hopeful than I was. I think my life would have been intolerable had I not experienced moments of joy and the possibility of hope, and that is bound to have been included in my poems—in "To Begin" I even make a virtue of loss.

INTERVIEWER: Can we take a brief biographical turn? When you first encountered modern poetry, whose were the works that seemed to define it for you?

STRAND: When I was a junior in high school we read Stevens' "Thirteen Ways of Looking at a Blackbird." It was very mysterious to myself and to the class, and the teacher could never really give us an adequate explanation. I never forgot it. I would read it and read it and read it, and it seemed impenetrable to me, yet in some way very attractive. Of course, later on, as I got older and read more Stevens and more modern poetry, it didn't seem as difficult. I think it had something to do with a gradual indoctrination into the world of poetry for me.

INTERVIEWER: And a love of Stevens has been a consistent factor in your poetry?

STRAND: Only a part of Stevens. The more meditative part I love, but the more playful part I don't really feel akin to.

INTERVIEWER: One frequently finds in your poetry lines which strike a strongly Stevensian chord—I'm thinking of those from *Reasons for Moving* ("What to Think of"): "You are the prince of Paraguay. / Your minions kneel / Deep in the shade of giant leaves. . . ."

STRAND: Yes, I guess those lines are very much the Stevens of *Harmonium*. Later on there are lines which I think take up the Stevens of *Auroras of Autumn* or "The Rock." Later still I think the influence of Stevens became greater; not in my recent poems, but in *The Story of Our Lives*, in which I'm trying to find the right way to say something, and worried about what it is that I'm trying to say. This is a preoccupation that follows Stevens throughout his poems: how to ask the question, how to answer it. He'll say the same thing ten different ways. He's always playing variations on a theme, and to a certain extent "The Untelling" is variation on a theme; it's four ways of writing the same poem. Similarly, in "To Begin," I'm worrying about how to say what it is that I want to say: one time I could say it differently, one time I could *say* it, but the person in that poem is paralyzed, depressed, unable to write, and the problem is how to begin. Stevens' problem is never how to begin, but how to finish. His arguments really break into two equal parts very often, and there is no real resolution—his resolutions are all rhetorical, they're never based on one side defeating the other. It's a rhetorical statement of disillusion very often, where night comes, and the pigeons float down . . .

INTERVIEWER: And we're left with suspended dilemma.

STRAND: Yes, or you have at the end of his poems the renewed presence of the imagination, in the shape of a giant, or the sky. It's an invitation to reinvestigate the subject at a later time. Stevens is one of those few poets you can read and discover new poems in all the time. Those poems are terribly beautiful, and the images are always igniting responses in my own imagination. Once I sit down to read Stevens it's not very long before I want to write my own poem. He's very important. It used to be that I would never take a trip without taking a selected Stevens along with me, to read in my motel room.

INTERVIEWER: This may seem one of the unanswerables, but I think it is a question one might have been tempted to ask Stevens, given the opportunity. To what extent do you understand your own poems?

STRAND: I think if forced to talk about them I can understand them pretty well, a lot of them. Some, I admit, I don't.

INTERVIEWER: Do you feel any compulsion to talk about them, to try to help people understand them?

STRAND: I don't feel that I have to. In fact, when asked to write about my poems I refuse to—to sit down and write something like that is very difficult. I'll give interviews because they seem easier, and even then I think they are probably most successful when I say nothing—when you get everything I've said and try to boil it down to some essential statement, you can't. The essential questions are unanswerable.

INTERVIEWER: These are things one suspects, and yet very often people expect, when they read an interview, or an article written by the poet himself, that some kind of essence exists which he is able to give them in that form.

STRAND: I believe that we understand so little about our world that it's unfair to put such pressure on a poem. If you ask a farmer why a certain tree is growing in his front yard, he may be able to tell you that it's growing there because he planted it, but if you ask him if he *understands* the tree, he'll look at you blankly:

"What do you mean, *understand* the tree?"

"Do you understand your wife?"

"What do you mean, do I understand my wife?"

"Well, did you marry her because you understood her?"

"No. I married her because I was in love with her."

"Does that mean you fell in love with her before you understood her?"

"I suppose so."

You try to tell that to an academic at a university—that you love a poem before you understand it—and he's likely to say "Look Strand, you're crazy. You're talking about life, and poetry isn't life." And there are many other objections that he could make. But the charm and power of poetry has very little to do with explanations, and much more to do with the *experience* of a poem, and the way the writer expresses his own poem. It's as if a voice were whispering in his ear. It's his own voice that he hears, and the writing of the poem is tinkering with it, adjusting it. The poem may be no more than the sound of the voice, and the words may be blurred, unimportant at first. What happens is very strange, but it *is* one's own voice one hears, in a very special way, and there are certain words one hears again and again. Sometimes one tries to retain the sound of the voice without the words—you leave out *mirror, stone, moon,* yet retain the sound. I've tried to do something like that in "The Garden."

INTERVIEWER: That is one of your most recent poems, and perhaps we could finish with a question about them: are you consciously trying to take a new direction in the poems since *The Story of Our Lives?*

STRAND: Yes. I think the newer poems are more open, easier going. There's more air in them, more light in them, and they are less intellectually directed, less riddling. I think some people will dislike my next book for that reason, call it a weak book, and too easy. They don't know that I'm working hard writing those poems. Some poems will be stronger, but there's not going to be any one poem in there as powerful as "Elegy for My Father." There's no poem like that in the new book—perhaps there shouldn't be.

Why I Write

ALICE ADAMS

A year or so ago my son went back to Chapel Hill, which is where I am from, on a somewhat problematical errand for me, to be combined with projects of his own, in New York (he is a painter, and wanted to take slides around). On his return to San Francisco, among other pithy remarks—he had been gratifyingly observant—he said, "Well, now I can really see why you're a writer."

His errand had involved the sale of the house in which I grew up, but which I did not inherit. I had been invited to choose certain things that I might want from the house, but although there were indeed a couple of things that I would have liked, I was withheld from making the trip myself both by reasons of sentiment, not wanting to revisit those scenes of disorderly family history—and by an experienced instinct which instructed me that the things I wanted would be mysteriously unavailable. Thus I readily accepted Peter's offer; he went to Chapel Hill, he stayed with a friend of mine, Max Steele, who teaches at the university there, and he spent time with various people who had been extremely important to me, including my childhood best friend, Josephine; and he met a woman whom I had known as the wife of another distinguished writer-teacher of many years back, Phillips Russell (I took a short story course from him, one significant summer, over thirty years ago). Thus, when Peter returned from his travels and said that he now knew why I am a writer I took him up very eagerly—he could have meant anything at all, perhaps some unravelling of dark familial mysteries. I asked, "Oh, *why?*"

"Well, writing books is all anyone ever talks about down there. Everyone is going to write a book, if they haven't already," Peter said.

Well, that was not quite the answer I expected, but as an observation it is absolutely true. Certainly during the thirties, the time of my childhood there, the town was rife with writers—past, permanent, and just passing through. Gertrude Stein even came from Paris, in 1932, with Alice Toklas, a visit arranged for by my mother, I believe. (I did not meet them because, humiliatingly, I had chickenpox at the time). Thomas Wolfe had been around almost the day before, as a student; his brooding, contradictory legend haunted the place. Paul Green, the playwright, was still there, and Prof. Koch, of Playmaker fame. And handsome Phillips Russell. And most local people knew at least a few writers from other places; my parents knew Allen Tate, who visited from Southern Pines; and Ralph Bates, the English novelist, who came to raise money for Loyalist Spain, in 1938. Everyone talked a great deal about all those writers, as well as distant William Faulkner and poor almost-discarded James Branch Cabell; they were our local folk heros, and heroines. Their drinking habits were endlessly fascinating, their lives were charmed—or so I interpreted what I was listening to, as a child.

The situation in my particular family with regard to writers and writing was slightly puzzling (as what was not). My mother had a considerable reputation as a literary woman, and was known to write poetry, which no one ever saw. But she was not a writer. I concluded that she wanted to be one and somehow had failed in that effort, which served to further exalt the calling, in my view; anything that my formidably intelligent mother could not do must be remarkable indeed, and it took a lot of nerve to resolve to exceed her, as I must secretly, unconsciously have done. My father was another sort of puzzle; he seemed to like writers, and he told a lot of writer stories, along with everyone else, but I never saw him read a book for pleasure.

Most people admired and were interested in writers, then, it seemed safe to assume, but the language in which this came through was highly ambiguous, as was much of the language that I heard, early on. In fact I was very slow to understand what could be called Polite Southern Conversation; it was years before I understood that the words, "Oh, if you're not just the smartest thing!" did not connote praise. To be smart, in P.S.C., meant to be out of line, somehow; if you were a woman, it meant that you were being most unwomanly.

Last summer in Alaska I heard Robert Stone speak movingly about early efforts to understand a schizophrenic mother. And I think that perhaps many of us began to write for somewhat similar reasons: to make sense of what seemed and sounded senseless, all around us.

Strongly motivated, then, I began to write small poems at what was considered to be a very early age. I found this an exceptionally pleasant pastime, all those nice words tidily arranged, and I was happily surprised by the attention and praise thus so easily acquired. A friend of mine has a theory that men who cook are often overpraised by women; for a man to cook at all still seems, in many circles, something remarkable. "Honestly,

Andrew made the whole dinner all by himself, I only cut up a few vegeta-
bles, and did the risotto." And so it often is, I believe, with child poets.
"Oh, what a darling little poem, and Alice is only six. Isn't she just the
smartest little thing?" (I took this remark at face value, of course, and was
awed by my own precocity).

This process of poems and praise, with a very young person, can continue for quite a while. I went on writing poems, literally hundreds of
them, for at least a dozen years, roughly between the ages of five and
seventeen. School magazines published them, I won prizes, and the notion of myself as a poet filled me with a sense of virtue that other areas of
my life did not (I was known by my parents and teachers to be 'difficult,'
'rebellious;' and they were quite right, I was). I was dimly, distantly aware
that what I wrote myself did not quite come up to the poems I read and
most admired; my sonnets, written at eleven or twelve, had no sound of
Shakespeare or Shelley, or even Edna Millay, but for a twelve-year-old to
be writing sonnets at all was considered both virtuous and unusual, by
everyone, including myself. I suppose, if I wondered at all about this gap
in literary distinction, I assumed that by the time I was twice as old, was
twenty-four, at least, my poems would be at least twice as remarkable, and
I would be a Poet. In the meantime I continued to write enthusiastically
about Nature, and in a more melancholy vein, of Love.

I went to a boarding school in Virginia where Polite Southern Conversation was elevated to an almost religious principle. There were no Jews in
the school, which was Episcopalian, because, "Of course," in P.S.C.,
"they would not be comfortable here." The headmistress of that school, a
most distracted lady who at sixty had married a handsome gentleman of
eight-two (was she or was she not a virgin? this was a popular topic for
girlish speculation), was fond of reading to us from *The Prophet* (her idea
of poetry, I guess) and she had a network of spies who reported to her on
girls who did not always speak in P.S.C., who were in fact overheard to
use words like 'damn' or 'hell'.

I hated everything about the school, the ugly uniforms and terrible
food, the lack of boys; I was often reported as using bad words, but I did
have some good friends, similarly rebellious. They were mostly girls from
Boston or New York who had somehow strayed down to Virginia, and
who seemed to speak a new and vigorous language.

Partly for that reason, my attraction to un-Southern and especially to
New England talk, I chose to go to Radcliffe, and there, almost at once,
everything in my life changed radically, for the better. My new friends all
spoke a language that I could at last understand. And the courses that I
took at Harvard were overwhelmingly exciting. I remember coming out of

Harvard Hall, from a course with F. O. Matthiessen in the criticism of poetry, and being almost unable to breathe, in that heady Cambridge spring air; I was so bedazzled by the brilliance of his lecture, and by sudden contact with poets I had not read before: Donne, Yeats, Eliot and Auden—to name only a few.

Reasonably enough, at about this time I began to recognize that my own poetry was pretty bad. The relative painlessness of this recognition now seems surprising, and I can only attribute it to my generally radiant mood of that time.

I still wrote an occasional poem, though, and I tried to enroll in a poetry writing workshop, to be given by Theodore Spencer; however the dean emphatically told me that my science requirement came first. And so I signed up for astronomy, and also for a short-story class. I began to read and to write short stories, and I fell totally and permanently in love with that form. I read stories by Elizabeth Bowen and Katherine Mansfield and Katherine Anne Porter, James Joyce and Henry James. Hemingway, Fitzgerald and John O'Hara. Mark Schorer and John Cheever. And I spent many happy afternoons in and around my writing classes in those distant lovely falls and springs.

Whenever one of us got an A or even a strong B+ we would instantly, with a wild and nutty gambler's optimism, whip that story off to *The New Yorker*. We could have papered our rooms with those politely printed form rejection slips.

I even took a writing course one summer vacation, at home in Chapel Hill, from Phillips Russell. He said that most short stories could be divided into three, or sometimes five sections, or acts; and he wrote outlines for both methods on the blackboard. I was impressed by his beautifully flaring eyebrows, but since he was so old (about forty, then, I think) and a friend of my parents *and* a most polite Southerner, I dismissed and forgot almost everything he said, or so I thought.

After college I went on writing stories, along with quite a few other much less rewarding occupations. The quality of the stories improved, over the years, although in a disconcertingly uneven way; I would write what I believed to be a fairly good story, and that story would be succeeded by others which were clearly much less good. Some of the stories were published, along with a novel that I wrote somewhere along the way. But it was many years, in fact almost twenty years after Radcliffe and those early writing courses, before I at last wrote a story that really pleased me, that I knew to be good. And that story, curiously, involved a return to Polite Southern.

The story began in my mind when two men whom I knew during the early sixties had a serious quarrel over money. They were both European, and had been intensely close friends since their own college days, at International House, in Berkeley. I was fond of them both, and I was strongly moved and disturbed by the nature of their quarrel. I first wanted and then had to write about it. In brief, what happened was that one friend, who had recently married, wanted to borrow some money from the other friend, who had just come into an inheritance. The would-be borrower offered a reasonable interest rate on the loan, and it was this that so deeply offended his friend, the offer of interest. "I would so gladly have given it to him," the wounded friend cried out, "and he offers me interest!"

For the purposes of my story I made the two men Southern, rather than European (and brothers rather than friends), both because a Southern background would come more naturally to me, and also because that particular, violently pained indignation seemed Southern: "You offer me interest!"—I could hear it in Southern voices. In my story, in fact, the two men often burlesqued Polite Southern. It was as though I could not learn to write until I had learned to master what was, after all, my earliest language.

Also, to cope with the long time span of their friendship, I used the Phillips Russell five-act outline, which fortuitously arrived at my mind, as I began to think about writing that story.

In any case, I thought it worked out, my story, and with some difficulty I persuaded my agent—at that time a most unimaginative young man—to send it to *The New Yorker* (he had me pegged as a 'woman's writer,' in those days a condescending term that precluded writing for good magazines like *The New Yorker*). *The New Yorker* bought the story, it won an O. Henry prize—and it was quite a while before I wrote another as good.

Several postscripts:

The things that I wanted in Chapel Hill were indeed unavailable, despite my son's valiant efforts to retrieve them, but I have written, at last count, three stories about the loss of an important house.

Phillips Russell's grandchildren and great-grandchildren now live here in San Francisco; one of the children has inherited his eyebrows, I think.

I occasionally hear my own voice complaining that many other people are rude, which is to say that they do not speak as politely as I grew up to expect.

These days, I write mainly because it is what I most enjoy doing.

"And A Great Amount of Joy in the Thing"

GRACE SCHULMAN

Marianne Moore said that the creative forces resulting in art had not changed, essentially, from Dante's day to her own. "Endless curiosity, observation, research, and a great amount of joy in the thing," accounted, she believed, for many forms of art. She spoke of those qualities in a Voice of America interview of 1963, attributing the comment itself to George Grosz, a caricaturist. On another occasion, she said: "My idea of research is to look at the thing from all sides: the person who has seen the animal, how the animal behaves, and so on."

Even before the nineteen-sixties, Marianne Moore had stressed those characteristics, and her remarks became my second important lesson in writing. My first had come from a family friend who, when asked for a book that would help me write well, gave me *Webster's Second Collegiate Dictionary,* a large abridgement of *Webster's Second Edition,* and one that contains many archaic words. I have traveled extensively with that edition, now covered with tape and shelf paper to keep the pages from crumbling.

From my childhood years, I thought continually of Marianne Moore's words. Curiosity and observation had been mine from the beginning. Having been raised on West Eighty-Sixth Street in Manhattan, in a steep, sooty, bricks-and-glass building whose windows had wrought-iron bars that were intended to keep my curiosity within safe bounds, I had an endless attraction to natural things. Trees, wild plants in flower, forests and bogs, were exotic fancies in my urban neighborhood, and they were magnets that compelled my deepest thoughts. Early on, I knew the oaks, the maples, the elms in Central Park, my childhood landscape. Later, I learned the precise names for my favorite trees: the camperdown elm *(Ulmus glabra)* near Seventy-Second Street and Fifth Avenue; the European linden *(Tilia europea)* near the boat pond; the black cherry *(Prunus serotina*) near the zoo. On a trip to Saratoga, I was dazzled by white pines, Norway spruces, hemlocks and arborvitae.

Language startled me in similar ways, and I remember the joys of finding words for emotions those trees evoked. What was more surprising, trees called back other images of people I had known and passages I had read. The girl who died of polio, my grandfather's voice, the first production of *King Lear* that I had ever seen, were among the many things that came alive when I saw branches and leaves. Elms, maples and *Webster's Collegiate Dictionary* were fundamental to my early years.

To learn names for things meant remembering objects that stirred me, as well as controlling the realities that lay scattered around. Calling wild plants by their names signified governing all I could. There was a mystery at the heart of every living thing; to give an object a name was to try to understand the luminous secret within. At the same time, I knew we give names to a thing because we do not understand it. I remember encountering Proust's comparison of trees to the process of memory:

> I feel that there is much to be said for the Celtic belief that the souls of those whom we have lost are held captive in some inferior being, in an animal, in a plant, in some inanimate object, and so effectively lost to us until the day (which to many never comes) when we happen to pass by the tree or to obtain possession of the object which forms their prison. Then they start and tremble, they call us by our name, and as soon as we have recognized their voice the spell is broken. We have delivered them: they have overcome death and return to share our life.
>
> And so it is with our own past. It is a labor in vain to attempt to recapture it: all the efforts of our intellect must prove futile. The past is hidden somewhere outside the realm, beyond the reach of the intellect, in some material object (in the sensation which that material object will give us) which we do not suspect. And as for that object, it depends on chance whether we come upon it or not before we ourselves must die.

As a child, I was convinced that Proust had shared my secret. My soul existed in the trees I named, just as some force within the trees named me. Stare long enough at a maple and memories will awaken. Then, too, my thoughts, passions and regrets were cast upon the elms, spruces and pines in my line of vision; they were painted on the maples that budded in spring, on the oaks that were taut as bowstrings in winter, on the spruces that raised up tiers of snow.

With the passing of years, curiosity and observation remained, but joy vanished gradually. I began to see trees in distorted ways. I concentrated on striated shadblows and twisted oaks near the sea, trees that grew grotesque above a level that was unprotected from salt spray. In pine country, the hemlocks became as deadly as their names. The arborvitae turned into a tree of death. Once I saw a spruce whose roots were exposed by an erosion of red earth on one side of its hill. The tree's roots were veins that burrowed underground. Outside my window in the woods, a starburst of white pine turned into a wounded mourning dove, then into the unfurled hand of St. James the Less, in a painting by El Greco. I remember seeing an illustration in Dante's *Inferno* of the forest of harpies, and knew that the horror of his living dead was benign when placed side by side with my own visions.

To this day, I do not know how the change came about. There are many possible explanations, of course, but none that satisfies. As a young girl, I could only subdue, or at least find equivalents for, the terrors of my imagination by finding adequate language to set them in order. And if words failed me, the unmanageable distortions were at large. Often the mind's Gorgons can lead to physical malady, and in time I had a perceptual disorder, astigmatism (whose literal meaning, "without stigmata," was no comfort in enabling me to think of visual disorders as visions), and an ailment with the intriguing name of tachycardia sinus arhythmia, or palpitations. These symptoms came when I looked at beautiful trees, plants and flowers.

Although I am not usually given to fears, my mind's dark terrors became overwhelming, and in my early adult years I stopped writing poetry to work on a daily newspaper in Alexandria, Virginia. I had to know that I was not easily intimidated. I covered the police department, and showed no qualms about asking Police Chief Dawes to tell me, in detail, the counts on which the owner of the local skating rink was charged with rape. I covered the Federal Court, and interviewed a gentle mathematician accused of stealing documents from one of the United States Government's security agencies. In the city jail, I spoke with a man who had been accused of poisoning his son, and I visited a family whose daughter had just been killed in a head-on collision. I investigated a Sanitation Authority proposal to filter sewage in the Potomac River, and sat in on countless boards of county supervisors. Those facts, those events of the living world were, I felt, more comforting than the bark and moss and brown leaves of my mind.

All too soon, however, I grew restless with the new-found world of information. Realities lacked reality. The sources of crime seemed less intriguing than, for example, the fact that fires and storms might actually favor stands of alder and birch. In covering news stories, I was unable to use words in any but prepared, formulaic ways. My language deserted me.

In time, I left my job as a reporter to try to summon the strength to step gingerly into the landscape of my imagination, to look at trees again and hold back fear. If necessary, I would resign myself to a difficult love. "Endless curiosity, observation, research . . ." Marianne Moore's words haunted me, "and a great amount of joy in the thing." There were, I supposed, different kinds of joy.

Then one winter day, years after I had committed myself to a sorrowful life that, nevertheless, seemed right for me, I was walking to my home on the northeast corner of Washington Square Park when I saw a blighted elm whose taut, bare branches appeared to be moving. Again, the palpitations, the double vision. At that moment, suddenly, it came clear: the branches seemed to be in motion because many tiny sparrows were leaping around them, investigating the tree's decay. When I stared at the branches, they were astir. But the sight of that elm and those birds had generated in me a fierce joy that had caused the arhythmia and the visual distortions: I perceived that dormant things wait for lively objects to animate them. The vaulting birds recalled the story of Christ pressing his face into Veronica's handkerchief, thereby imprinting an image with the stains of his tears and blood. Shortly after that, I composed this poem:

Birds on a Blighted Tree*

Free things are magnets to the moving eye,
Beckoning the mind to rouse the dead;
Under a cloud's passing power
A spire sails—a mast.
These birds antagonize a tree:
Scavengers invade decay
Winter's engraved in air.
Defiantly they strain for light and fly,
Tightening branches to bows.
Iconoclasts impress indelible
Veronicas on living things,
Leaving a branch leafless.
Free things breed freedom;
That dead arm beating.

Some time later, in a poem called "Double Vision," I wrote the lines: "My heart's arhythmia, my double vision / are handicaps. They are all I have." What I knew then was that language was all I had, for I learned, at last, the meaning of "a great amount of joy in the thing."

---

* "Birds on a Blighted Tree" was first published by *Antaeus* and later collected in *Burn Down the Icons* (Princeton University Press, 1976).

First Person Singular

Writers On Their Craft

compiled by
JOYCE CAROL OATES

Here is a remarkable gathering: twenty-nine outstanding North American writers speak frankly of the secrets of their craft in highly original and provocative pieces, many of them never published before in book form. Saul Bellow discusses the role of the writer in a Philistine culture; Adrienne Rich tells of a new "psychic geography" to be explored, especially by women writers; John Updike confesses that "success breeds disillusion as surely as failure" and asserts that the writer in mid-career must be born again; Cynthia Ozick tells of her long and painful apprenticeship to Henry James; E.L. Doctorow discusses the moral obligation of the writer in "post-humanist" America; Francine du Plessix Gray speaks of writing out of "a desire for revenge against reality."

A rich and varied collection of essays and conversations, **First Person Singular** also includes Margaret Atwood, Hortense Calisher, Gail Godwin, Mary Gordon, John Hawkes, John Hollander, Maxine Kumin, Howard Nemerov, Joyce Carol Oates, Reynolds Price, Ned Rorem, Dave Smith, William Stafford, Anne Tyler, Eudora Welty, and others.

cluding *The Best American Short Stories 1979* and *Night Walks: A Bedside Companion*. Her new novel is *Mysteries of Winterthurn*. She teaches at Princeton University.